My Dream Time

GEORGIA -

You knew I had to find a long book for you to finish your Pomona time with us! I cannot thank you enough for the countless hours of backhands, hard conversations, relentless competitiveness, and culture changing competitive edge you have helped the team with. Want it sounds cliché, the belief you have instilled in this program has been incredible.

Thank you always,

MIKE

My Dream Time

Ash Barty

HarperOne
An Imprint of HarperCollinsPublishers

HarperCollins books may be purchased for educational, business, or sales promotional use. For information, please email the Special Markets Department at SPsales@harpercollins.com.

Originally published as *My Dream Time* in Australia in 2022 by HarperCollins Australia.

FIRST HARPERONE HARDCOVER PUBLISHED 2023

Designed by Mark Campbell, HarperCollins Design Studio

Unless otherwise noted, all photographs courtesy of the author.

Library of Congress Cataloging-in-Publication Data has been applied for.

ISBN 978-0-06-328353-4

23 24 25 26 27 LBC 5 4 3 2 1

For Mum, Dad, Sara and Ali.
Without their love and sacrifice,
the best journey of my life never begins.

For you,
Be brave
Be courageous
Be authentic
and most importantly,
Enjoy your unique journey.

Contents

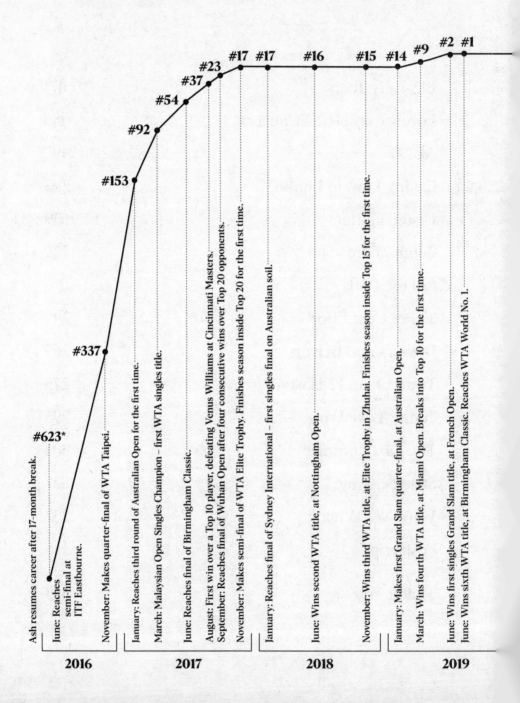

Ash's journey to
WTA World #1

#623*

#337

#153

#92

#54

#37

#23

#17   #17

#16

#15

#14

#9

#2   #1

Ash resumes career after 17-month break.

June: Reaches semi-final at ITF Eastbourne.

November: Makes quarter-final of WTA Taipei.

January: Reaches third round of Australian Open for the first time.

March: Malaysian Open Singles Champion – first WTA singles title.

June: Reaches final of Birmingham Classic.

August: First win over a Top 10 player, defeating Venus Williams at Cincinnati Masters.
September: Reaches final of Wuhan Open after four consecutive wins over Top 20 opponents.

November: Makes semi-final of WTA Elite Trophy. Finishes season inside Top 20 for the first time.

January: Reaches final of Sydney International – first singles final on Australian soil.

June: Wins second WTA title, at Nottingham Open.

November: Wins third WTA title, at Elite Trophy in Zhuhai. Finishes season inside Top 15 for the first time.

January: Makes first Grand Slam quarter-final, at Australian Open.

March: Wins fourth WTA title, at Miami Open. Breaks into Top 10 for the first time.

June: Wins first singles Grand Slam title, at French Open.
June: Wins sixth WTA title, at Birmingham Classic. Reaches WTA World No. 1.

2016   **2017**   **2018**   **2019**

Career Highlights
3 Grand Slam singles titles
1 Grand Slam doubles title
12 WTA singles titles
11 WTA doubles titles
Olympic bronze medal
  for mixed doubles

Ash held the WTA World No. 1 ranking for 114 consecutive weeks, the fourth-longest streak in tour history, behind Steffi Graf (186 weeks), Serena Williams (also 186) and Martina Navratilova (156).

In all, Ash spent 121 weeks at No. 1, the seventh most in WTA tour history, surpassed only by Steffi Graf, Martina Navratilova, Serena Williams, Chris Evert, Martina Hingis and Monica Seles.

#2 #1 #1   #1 #1   #1   #1   #1 #1 #1 #1   #1   #1 #1 #1

August: Drops to WTA World No. 2.
September: After US Open, returns to WTA World No. 1.
November: Wins seventh WTA title, at WTA Finals. Finishes WTA Year-End World No. 1 for the first time.

January: Wins eighth WTA title, at Adelaide International – first WTA singles title in Australia.
January: Makes semi-final at Australian Open for the first time.

From March to November: Does not compete due to Covid-19 pandemic.

November: Finishes second consecutive year as WTA Year-End World No. 1.

January: Wins ninth WTA title, at Melbourne Summer Series.

April: Wins tenth WTA title, at Miami Open.
April: Wins eleventh WTA title, at Porsche Tennis Grand Prix in Stuttgart.

July: Wimbledon Ladies' Singles Champion – second Grand Slam singles title.
August: Wins thirteenth WTA title, at Cincinnati Masters.

November: Finishes third consecutive year as WTA Year-End World No. 1.

January: Wins fourteenth WTA title, at Adelaide International.
January: Wins Australian Open – third Grand Slam singles title.

March: Announces retirement from professional tennis.

*WTA rankings as per the ranking cycle following that tournament.

2020   **2021**   **2022**

The Wolves of Wimbledon

I hear two voices when I'm playing tennis. I always have. One whispers, 'Ash, you're not good enough,' and the other replies, 'Yes, you are – come on, Ash!'

Those sentiments both sound true because both belong to me. They're distinctly my own. One voice cuts deep into my confidence, undermining whatever goal I want to achieve. The other lifts me up, underpinning everything I've achieved so far. They're so familiar, so convincing, so confusing. Both can have an impact in those fleeting, dramatic moments between big points.

So which version of myself do I listen to? That depends on timing, and circumstance, and mood. It depends on which voice calls to me more loudly. On which one wants to be heard. Or *demands* to be heard. Maybe what matters most is which version of me is listening on any given day. Today, Saturday, 7 July 2018, on the No. 3 Court at the All England Lawn Tennis and Croquet Club, all I'm listening to – at least, all I can hear – is: 'Ash, you're not good enough.' I want to cry.

Why does it have to be this way? Why do *I* have to be this way? I love this court. The stands surrounding it hold a couple of thousand spectators at most. You look up from the manicured grass here and see green bleacher seating and blue sky. It's the very definition of British pleasantry. It's not as if the setting is daunting – it's no cavernous modern cauldron of flashing lights, incessant advertisements and unruly crowds.

This is Wimbledon, that tournament where etiquette and decorum still reign, and civility and gentility count for everything. It should be one of the joys of professional tennis to play here. It should be a pleasure and an honour – something not taken for granted.

It's not for me today, though, in this third-round match against Russian tyro Daria Kasatkina, not with that hateful, doubting voice droning away in my ear, getting louder and louder, drowning out any hope or belief.

Have you heard the Native American tale of the two wolves? It's a Cherokee proverb – a story about a young man who asks his grandfather about the painful struggle and fight between the two growling animals inside of him. One wolf is evil – it is anger and greed, arrogance and self-pity, ego and sorrow. The other wolf is good – it is faith and compassion, joy and love, humility and hope. They are both biting at one another, trying to control the young man.

The young man asks: 'Which wolf will win?'

The grandfather answers: 'The one you feed.'

There's always a choice to be made between fear and faith, between inferiority and belief, between 'Ash, you're not good enough' and 'Yes, you are – come on, Ash'.

Today, I feed the wrong wolf.

In truth, I've been doing this for a while. This crisis has been brewing for months, remaining largely invisible to everyone but those in my inner sanctum, but now it spills over in the very public spotlight of the British grass-court season. What's happening? In tennis terms, I'm redlining. In layman's terms, I'm pressing, pushing – panicking.

It's a moment you might recognise in any sporting contest: a competitor is blinded by the scoreline or the flow of the contest, and they abandon their process and start taking short cuts. Not content to go step by step, they attempt giant leaps – speculative strategies and 'Hail Mary' plays. And, almost inevitably, they fail.

I notice this in myself nine days prior to Wimbledon, at the Eastbourne International, held at the quaint Devonshire Park Lawn Tennis Club. I usually love this time of the year, when I finally step off that clay-court season of the European summer and onto English grass, heading first to the Nottingham Open and then to the Birmingham Classic. I love the way the spongy soil cushions every step I take, the way the courts reveal their wear and tear, showing you little goat tracks and pivot points where the greenest blades of grass have been worn down to dirt through the effort and application of the best tennis players on the planet. But I can't seem to enjoy any of that on this day at Eastbourne, against Danish star Caroline Wozniacki.

Caro is the number 2 player in the world, yet it's not her power or shot-making ability that worries me so much as her biggest weapon: she just doesn't miss. She hits the ball where she intends. And she intends to put me in positions on the court that I don't like. There are other players who do this too. Simona Halep and Agnieszka Radwańska come to mind. They're happy to stay out there all day, play a thousand balls back at me – *thump, thump, thump, thump*, like a bloody metronome – boring me to death and wearing me down.

Against those players, I find myself thinking more than I ought to, plotting a path to victory and fretting when it doesn't immediately appear. I push harder than I should, forcing each moment, pressing when I need to remain patient.

I can feel myself doing that now against Caro, getting anxious and overplaying my shots, barrelling ahead with a ferocity I can't control or sustain. I gift her points and stress over that. I play higher-risk tennis and start to lose games, then I lose the match altogether. Straight sets. Her experience has taken advantage of my immaturity. This is happening to me more and more – and it keeps happening in big matches. The ones I want the most. I don't get it.

The short drive to the fringes of London for Wimbledon does little to ease my anxiety. This tournament above all others has seared a hole into my consciousness. It is the only one I watched as a little girl, and the one I dream most of winning. But for me, ambition leads to apprehension. And that leads to stress and distraction, and to cracks in my mindset. And through those cracks creep all that extra noise and bullshit that accompanies any and every Grand Slam.

I try to stay away from all that. I like the nice little home I'm staying in here, for instance, with the nice little pub around the corner. I like meeting the other girls on tour and training on the ovals at Roehampton. I like the fact that my coach, Craig Tyzzer, has forgotten to bring white shorts with him, and has to make a run to TK Maxx and Sports Direct, and all he can find there are these big, baggy white soccer shorts. Tyzz doesn't like it, but he has to pull them up, fold them over and tighten the drawstring, because he won't be allowed on the courts of Wimbledon otherwise – and this is very, very funny to me, because I'm juvenile if nothing else, and the old guy looks ridiculous. We both laugh.

We walk through the gates of the All England Club earlier than most, and find it eerie and still. The ground staff are only just setting up, mowing the ryegrass and testing the soil moisture and marking the lines, all so we can step onto a living, breathing arena. I have a hit with Jo Konta and it's heaven. I feel good about this Wimbledon.

In the first round I play Stefanie Vögele, a Swiss girl who's older than me and whom I should beat. We're good friends – during my first year on tour, she always put her hand up to hit with me. We know each other well. She couldn't get near me in Nottingham only a few weeks earlier, yet she troubles me in this match. Why? Perhaps she's had a good look at me, and now, on No. 12 Court, she has nothing to lose. I have to dig in and fight for this one.

I'm loose, yet frustrated. I slam my racquet into my leg, though I know I shouldn't. I *shouldn't* let my opponent know

I'm bothered, and I *should* know that my thin skin bruises like a peach. The difference between missing a ball and making a ball shouldn't mean so much to me, but in every tiny error I see a colossal failure. I'm blowing everything out of proportion.

I come off court with a win but feel tired and frustrated. Not a good sign. I head home immediately; even at the best of times, I don't feel like socialising at the Slams. My eyes are stinging. My body is slumping. I need rest.

Next I play Genie Bouchard, and the media builds the match up, for no other reason than we both once won the Junior Wimbledon title, and she'd made a Wimbledon final in 2014. We were both comfortable playing on these courts. I know it's a flimsy news angle, yet I get caught up in that narrative – another sign that things aren't quite right. I begin to imagine how it will be a gripping contest, a telling and compelling match. Usually, I read nothing about myself. I listen to nothing. I turn off the television. Now? I'm drawn in, or sucked in, perhaps looking for something to motivate and energise myself. I'm not sure.

We play on that No. 3 Court, right beneath the view from the players' restaurant. I start incredibly well, missing only a handful of first serves through the first set. In the second set I get broken out of nowhere, and the familiar and unwelcome stress builds. A few cheap points get me out of trouble, and I end up with a series of match points. I try to hit my flat, wide serve to second court but instead slap it into the net. Two, three, four times I miss the same serve.

There are two voices inside me now. One sounds wise – 'Change your positioning, throw something unexpected her way, apply the pressure to her weaker side' – but the other is stubborn – 'Nah, I like my patterns, I'm keeping them, because I want to make this particular serve.' I get distracted, even looking up into the restaurant to see who's eating there. Somehow I scrape through and win the match.

I'm flustered but I'm also hitting the ball well, and now I must face Daria Kasatkina, a prodigy and a tough opponent. The prize on offer is a place in the fourth round. That's uncharted territory for me at this point of my career: the chance to advance to the second week of a Grand Slam has arrived. And to make it more exciting, it would be Manic Monday at Wimbledon.

I feel the match flowing for me early. I'm quickly up 4-1, and a sense of entitlement washes over me. That's always there too. It'd be wrong to pretend otherwise. I like to think I'm a humble person – gracious, kind and complimentary of others. But those traits have no place during a competitive match. When you're staring across the net at someone who is trained to beat you – to break your game down by exploiting the frailties in your brain and body – you can't help but find another side of your psyche. I begin talking to myself. *I know I'm a good grass-court player*, I think. *And I know I'm a better grass-court player than her.*

I feel fresh, and I'm controlling this match, but I know I have to guard against arrogance just as much as doubt, because either one can bring me down. Grass-court tennis is quicker, with lower balls and fewer rallies, and I love how swiftly and smoothly this match is unfolding for me. My expectations build because I'm cruising – and then something shifts.

Kasatkina begins using shape. She slows down her ball speed and controls her racquet-head speed. She hits it high and slow over the net. She puts the ball into my backhand corner, and does so again and again, just like Caro would. She's not trying to hit winners, only to dictate the tempo of the play. This is designed to annoy me – and it does. Her looping shots give me no pace to work with. Her depth and placement give me no angles to exploit. All I can do is go neutral, hitting the ball back, and back, and back. *Thump, thump*, again and again. She takes control of every point. She denies and frustrates.

Tactically, the shift is minor, and only mildly surprising, yet it throws me off course. I'm too fragile to tweak my plan, too stubborn to see its flaws, too flustered to reroute my path to victory. I have no clarity in this moment, no answers, not even a process for *finding* some answers. All I have is a rising anger.

This grows over two or three points, and once I'm tipped over that edge, I'm gone. When Kasatkina finds a lucky net cord winner to break back in the seventh game, it's like I'm falling off a cliff. I should walk off the court right now.

The issue is that my good is great, but my bad is horrible. When I'm winning, I look like a million bucks – like I'm toying with people – but when my tactics aren't working, I lack the maturity to solve my own problems. Basically, when Plan A isn't getting the job done, I can see no other options, even if Plans B, C, D and E are right there in front of me.

Plan F – swearing and sniping and muttering and grumbling – seems simpler. So that's what I do. 'Fuck this,' I mutter. 'This is shit.'

I'm a 22-year-old highly trained professional athlete, but in this moment I decide on a public tantrum. As the points and games fall Kasatkina's way, I shake my head and grimace, and I backchat with my box – with my family and friends and supporters, and mostly with my coach. It's always like this when I'm cornered. I get snappy. I'm not really saying much at all, just venting but with venom. There have been flashes like this before in other matches, but my natural game has saved me. Nothing can save me today.

Today, on day six of the championships. I have 24 unforced errors. I drop 12 of the last 16 games. After being 4-1 ahead, I lose the match in straight sets: 5-7, 3-6. A gift to Daria.

Today, my childhood dream dissolves and I sink into the loss. I swallow it whole and can feel it in my stomach, which is sick and swollen with something sour – not just losing the match and losing my shit, but losing my dignity too. I shun my closest supporters and cry myself to sleep that night, embarrassed and ashamed. Bereft, really. I can't look at myself in the mirror.

I don't speak to Tyzz – by which I mean Tyzz doesn't speak to me. He leaves immediately after the match, without a word. He usually stays a ten-minute walk away from Wimbledon, and I later learn that he left the courts where I'd sworn at him and publicly rejected his help, and stopped for a think down Dairy Walk, a little country lane with an old white wooden Wimbledon turnstile. There he composed his thoughts before flying home to Australia the next day.

Tyzz took me on two years earlier, when I was coming back to tennis after a hiatus – when I was an unranked and unquantifiable risk. Now I've just treated him like garbage, messing up the relationship, ruining everything, over a match, over a point, over a moment when I stopped acting like an adult and instead lashed out like a selfish child.

I can't bring myself to call him, so I send messages, texting rapid-fire apologies over and over.

His response is swift and short: *We'll talk about this at a later date. We'll work through this.* He asks a few questions, too. What was the message I was trying to get to him when I was on the court? What was I yelling? What the fuck was I trying to say?

I call him days later, to apologise and explain.

'One voice' – that's what I was trying to say. I was trying to say that I wanted to hear from Tyzz and Tyzz only. Not to hear cheering from my manager. Not to hear encouragement from my boyfriend. Not to hear barracking from my trainer. Not to hear 'Come on, Ash' or 'Let's go, Ash' or 'You've got this, mate'. I didn't want general support. I wanted specific direction. One voice.

Tyzz pauses before answering. He has his own theory about what's going on. He thinks I don't believe I'm good enough. He thinks that I think I'm letting everyone down. He thinks that in those moments on court when I have no answers – when the win I want is being snatched away – I wither and withdraw and despair. He has a mental filing cabinet full of such moments, and he shares a few with me now.

Only a year earlier, Tyzz reminds me, he saw something that simply wasn't normal. I was playing in the 2017 French Open doubles with my mate Casey Dellacqua, and we were playing powerful tennis. The conditions were great and we started well. We were playing the top seeds, Bethanie Mattek-Sands and Lucie Šafářová, and thought maybe that day was our day. Three games in, Tyzz recalls, we played one bad game – just one – and he saw it. We shrank on court. Shrivelled and withered. We might as well have dug a hole in the clay. Bethanie saw it and put the hammer down, and after that we didn't get close. It was all over in 66 minutes: 6-2, 6-1.

But what stood out most to Tyzz, he tells me now, was our reaction. Casey started crying on court before the match was even over, and I followed suit. We soaked the rooms in uncontrollable sobs. Our fifth Grand Slam final together and again we had failed. The only explanation Tyzz has is that we simply expected things to go our way, and we weren't remotely equipped for the possibility that it might not come easily. He wrote a long message to me later, and summed up his message simply: 'In the end, there's no fairy tales. You have to win it.'

He saw something similar later that year, in Zhuhai, when I was playing Coco Vandeweghe. I was ranked 16 and Coco was 10, but my game was better, and growing, too. Coco has a big serve and a big forehand, but if you keep the ball in court long enough, and make her hit enough shots, that's where she can falter. That's how you put her under the pump. I knew that, yet I let that big serve and big forehand intimidate me; I shrank onto my back foot and allowed her to dominate. Afterwards, Tyzz suggested that Coco and I pair up in doubles – he was hoping some of her confidence might rub off on me. He also knew that our game styles would complement each other. He knew my problem was becoming a pattern, and that it had nothing to do with how I hit the tennis ball.

But we're not talking about that right now. We're talking about my outburst – my brain explosion at Wimbledon. We're focusing on my fury, how I'd waved him and everyone else away. This is exactly the kind of behaviour he won't tolerate. He never has. It's a dealbreaker for him – as close to a non-negotiable as they come.

'What it looked like to us,' he tells me, 'is you telling us all to fuck off.'

That breaks my heart. Completely destroys me.

Tyzz explains something carefully to me now. He can't watch this show on repeat any longer. He's sick of the ending.

Something needs to change, and he's not the one who can change it. Why do I always look like I'm about to take off and then stumble? Why do those stumbles always turn into ruinous collapse? Why am I so emotionally distraught over wins and losses? Why am I not performing as well as he knows I can – as I know I should?

Why can't I feed the good wolf?

'You are as good as every one of these girls,' Tyzz tells me now. 'You can compete with these girls. You can *beat* these girls.' Then he's silent for a moment. 'But there is something going on in that bloody head of yours that I have no idea how to fix. We need help.'

Something needs to change.

Before Anything and Everything

I was born at Ipswich Hospital on 24 April 1996. I arrived four days late, and with no great excitement or drama. I suppose there was one concern. I did have congenital dislocation of the hips as a baby. Basically, your hip socket doesn't form properly – it's too shallow and can slip out of the joint – so you have to wear these stirrups that keep your little knees up above your waistline, as if you're in a squatting position at all times.

I'm told I hated those bloody stirrups, pushing and kicking against them, always trying to get free, itching to run before I could even roll over. Once my hips settled down, I was put in a Jolly Jumper, and apparently that was my first love. If I caught sight of that thing I'd immediately cry for it, wanting it hung up in every doorway or fixed to the bough of every tree. I was a bouncy little bugger, I guess, eager to fly up and see beyond my horizon.

I was raised in a low brick house, where my parents still live. Orange brick walls, brown tile roof, cream-coloured trim and beige carpet. We lived at the end of a short cul-de-sac in a place called Springfield, half an hour southwest of Brisbane. It's the kind of neighbourhood you only visit intentionally, with no big busy roads cutting through it – a lush and quiet pocket filled with jacarandas and palms and spindly gums, and a small pocket park to play in only 20 metres from our front door.

My parents met not far from here, while playing a social game of golf at the Gailes Golf Club in 1983. My mum, Josie, has always played recreationally, but my dad, Robert, took the sport a little more seriously than most. Dad's a country boy from Bowen, in north Queensland, and he was driven hard by his father, who was strict. In a way, Dad was pushed too far, and then finally not pushed far enough.

As a young man, Dad was ready to take that last big step to becoming a professional golfer. He was set to play for the University of Houston, a springboard to a professional career, until his father stepped in: 'There's no way you're going to America – you'll end up getting shot.' The boy who took Dad's place was named Steve Elkington, and he went on to join the international tour, even winning the 1995 PGA Championship. Meanwhile, Dad's dream was snuffed out before it caught fire. Being the stubborn person he is, he let the spark subside: Dad barely picked up a golf club for 25 years. He went on to build a career at the State Library of Queensland.

Mum is one of six kids of English migrants, and for most of her professional life she was a radiographer working at Ipswich Hospital. She's the emotional member of our family unit. The one who cries at the drop of a hat. The clumsy one. The one who needs reminders. In our house when I was growing up, there was a rule: 'If you're five minutes early, you're ten minutes late.' With that in mind, we made fun of Mum, who was the relaxed one, the laissez-faire one – but in truth she never showed up late for anything. She just had little interest in being 15 minutes early!

Importantly, she was the person I sat with when I was sad, who would scratch my head and hold me in her arms. In all of my worst moments, nothing ever calmed my breathing and warmed my heart like Mum's fingers running through my hair.

When I wasn't inside watching *The Simpsons* or *The Brady Bunch* or *The Nanny*, or playing Pokémon on my Nintendo Game Boy, I was out in the garden with Mum. We would go for drives on the weekend – often on a Saturday, after tennis – and we'd almost always end up at a local nursery, where I could pick out a $1 flower and then go home and plant it in the garden. I'd tug at a few weeds, mow the lawn and scrape the moss from the grout between the concrete slabs of the carport. Mum would potter around and water and I would play with the dogs, or we would read together in the shade. It was simple and comforting, and sparked my love for this sort of life – finding happiness in small things. Mum used to go for morning walks – she still does – and always with her earphones in. She strolled the streets, humming and softly singing to herself. I would tell her she looked like a lunatic, but she would just smile serenely because she knew what worked best in her world. She knows the secret.

Mum hates conflict, though, and tough conversations, and that's alright because that's Dad's domain. He was always the organised one. The structured one. Methodical. Rational. Clean. Efficient. Play a round of golf with Dad and you'll understand immediately why it appealed so much to him. It requires the patient marking of a mental checklist for every stroke, meaning hours spent drifting in and out of a state of meditative focus.

I have that in me too. I'm the kind of person who gets home from a trip and unpacks everything before doing anything else. All bags emptied – immediately. I'm the kind of person who knows at all times where their phone and purse are. I do not lose my keys. I don't lose anything. I pack my tennis bag in the same order every time, and I don't like anyone touching it. And if I change bags, I transfer everything right away, so everything immediately has its new home.

Some people call it fastidious, others call it obsessive-compulsive. The latter term gets thrown around loosely, but not with Dad. He told me once that back when he was a teenager, he needed to learn a particular bunker shot. His coach told him to stay in the sand trap practising that one shot until the action was muscle memory. Dad took that more seriously than he should have, and kept swinging until his hands bled. He's struggled with that mentality his whole life, and with depression. We have that in common.

I think Dad saw a lot of himself in me as I grew up, and while he enjoyed watching me walk my path to professionalism, he was wary and nervous too. I remember a time in my teens when I wasn't feeling myself, and we found it hard to relate. We would sit on the couch together watching the footy, and not speak a word. We were too stubborn to be vulnerable with one another. Not knowing what to say, we instead said nothing at all.

Dad is trusting and trustworthy, and he struggles if someone breaks that bond. He gave that to me: the notion that loyalty and respect are given generously, yet thrown away swiftly – and impossible to get back. Does he forgive? Mostly. Can you forget? Never. But mainly I recall my connection to him through sport, sitting up into the early hours of the morning, watching the Ashes together. He was a big softie, really, who wanted nothing more than to see me have fun, laughing and smiling and carefree. I guess he was just my best mate.

I suppose my big sisters were my mates too. But I used to annoy Ali and Sara as much as possible. Do you know the game called 'corners'? It's not much of a game. I would sit in the middle seat in the back of the car, and every time we turned at a roundabout or took a sharp left or right, I would hurl my body in the opposite direction, trying to crush one sister or the other into the car door. 'Ash, stop it,' I'd hear. 'Ash, stop it,' they'd groan. 'Ash, STOP IT!' they'd snap. And that was when I knew I had them. *Here we go*, I'd think, practically rubbing my hands together. *Let's see how far we can take this.*

That was particularly true for Ali, the middle child, who is three years older than me. We grew up sleeping in bunk beds: me on the bottom, her on top. Ali is the kindest, most beautiful, sensitive soul – and I exploited that without mercy. What did we fight over? The breakfast bowl we wanted to use. The first piece of chicken at dinner. The choice of TV show at night. *Whatever you have, I'm going to take it*, I would think. *Because I know you won't fight for it.*

If it was time to clean up, I would hide under the bed and, when caught, pretend to be cleaning under there. I threw an animal encyclopaedia at Ali once – helicoptered it right at her head – but I missed and put a hole in the wall. We joined forces briefly to hide the evidence, covering it with a poster. *Job well done. Shake on it, mate.* Mum immediately identified it as hung in a strange place, and I betrayed my sister instantly: 'Ali did it!'

We went to Woodcrest State College, a Prep to Grade 12 school three kilometres away from home. At some point on the walk home most days, I would drop my schoolbag and simply walk away, or run off. I didn't want to carry it, and I knew that Sara, five years older than me, would have to chase after me – I couldn't cross the street myself, after all – meaning Ali would have to carry my bag.

Ali gave up a lot for me. When I started playing tennis, she gave up netball and decided to learn tennis instead, because it would be easier for Mum and Dad to drive the two of us to the same place. Later, when I needed more coaching but we couldn't afford it, Ali gave up her private lesson so that I could have a second session every week. Ali was the last person in the family to beat me at tennis, when I was eight and she was 11. And she never played me again. She retired against me with that win forever in her pocket – and while that makes me seethe, if anyone is going to hold victory over me forever, I'm glad it's her. She earned it.

I never clashed with Sara, and not just because she's older. She's simply stronger than me, and smarter than me too. Far smarter, in fact. I never wanted to chance being pitted against her, but I also genuinely can't recall there being any friction between us. We've never had a fight in our lives. Sometimes similarity causes tension – two bulls in the same paddock – but with Sara I felt only as though we saw one another clearly from the beginning. I watched her in awe. She's my hero.

When you're a little kid, your big sister is the one doing everything for the first time. The first to have issues with friends at school. The first to have a boyfriend. The first to go to university. The first to solve every problem. Whenever I met a bumpy road I didn't know how to negotiate, I knew Sara would show me the way. She's the tough one. The pragmatic one. She wants certainty. She wants things fixed. When things get hard, Sara is the person you want in your corner – an emotional ear but a logical sounding board. She tells you how it is and what to do. She will sympathise and she will not judge.

But our family was far more than just the five of us. With a large flock of relatives on both sides, I grew up with a feeling of natural insulation from the outside world, by sheer weight of numbers. My cousins were my mates, and there were dozens of them, and we saw them every weekend. Family before anything and everything – that's what we were taught. The lesson wasn't explicit or even said out loud; it was simply assumed and understood, without need of reminder or reinforcement.

We felt that most keenly every spring school holidays on North Stradbroke Island. A trip to Straddie meant camping in tents or staying in caravans and cabins, and scores of children with nothing to do but chill and swim. I would go fishing with the boys – my uncles – from early morning to late afternoon. They would invite me and often not the other young cousins, because they knew I wouldn't lose interest or bellyache, and that I would bait my own hook and help pump for yabbies on the flats, and reel in the whiting and the bream from the blue water off the white-sand beaches.

I hated girls' clothes and loved my Straddie uniform: long board shorts, no shirt and a backwards cap. When Mum finally forced me into a top, it was one of those ugly long-sleeved fishing ones with garish colours and brand names like Wilson and Shimano, and covered with pictures of big game fish.

For ten days every September it was heaven there. We'd be up at dawn, explore all day, then we'd have 'foursies'. Just after three o'clock, we'd sit around and slowly prepare a long snack – maybe a cheese board and crackers – and we would talk and laugh. That was the signifier that 4 pm was approaching and playtime was over. You have your foursies, you have your shower, you eat your dinner, you go to bed. You close your eyes and dream deeply, and in the darkness the water laps at the shore and the Milky Way dances up above and the Earth spins and the sun returns and you do it all again.

Finding happiness in small things.

Attacking the Bend

I need help. It's July 2018, post-Wimbledon.

I know what will happen if I let this moment slip. If I try to sweep aside this Wimbledon loss – this emotional unravelling – it'll happen again. And again. Then maybe it begins happening four or five or six times a year, always in the spotlight, always when I'm on the cusp of something bigger and better. Then maybe I become just another average tennis player, one who doesn't enjoy the game and isn't grateful to play it for a living. I need to figure this thing out, yet I can still hear Tyzz in my mind: *There is something going on in that bloody head of yours that I have no idea how to fix. We need help.*

One thing Tyzz does know is who can provide that help. His name is Ben Crowe, he tells me, a leadership expert and mind coach – whatever that means. I learn that he went to university in the 1980s and studied Philosophy and Anthropology and Literature, and that he wondered what he would ever do with such disciplines. In fact, he was years into his career in sports marketing before he realised that those subjects he had been studying could just as easily be called Wisdom and Human Behaviour and Storytelling.

Crowey worked at Nike, and was their youngest ever executive. He spent decades helping athletes understand their own narratives, improving them as people and competitors. From there he began mentoring C-suiters and administrators and coaches. He focused on authenticity and vulnerability and connection. He developed deep and abiding relationships with world champion surfers and Olympic gold medallists, Fortune 500 executives and special forces soldiers.

And that all sounds great, but I don't know this guy. Until this moment I've never heard of him. I'm back in Brisbane and muddling through a week off from training, recovering mentally as much as physically from the loss to Kasatkina, and Tyzz calls again. He tells me he's been thinking about bringing Crowey into the fold for a while now, but now is the time. Why? I needed to hit 'rock bottom' before he made that call.

Rock bottom? The term makes me think of people with addictions or compulsions, drug problems or drinking problems, but Tyzz thinks the same principle applies. 'There is no point in you talking to someone if you're not ready to hear what they have to say, or if you're not going to acknowledge what they're saying,' he tells me. 'You weren't ready to accept help. Now you are.'

He's right. I needed to know I couldn't do everything on my own, and I can see that now – it's become abundantly clear to me that I cannot go it alone – but still Tyzz can hear trepidation in my voice. He isn't sure that I'm sure.

'Ash, this is how we can improve,' he says, 'but you've gotta be all in. You've gotta invest. You've gotta trust me.'

Of course I trust him. Tyzz is the person I trust most.

And so, one Saturday in July, I fly down to Melbourne and drive to Crowey's office. It's winter, bitingly cold and bitter, and I'm glad to step into the warmth of his quarters in leafy South Yarra. It's a slick space, and he seems like a cool person. He wears a thin woollen jumper with the sleeves pushed up to the elbows, and he gestures to a couch. He smiles, then he looks me in my eyes and holds my gaze. I look away, and my gaze settles on his walls.

There's a picture of Andre Agassi. A cricket shoe signed by Shane Warne. A replica of the suit worn by Cathy Freeman at the Sydney Olympics. These things might look ostentatious to an outsider, like trinkets bought from a memorabilia store. But they're not. They're so much more than that. Agassi? He became first a close friend of Crowey's, and later a trusted business partner. Warne? A bloke Crowey once took on a tour of America, and who became a great mate. Cathy? A living legend whom Crowey sponsored when he was working at Nike.

They say it's not what you know but who you know, and for me, who Crowey knows counts for everything. Understanding that these great sportspeople worked with him – that they trusted him – helps me offer up that same trust now. I ask him about them, trying not to pry too much, and I soon realise that Crowey has a deft way of framing their frailties as lessons.

In her documentary about the 2000 Olympics, Cathy tells how she segmented her stunning gold medal race. She worked with an acronym – FLAG – that helped her break up that famous 400-metre dash into four 100-metre sections. F stood for 'Fly out of the blocks'. L was for 'Leg speed in the back straight'. A for 'Attack the bend', and G for 'Go girl, go'. Crowey tells me how she developed an entire framework for success that night, including a mantra, which she repeated over and over again as she walked onto the track and up to the starting line: 'Do what you know. Do what you know. Do what you know.'

This is called a 'courage mantra', Crowey tells me, and he explains that you can develop your own by asking yourself three personal questions.

The first is: 'How do I show up when I'm nervous?' Do I go to silence or violence? Fight, flight or freeze? Do my cheeks go red? Do I hope no one asks me a question? Do I name-drop? Do I argue?

All I can think in this moment is, *Do I swear at the ones I love?* and *Do I push them away on the No. 3 Court at the All England Lawn Tennis and Croquet Club?*

The second question is: 'When does it happen?' Is it when I feel judged? Is it when people are staring at me? Is it when I feel like I'm losing control of a situation, or a match?

Again, all I can think of are those moments within games when nothing will break the way I want – when Caro is relentless with her pressure, or Kasatkina is putting me in uncomfortable corners of the court.

Finally, Crowey says, I need to ask: 'What can I say to myself in real time, the next time it happens?' What can I *think* that reminds me of strength, and not weakness? What can I *say* to myself to make me go tall and not small? What is the offering I can hold up high that the bad wolf will ignore and the good wolf will eat?

This is the essence of the courage mantra – the words that will make you a warrior and not a worrier. The Richmond Football Club's superstar midfielder Dustin Martin repeats three words to himself in those moments when he experiences even a trace of doubt: 'Strong. Aggressive. Unstoppable.' World champion surfer Steph Gilmore says to herself, 'I love this challenge' and 'Breathe in the energy around me'.

Crowey explains to me that in embracing these kinds of maxims – from 'I'm imperfect but I'm worthy' to 'I'm enough' – you can find a way to overcome doubts and distractions, and to do so again later. It becomes a form of pattern recognition – an understanding and a reminder that there is a way through everything, including whatever confronts you now. He tells me all this – about his life and his work, about who he is and what he does – and then he smiles that same smile, and holds my gaze once more.

Now Crowey pushes a box of tissues towards me on the coffee table between us, rests back in his chair and gestures to me. 'Ash,' he says, 'what's your story?'

For the first time in my life, I tell someone my tale. I walk through it all, from the time I first picked up a racquet, to packing my things away at Wimbledon less than a fortnight ago. I cry throughout. Truthfully, I weep. I *talk* and I weep. I *weep* and I talk. For four hours. Through pivotal moments and crucial relationships and a second box of tissues. I say it all out loud, and Crowey listens. It feels like an out-of-body experience, as though I'm watching myself behind my eyes, and hearing each word as it spills faintly from my mouth. It is incredibly powerful, and absolutely terrifying.

When I finish speaking, Crowey thanks me. I feel heard, understood by this man, and I feel also as though I understand myself better too. I sip water and sigh now, and breathe deeply, emotionally exhausted.

Crowey explains that what I'm experiencing is common in elite athletes. 'Athletes have a bad habit of coming to understand their life story only through their career,' he says, 'mistaking the games we play for the people we are.' He tells me I need to forgive and change and reframe. Now that I've told my full story, he says, I need to find my *true* story. When I go to bed that night, I sleep the sleep of the dead.

The next morning the world seems new, but it's disorienting too. I meet Crowey for breakfast on the affluent Toorak Road strip. I'm still spent, but we have work to do. He has important questions for me to answer – 'Who am I? What do I want? What are my values?' – but I'm stuck for a response.

He probes and prods, approaching me from all angles, giving me every chance to find my voice. 'What are your dreams, Ash? What are your needs? What motivates you?'

I look away and strain for something to say. I hold on to a half-thought but it slips away. I stare back at him, flustered and apologetic. I've got nothing. Later that day I fly home to Brisbane.

My manager, Nikki Mathias, calls Crowey, excited and nervous, wondering how our meetings were. He tells her the truth. 'It went incredibly well but … something is still missing.'

Confirmation, maybe? Enthusiasm? Acceptance? 'I don't know where she wants to go from here,' Crowey says. 'I don't know if she's ready. Does she actually want to do this?'

A few days later, he gets in touch with me directly. He's summarised our sessions. He's looked at my issues and framed everything from a high-performance perspective. He tells me exactly what happened on those grass courts in England.

I hadn't simply stumbled on a crack in my game, he explains, but rather I was cracking up. And for it to happen in such a pronounced way – for me to turn into a monster, to feel uncontrollable anger, to lose the plot, knowing I was hurting someone and yet not caring – was not unexpected either.

It's about self-worth, Crowey tells me. If we don't reconcile our self-worth, we tell a story of shame. We develop imposter syndrome. Or we put up ego defences. We deny – 'I'm not really losing this' – or we rationalise – 'I'm not getting the advice I need from my team'. And once those excuses don't work, we melt down. We criticise and judge, bully and blame. We transfer that pain out of our body onto something or someone else.

When that doesn't work, we might turn to addictive behaviours – alcohol, sex, drugs, exercise, shopping, social media. It's not the behaviour we're addicted to but the feeling it gives us, or the lack of feeling – that delicious numbness. And it never works, he says.

Rock bottom? Yep, that was me.

Crowey has talked with Tyzz, too, because my coach needs to understand what happened out there. He needs to know why I began tearing into my closest supporters.

'You understand what Ash was doing?' Crowey told him. 'She was striking out at the ones she loves, because you were the nearest and dearest thing. Think of it like being out in the ocean, and Ash is drowning. Who is she going to reach out to? Is she going to reach out quietly?'

I begin to feel something shift now, and not just because someone has helped me have an epiphany, but because Tyzz and Crowey have spoken. It feels as though we're forming a team, and reaching a common understanding. As they say, a problem shared is a problem halved, and then it's a problem quartered or cut into smaller pieces again. It's as though I am finally recognising that I have this group of people who can help me walk this road, and who will do so not just because they love me but because they enjoy the view – because they want to go where I'm going.

After Crowey presents his findings to me, he asks me a question: 'Do you want to continue working?'

I grin as I speak into the phone: 'Absolutely.'

It's about self-worth.

My Mr Miyagi

Jim Joyce talks fast. Really fast. He's irrepressible, actually. And funny. And direct. And he never shuts up. Even with kids. I met him for the first time when I was four, almost five.

My sisters had played netball but I didn't want that. I thought it was a girls' sport. I saw a hockey field on the way to their match one day and showed an interest in that – I liked the idea of hitting people with a stick – but there was no way Mum would get on board. Not many girls played cricket in those days, but I knew there had to be a bat-and-ball sport for me.

Mum had always watched tennis and loved it, but she'd never played. Dad had shown interest in watching it like many Aussies do, when the Australian Open rolled around each summer. They had heard from a family friend about this bloke called Jim Joyce, a tennis coach. He was apparently a good man, running a sound local business. And so Dad drove me one morning down to the West Brisbane Tennis Centre.

The name makes it sound like a gleaming modern training facility – perhaps an air-conditioned space over plexicushion hard courts, and a concrete-and-glass structure with a cafe and gym and locker rooms. But it's not that. It's so much better than that.

The West Brisbane Tennis Centre sits in the suburb of Richlands, not even ten minutes drive from where I grew up. It's a plot of green suburban land, and on the front corner rests an old homestead, built before Federation. That's where Jim grew up. The first tennis court there was made by his dad in the 1950s – an old ant bed court made of decomposed granite, built for family and friends. His father had people over every weekend for tennis parties, meaning young Jim would have to water and roll and mark the unpredictable surface.

Jim's brother, John, became a top-level player, and so they built more courts in the 1970s. Jim was good too, but he reached that point some tennis players do where he didn't love the training anymore, and so he became a coach instead. Soon they had new concrete courts with synthetic grass on top. Tennis in the 1980s was booming. You couldn't get a booking at his club.

The area was different then too, and not at all affluent. It was once all poultry farms and vineyards, not grapes for wine but for eating. Italians and Greeks had settled the housing plots between the big semi-rural blocks there, and then the area became slowly zoned for industrial use. The drive from my house took us past freight terminals and auto parts manufacturers. Even when I first saw the courts, around the turn of the millennium, they had cow paddocks on one side and a drive-in theatre on the other, with factories popping up in the distance beyond.

The space itself was magic to me. You drove in along a sandy gravel track, past manicured little garden beds and under massive century-old poincianas, planted by Jim's mother.

Jim used to knock back kids who wanted to take lessons, and that's what he flatly told Dad when we arrived: 'I don't take them that young.' He believed young children should develop themselves by playing all sports, and be coordinated enough to throw, catch, kick, jump and swing before deciding to do one thing to the exclusion of all others.

Interestingly, there's a book called *Range* in which the author, David Epstein, backs up this idea with science and anecdote. Tiger Woods and Roger Federer are the extreme examples: Tiger focused on nothing but golf his entire life, from his earliest years, while Roger didn't settle on tennis until he was older. Both methods can produce a champion, clearly, but which one is healthier for the individual? Jim felt he knew the answer.

'But I'll take a look at her,' he told Dad, 'and tell you what you can do to practise at home until she's ready in a few years.'

I've always been small, but I must have seemed beyond tiny to Jim that day, standing there with my racquet in hand. I remember its weight and shape even now. Slazenger, 23 inches, green and black. With one string that was broken, repaired and replaced with a single rainbow-coloured thread.

I stood on the service line of Court 4 and Jim tossed me a ball. I sent it whizzing back past his ear. That story grew into legend later, thick with mayo. The light toss from Jim became a vicious half-volley. The soft whack from me turned into a screaming missile that slammed against the chain-link fence behind the court. It was neither, but I definitely middled it.

The next ball Jim picked up was split, so he tossed it to one side of the court as rubbish – but I dashed after it and smacked it too. There was something about that combination that grabbed Jim. It was the hand–eye coordination of the hit, yes, but also the desperation of the chase. He looked at me and said, 'You can come back next week.'

Soon tennis was all I could think about. Between our front and back yards at home was an open carport, under which we loved to play. Young athletes make do with what they have around them, don't they? Don Bradman used a stump to practise hitting a golf ball against a tank stand. Lance Franklin pretended the karri tree branches were goal posts. For me, it was a bit of masking tape Dad stuck up on the garage wall at the height of a tennis net. I was little, but I hit it against that wall and over that masking tape net relentlessly. I served and volleyed. I played points against myself. I had to be forced to come inside. Mostly it didn't bother anyone – except Ali, who would be sitting at the kitchen table doing her homework, hearing that soft *donk, donk, donk*. The neighbours probably didn't love the early-morning starts either.

I was dedicated, or at least determined, not that I knew what those words meant. I just enjoyed hitting that yellow ball. I liked tracking it in the air, and bringing my racquet around my body to meet it. I liked that I could imagine where it should go and then make it go there, as if I were controlling something elemental. I became addicted to the creativity. There was magic in that, somehow.

I went back to the West Brisbane Tennis Centre a week later, on the Saturday morning after my fifth birthday. Mum made cupcakes to share. And then the lessons began. There were different age groups and different ability levels. The little ones in the morning, before the heat of the day became too oppressive. Five courts in total, with about eight kids on any given court. I loved the sound and energy – the pop of a few dozen balls hit in staccato waves, and the peals of laughter from everyone there. Immediately I understood the age group hierarchy, and wanted to climb each rung. *Gotta get to the next group*, I thought. *Gotta get to the next group.*

Jim picked up on that too, and I progressed through lessons with kids aged six and seven and eight, and soon enough with kids aged nine and ten and 11. He says it was in my eyes – they never left him. He would walk and talk and opine and explain, and my eyes tracked him like the pupils in a portrait on the wall. I think I was just being respectful, listening intently to an adult, a teacher. But he noticed too when we gathered up balls at the end of the session and I balanced half-a-dozen on my racquet, like lemons on a plate. I thought I was just doing what he showed me. He thought of it as a unique kind of focus.

There were the fundamentals, of course. Forty minutes of forehands, backhands, slices, volleys, and then – always – 20 minutes of serving at targets. You'd put all the balls in a basket, and serve every one – maybe 70 or 80 balls. Repetition is everything.

Jim found ways to challenge me, though, even if I didn't know I was being challenged. He would try to get me to hit a kick serve when I was nine years old, for instance, even though no nine-year-old is strong enough to hit one. In a kick serve, the racquet face comes from the back over the top of the ball, striking it between eight o'clock and two o'clock, giving it topspin. That spin is what gives it a kick – when the ball bounces, the rotations fling it up and forward, which is why it's also called a 'hopper'. But it's an unnatural motion, requiring serious racquet-head speed.

I found a way to mimic the right technique, but I didn't have the strength to make it hop. When I thought at last I could hit one, Jim would stand about a metre and a half in front of me, facing me, and tell me to serve it over his head. Talk about trust! I was much shorter than Jim, so I had to propel the ball up before it even came down. One day I finally hit one sweetly. 'That kicked!' I said.

Jim just looked at me with a smile. 'But did it? Really?'

He began teaching me the slice backhand too. In many ways, it became the shot that would separate me from other professional women. My point of difference, my trick – although there's no real trick in the technique. It's nothing more than the extension of a standard backhand volley, hit with enough angle and speed to generate a fade, and – importantly – producing an unpredictable low bounce. The trick is learning to use it in different ways. Your aim is to be precise in your placement, as then you can force your opponent to panic and make poor decisions.

Jim taught me the shot in stages, bit by bit. I remember him standing behind me, holding my arm and showing me the flight path of the racquet. 'This is what it feels like,' he said. 'Now we're going to do it with a volley.' Then we would do it with a bounce. Then we would repeat. Bounce, hit, bounce, hit, bounce, hit. Then he would instruct the boys I was playing against at the time to only hit slow, loopy balls to me, which forced me to figure out a way to generate enough pace to make the slice move. The slice quickly became my favourite shot. I was completely obsessed with trying to master the stroke.

In one match, I struggled with my smash. I told Jim I had the yips. He told me to show him, and I hit one sweetly. Bang. He made a few adjustments, but never so many as to overwhelm me. 'Just tilt your shoulder, and adjust your frame,' he said. 'Good, you can smash.'

Later, he told everyone who I played against: 'When she comes to the net, make Ash smash.' And he told me: 'When you see it up there, you smash it, until that becomes what you do.' I remember so many of these 'Mr Miyagi moments'.

Jim's techniques were a little different, but always effective. I would use the same racquet for months and months, for instance, until it was about to break a string. And then, right before a tournament, he would give me a different racquet to use. He knew I wouldn't be comfortable with it – that it wouldn't respond to me in the same way – and that meant I'd have to figure out a new way to hit the shots I wanted. And quickly.

He would question me too, knowing that the answers would stick better if I figured them out for myself. The first time I played on clay, Jim didn't warn me what to expect, and when I came off the court he didn't explain why the game had unfolded differently from what I'd experienced on other surfaces. He just asked me a question: 'What did you feel?' I knew the answer immediately: the flat ball doesn't work as well, spin is your friend and the slice is even more receptive. He just had a gentle way of encouraging curiosity.

We would do lessons where I wasn't practising any fundamentals at all – when Jim was just putting the ball in difficult
places. I thought we were having fun, breaking up the grind,
but really he was teaching me how to hit a high backhand volley or a low defensive lob. He knew how to bait me and test me
as well as nurse me and praise me. He demanded better of me,
but even more he made me demand better of myself. He built
me up from scratch, and quickly became a father figure.

In so many little ways, Jim was teaching me to play and think
differently from everyone else. I came in one day and started
making noises when I hit. Just a little grunt or a groan. He asked
me if I was sick, and I said no. We went back to hitting and I
kept on grunting, so he asked me what I was doing. Sheepishly,
I told him I had heard it would give me more power.

'Asho, that's absolute rubbish,' he replied. 'You do *not* need
to grunt, right? You haven't before. You're not doing any better
with it. You're concentrating on grunting instead of hitting. If
you grunt again, I'm walking off this court.'

One day I went to practice and was holding the racquet
differently. Jim tilted his head askance. 'Who are we today?' he
asked. Wimbledon was on at the time and I'd been watching
Andre Agassi, and I'd decided I should emulate his game and
even his grip. Jim just sighed, and spent 15 minutes undoing
every lesson I'd learned from the TV. But he did it with the
same good-natured effect: 'You're not doing that anymore.'

He made tennis fun, too. And I don't mean funny. Or jokey.
Or even easy. Jim wanted me to play the game for its own
pleasure, to find love in the marriage of movement and timing
and speed and strength and guile and nerve. Jim always said he
had a 95 per cent return rate for kids who came to take a lesson,

because while tennis was serious to him, it was also – always, completely and unmistakably – a game.

Jim also found ways to keep me grounded. I played my first competition when I was six going on seven. I was so excited. I'd been practising for almost two years. I was going to win – I was certain of it. Jim made me lose. I was beating kids my age and older too easily in practice, and he didn't want that. There are few lessons to be learned from an easy win, except maybe arrogance. He wanted to pit me against people who would make me work, who would force me to be better, and humble me too. He found an older girl with the weapons to play me clean off the court.

This philosophy extended to everything I did. Occasionally Jim came along to tournaments, but not exactly to revel in them. I remember climbing out of my age group, competing when I was 11 against a 14-year-old girl. Jim went to her mother – a competitive parent – and told her how to beat me. 'Play to her low forehand,' he told them. 'Hit a short slice.' These were shots that would bring me unstuck – which meant they were also elements of my game he wanted me to work on. He knew I would pay more attention to my deficiencies if they led to losses. I won anyway.

And even when I was successful, there were lessons to be learned. One time I won a tournament on the road and got a tall golden trophy, two feet high. I took it into the tennis club to show Jim. I must have been beaming. He held it up, turned it around in his hand, studying it and nodding. Then he walked over to the bin, at the corner of the outdoor court, and dumped it inside. 'That's what that trophy will mean to you down the track,' he said. 'You've got so much further to go.' He smiled then and took it out of the bin again, but the point was made. And at a good time, too.

I began winning quickly, and he kept holding me back – not from chasing my potential but from chasing rankings and points. I still won trophies – so many trophies – and he had the idea that we should donate them to less fortunate tennis clubs, which could recycle them with new name plates. There were many competitions open to those willing to travel, but Jim could see that wasn't what I needed. I needed opponents who would challenge me.

When I was 13, he began lining me up against adult men. It wasn't just to pit me against better players but to force me to find new ways to beat opponents who were stronger and faster than me, and to see if my technique and shot selection and composure could prevail. I felt bad for those guys sometimes, as if I was embarrassing them, somehow upsetting Jim's customers. He had to tell me it was okay to win.

After some matches I cried to him, too. I was playing at St Lucia once when I was 12, in a tournament held at the University of Queensland. Jim had done his usual dirty trick – telling my opponents how to beat me – and one of them did. The tears fell this time and I was inconsolable. 'I couldn't do it!' I wept to him. 'I couldn't figure her out!'

'It's alright, mate,' he said, giving my shoulder a squeeze. 'You have to learn how to lose.'

There was one girl in particular, Lyann Hoang, who was my best mate and greatest competition. For years we were the best two junior players in Queensland. We both trained with Jim, but she was always the clear number one. Hoangy was a head taller than me and much stronger. I was forever chasing her, endlessly losing to her power. Jim loved seeing me challenged this way – until I cried again, and then he would just tell me to keep trying. 'Keep going,' he said. 'One day you'll catch her.'

Finally I did, and I turned to him with a look that was equal parts delirium and deliverance.

Jim was as deadpan as ever. 'Yeah, Asho, but it's just one match. Let's practise again tomorrow.'

I can see why he did it. The ego is a hard thing to keep in check.

We played matches at the tennis centre all the time, testing ourselves against one another. We called this 'fixtures'. One night I found myself dominating against everyone, no matter how much older, no matter girl or boy.

Jim came walking over, and I was expecting a cool whistle, or even praise, but he just shook his head. 'Your attitude was shit. You can't play like that,' he said, not even looking me in the eye. 'You have to be able to respect every opponent. You can't walk or talk like you're better.'

But such messages take time to sink in. I was playing a match one night after school on the top court, the old one by Jim's family home, and facing off against a boy who was older than me, but who I knew I could beat. We were playing first to four games, and it was two all. I was grumpy about this because I thought I should be in front. I was maybe ten years old, but was trying to make it understood that I was the alpha here, and that this guy should be flattered to have stayed with me this far.

In anger I bounced my racquet, whipping it down onto the concrete surface – and then I heard Jim roar: 'Stop!'

He walked onto the court and pulled me out of there, and instantly I knew I'd screwed up. 'You can't tell Mum and Dad,' I begged. 'They'll yank me out of here by my ear!'

'I know, mate,' he replied. 'But why are you so angry?'

'I should be beating this kid.'

'You never *should* beat anyone. You're not *entitled* to win. You've gotta do it. And that's all.'

'Yeah, but …'

'No. You can't just walk on the court thinking you're gonna wipe the floor with someone. Not with *anyone*. You have to be a better person than that.'

It's easy to see how Jim became part of the family. Mum and Dad trusted him implicitly. It helped, I suppose, that they knew nothing about tennis, so they were forced to entrust my lessons to someone with the right skills. But I think they'd judged Jim's character, too, and they knew he was a good temperamental match for me. That much was clear only a few weeks later, when Dad offered his own version of the lesson, after hearing about my little outburst.

'That's your racquet,' Dad said. 'Just to be clear: if you break it, you're not getting another one.'

'But what am I going to play with?'

'Nothing. You're just not gonna play.'

I didn't need to be told off again. I knew I'd crossed a line. I'm as stubborn and competitive as Dad, but I also want to be the conciliatory good girl like Mum, too. I didn't want to get in trouble. I just wanted to keep playing, and to keep going back to the West Brisbane Tennis Centre, because I loved it there.

Nothing could keep me away. A tropical thunderstorm might whip through the region, drenching everything and ripping down palm fronds, but Dad would drive me to Jim's anyway, past all those engineering warehouses and building supply distributors, and we would roll in over that gravel driveway and past the grassy lawns and the little wooden shack and under the tall jacarandas, and I would leap out of the car and head straight onto the court with Jim. We couldn't run because it was too slippery, but I could still hit volleys and practise my serves, and he could still feed me balls to hone my drop shots and smashes. Most important of all, he could still teach me lessons, whether I won or lost.

Toothaches and Toilet Breaks

I'm a sponge now. My mind craves the messages Crowey delivers, even if it's not easy to adjust to a new way of thinking. He warns me about this in the first text message he sends me, telling me it will be messy and confusing as I reframe my mind – I will need to build it up like a muscle. *Don't be in a rush,* he writes, *and have compassion for yourself. Remember: 'I am Imperfect and Worthy'*.

This is how I feel now, in my first match after last month's Wimbledon meltdown. I play a tournament in Montreal in early

August 2018 – the Rogers Cup – and first up I'm facing Irina-Camelia Begu. The Romanian is five years older than me, and fiery, and not in a pleasant mood. It's been raining all morning and we've both had barely ten minutes to warm up. Late in the third set I'm down a break, and we fight over one long point. I scrap and chase and cover every inch of the playing space, and finish with a cross-court forehand pass on the run, and I know in this moment – I'm quite certain, in fact – that I will win.

This little victory – on a hidden court, in an inconsequential match, during a second-tier tournament – means nothing but stands for everything. I play Alison Van Uytvanck next. I beat her 7-6, 6-2. I was sharp. Then I play Alizé Cornet – a French woman not to be underestimated, who once beat Serena Williams three times in the same year – but I knock her over 7-6, 6-4. After that it's Dutch top ten player Kiki Bertens. She's just come off a quarter-finals appearance at Wimbledon, but I roll her easily: 6-3, 6-1.

In the semi-final, I think I'll be up against reigning French Open champion Simona Halep – I've just watched her beat Caroline Garcia in the first set – and I message Crowey, anxious and looking for reassurance.

'Already I'm thinking about trying to figure out a way to try and compete with a world #1,' I type into WhatsApp. 'And she hasn't even won the match yet …'

'Is it strategic thinking or stressful (distracted) thinking?' Crowey asks.

'Stressful. Because already I feel like it's a different level. And I don't know if I can even compete with her.'

'This is a great test for you,' he replies. 'This is where acceptance and letting go come into play again. You have no control over Halep, so focusing on something you have no control over is stressful. This happens when we let our ego mind switch our attention to B factors (opposition, results, rankings, etc.). Fuck that. Fuck the result. And Halep. Don't give her any more kudos than she deserves. Respect her, yes. But then let it go. Her ranking is irrelevant. So is yours. Remember – no expectations, other than your words (calm, clear, present, sharp, etc.). That way you've got nothing to lose and everything to gain. You lighten up and just play – and the rest will take care of itself. You are a bloody good person, Ash Barty. And a bloody good tennis player. And you are worthy!'

I lose to Halep in the semi-final but I learn. Immediately I want to play her again. I don't want to hide away, or sulk or fret. I play her again in Cincinnati a week or so later – after wins over young Czech left-hander Markéta Vondroušová and Estonian veteran Kaia Kanepi – and she beats me again. But coming off the court, all I want to do is work. I'm not seeing the defeats anymore – only the challenge. Something inside me is changing. The opportunity for growth. Those bromides you read on motivational posters – about enjoying the journey and not the destination – are worth paying attention to sometimes. I feel my sense of perspective expanding and my self-talk changing. I'm getting better at considering process, not product.

We go to Flushing Meadows soon after. Every tournament, to some degree, takes on the personality of its home city, and nowhere is this truer than in New York. The event becomes a microcosm of the sprawling metropolis. The fans – like the city's residents – make their feelings known. Inside Arthur Ashe Stadium they sometimes seem as loud as the 747s taking off from nearby LaGuardia Airport. There's a frenetic pace here, and a kind of stink, too, as the smells of car exhaust and industry mix with the aroma of Momofuku fried chicken and Pat LaFrieda steak sandwiches. The fans sit for hours in the heat, craning their necks and perspiring, cooled only by icy $20 Honey Deuce highball cocktails. It's sweaty and noisy and glorious – or at least that's what it looks like to me. I only get to see all that from court level, and never for too long.

I haven't been past the third round here, but with wins over Ons Jabeur, Lucie Šafářová and Karolína Muchová, I go into what is probably the biggest match of my Grand Slam career so far, against Karolína Plíšková. Typically, our matches are separated by small margins – she's always been a good test for me. Today, it's an anticlimax. I lose 6-4, 6-4 but walk off the court at Louis Armstrong Stadium disappointed but thinking clearly, dissecting the play, focusing on what I did well as well as what I did poorly – how I missed my margins by metres early on, but fought back and stayed with her. *Yep, I lost that tennis match*, I think to myself, *and it's okay*. I move on quickly.

What I'm learning and practising and experiencing for the first time is acceptance. It shines through in all the quotes Crowey and I share with one another. Some of the lines are modern, like that of American soccer icon Mia Hamm: 'Somewhere behind the athlete you've become and the hours you've practised and the coaches who have pushed you … is the little girl who fell in love with the game and never looked back. Play for her.' Others are historical, like that of former US First Lady Eleanor Roosevelt: 'The future belongs to those who believe in the beauty of their dreams.'

The thread running through them all is that everyone is human, and imperfect, and that's okay. It's *better* than okay, actually, because it means we're all unique, all fallible and all with our own foibles. We're all just finding our way in this world together. I'm going to miss a bunch of forehands. I'm going to shank a few backhands. When I most need to win, I'm sometimes going to lose. That's me and that's life.

My favourite quote is almost a cliché. It's known as 'The Man in the Arena'. US President Theodore Roosevelt delivered it within his 'Citizenship in a Republic' speech in Paris in 1910. It's about coming into contact with life's many and messy realities.

> *It is not the critic who counts; not the man who points out how the strong man stumbles, or where the doer of deeds could have done them better. The credit belongs to the man who is actually in the arena, whose face is marred by dust and sweat and blood; who strives valiantly; who errs, who comes short again and again, because there is no effort without error and shortcoming; but who does actually strive to do the deeds; who knows great enthusiasms, the great devotions; who spends himself in a worthy cause; who at the best knows in the end the triumph of high achievement, and who at the worst, if he fails, at least fails while daring greatly, so that his place shall never be with those cold and timid souls who neither know victory nor defeat.*

Here's the thing. That speech is so popular with athletes, and I think that's mostly because they see themselves as protagonists – the doers of deeds – and they see the critics as the writers or commentators or the many multiplying voices on social media. Athletes enjoy the Roosevelt quote so much because the passage speaks to their unique isolation: they are in a battle against everything and everyone that no normal person could understand.

But I like it for another reason. I like it because the hero has moments of failure. Look deep into the words. The strong man stumbles. He errs. He comes short again and again. Despite shortcomings, he strives. He knows triumph and failure. He knows great devotion. And that's me, in my life and my career. It is what it is. I am who I am. Whatever happens, the universe is working for me, not against me. The 'Man in the Arena' quote reminds me that I can put my hopes and dreams into the world and just see what happens.

And what happens is victory, finally, in Zhuhai in November 2018. I find myself in the final there against local favourite Wang Qiang, and win the biggest tournament of my career so far – the WTA Elite Trophy. I take out the match in straight sets, and walk off court happy with the way I played, knowing that the win or loss doesn't at all change who I am.

I'm getting ready to do my press conference when Tyzz confirms this, slamming a beer down in front of me and grinning like a loon: 'You're going to finish the year as the number 15 player in the world.'

*

I did not imagine ringing in the New Year or the new season from a hospital bed, but here I am at Royal Perth Hospital on the afternoon of 31 December 2018. It's my wisdom teeth. I had all four removed in late November, in an attempt to eliminate problems further down the track, especially if we were in a foreign country. It turned into more of an issue.

Antibiotics settled down the initial infection, but the irritation had worsened. I've been playing in the Hopman Cup, which I should probably have skipped, and perhaps the bacteria have taken advantage of my tiredness. I'm at a women's cricket match with my boyfriend, Garry Kissick, when the pain settles in and sends me to the emergency room.

I've never had a needle in my mouth before, and I'm shit-scared. I demand that the dentist apply some numbing gel before giving me a local anaesthetic injection. Children's numbing gel. My physiotherapist is with me and is laughing loudly at my cowardice. She knows I'm a wimp.

I go to the tournament's gala ball that night with my mouth restitched and swollen. I try to eat but my lips are still numb. I give an interview on the red carpet and have to concentrate hard to avoid stumbling over my words. I pretend I'm back on tour in Europe, where I always try to take extra care when speaking, enunciating clearly and playing up my accent. 'It's so greaaat to be here. Everyone has been awwwwesome.'

This is not the ideal preparation for an assault on the Australian summer of tennis, but I roll with the moment. Sydney is where I try to find my form. The conditions are close to what the Australian Open is like: sweltering and windy, the warm air having travelled over the dusty interior of the country before landing on this city like a floating furnace. Everyone says a dry heat is better than humidity, but playing inside the Ken Rosewall Arena is like playing inside a fan-forced oven. It's gusting and swirling, and a number of players wilt and fold as the mercury rises.

I do what I always do when the temperature soars and the breeze kicks up – I think of Jim Joyce. I remember what he said to me when I was discovering new conditions like these. At the time, he seemed excited for me. 'You'll love playing in the wind, mate,' he said. 'You can adjust at the last minute, you can use your slice, use your mind and use the wind to your advantage. You have to let it be your friend and not fight it. You'll love this stuff.'

I scoot around through the hot draughts and baking eddies and warm whirlies, and beat the number 5 player in the world, Jeļena Ostapenko, which gives me another shot at Simona Halep. Simo is returning from a back injury, but beating her still gives me a jolt of confidence, and then I get more by knocking over Elise Mertens and then Kiki Bertens. I'm in the final but can't get past Petra Kvitová. I do nothing wrong. We go to three sets, and she plays more aggressive tennis in the deciding tie-break. Sometimes you just have to tip your hat and move on – which in this case means moving on to Melbourne Park and the Australian Open.

We have a problem, however. Tyzz is ill. He was as white as the baseline during the tournament, and before the final went into hospital in Sydney where he was diagnosed with pneumonia. He wants to get to Melbourne, though, so he discharges himself and gets on our flight, pale and sweating.

We share a jet with Petra and her team, and she is immediately shocked. 'Oh my God,' she says. 'This guy should be in hospital.'

Tyzz rests for the first week while I play, and we joke that this is because he has become a 'big-time coach' who doesn't get out of bed for anything less than the second week of a Grand Slam. He is gaunt, having lost seven kilograms, but assures me he is fine. 'Don't worry about me,' he says. 'You've got a tournament to play.'

Do I ever. It always feels as though the entire country is waiting to see what unfolds at the Australian Open. It's a stunning summer spectacle, but there's a psychology that needs to be navigated. The hope of the nation can become a burden, a weight of expectation – or you can let it lift you up, with the lightness of anticipation.

There's no point pretending the Australian Open is a tournament like any other, because it's not. It's hard to get practice courts, and impossible to get time alone. Your ever-expanding circle of friends and family, contacts and sponsors seems to swell from four to 40. Everyone has a question. Everyone sends a text. Everyone wants that interaction, that reply, that acknowledgement, and if you give a little piece to all of them – pausing for each conversation, stopping for every selfie, answering all those DMs – then soon you don't have anything left for yourself. The attention comes from a great place, but it can be tiring.

The turbulence we've experienced just getting here, however, means that this year my Australian Open experience feels bizarrely calm. I train. I play. I do media. I leave. That necessary schedule can turn into a vicious cycle, where you look at your watch and four hours has somehow elapsed and the next pressing itinerary item is upon you. But I feel none of that.

My first-round match against Thai trier Luksika Kumkhum is a settler. In the second round, I'm posed no problems by Chinese player Wang Yafan either. Maria Sakkari has a beautiful game – one that I know can burn me if I don't plan and execute well – so I adjust my string tension, anticipating that the play will be slower and heavier under a closed roof, and I dispatch her solidly in the third round. Momentum is building, and I'm about to face Maria Sharapova.

I've never felt excitement like this before. I'm almost not myself. Maria is a champion. A figure in the firmament. She's an aggressive, first-strike player and loves getting in your face. Back in 2012, in Brisbane, an injury robbed me of the opportunity to play her. I want this match-up – badly.

In the first set, I'm feeling like I have to play the best match of my career to win. I press too much, and lose my way. Maria is a great front-runner, one of the best in the game. In the second set I have to fight and adjust. I read her patterns better, sit on her serve and change the dynamic, and I win the second set. I offer a big fist-pump to my team: *I'm not going anywhere!* The noise and energy in Rod Laver Arena is extraordinary. I have never played in an atmosphere like this before. I am so ready.

Now Maria takes a bathroom break. I think I've taken all of two bathroom breaks in my life. I'd love to know how many players genuinely go to the toilet, and how many are simply using the break to arrest negative momentum and recover. I don't hate the gamesmanship – it's within the rules, after all – but often it's questionable. I go back to another Jim Joyce saying from my youth: 'If you're going to let something that trivial rattle you, then you're probably not in the right frame of mind to win anyway.'

Not everyone sees it that way. After the seventh minute, this break from Sharapova begins to feel tactical – and the crowd don't like it. I have to tell myself not to look over at my box, because if I make eye contact with Tyzz I'll laugh, and that laugh will be picked up on camera, and then people will think I'm smirking while the home crowd jeers. Finally, Maria walks back onto the court and I can't help but grin, and that syncs up with the booing of the crowd. But I don't care anymore. Fuck it.

When I want to stay in the moment on court, I often use a little breathing exercise: I briefly close my eyes, inhale and smile. But I have other ways. Right now I see the Spidercam zooming above me on its cables. Sometimes I try to hit it during warm-up, and now I chuck a ball at it for the same giggle. As Crowey likes to say, 'Lighten up or tighten up.'

I'm ahead in the third set now, 4-1, and feeling strong. In control. Close to the finish line. But it soon becomes 4-2. Then 4-3. It's 15-40 on my serve, threatening to go 4-4, in front of my crowd, in the heat on Rod Laver Arena. But against the imperious might of the towering Russian five-time Grand Slam champion, I play brilliant tennis. I lighten up and hit aces. She tightens up and hits double faults. I scream to my box – 'C'mon, mate!' – as the ascendancy becomes mine, and after two hours and 22 minutes I win. I'm through to the quarter-finals – the first Australian woman since Jelena Dokic ten years ago. I am 22 years old, and this is the most satisfying victory of my career so far.

There's no fairy tale for me in the next game, though, against Petra. On a cool evening, she coolly hits everything out of the middle, and I can't find myself. She crushes me. Simply put, Petra has my measure – but whenever you walk to the net after playing her, you instantly forget who's won and who's lost because there's always a smile.

I wave goodbye to the crowd and do my interviews. I have a beer and a pizza. I sleep and fly home to Brisbane. I unpack and reset. Every tournament ends this way – like some sort of fly-in, fly-out stealth mission – but the Australian Open is always such a whirlwind. You lose and leave, and love the experience anyway.

Besides, I'm not dwelling on the loss. I'm thinking about how our limited and interrupted preparation didn't unsettle me.

I'm thinking about toothaches and hot winds and pneumonia. I'm thinking about finally beating Simo. I'm thinking about knocking over Maria Sharapova in an epic, and I'm thinking about what Crowey said to me in the gym immediately afterwards: 'That's one of the strongest displays of performance mindset that I've seen.'

More than all that, I'm thinking of the play itself – the points I won when I needed to save the match, and the points I won when I needed to control the tempo – and about how I recognised something in myself before there was any win to celebrate or loss to mourn, when it was just me and a baking tennis court, with a ball in hand and an opponent across the net. It's what I love to do the most.

I'm a different player now, I think to myself. *I'm a different person.*

Don't be in a rush.

Schoolwork and Broken Hearts

When I was ten years old, a normal week for me might have looked a little abnormal to you. I would come home from school, drop my bag in the middle of the living room floor, ask Mum for some food, go get changed into shorts and a T-shirt, and ask for a lift to Jim's. And that wasn't just most nights, it was *every* night. Monday was fixtures, Tuesday was squad training, Wednesday was a private lesson, Thursday was more squad training and social tennis, Friday was more fixtures, Saturday morning I played idly, and Saturday afternoon was

Super League. Sunday I was supposed to have off, but I played anyway. Every single day was tennis.

The only person driving this obsession was me, although the person driving the car was usually Dad. I went on my first road trip with him when I was eight, to Rockhampton. It took eight hours to get there, but I won the state national title for girls aged ten and under. I won the ladies' trophy in Toowoomba when I was 11 – but I looked all of nine, and people there found it hard to believe. One time I won a tournament in the Brisbane suburb of Wynnum, and because I was as small as the ball kids and dressed in similar colours, it seemed as though some plucky youngster had been called up from the edges of the court to fill in for an absent player, and stumbled on to a win. I was so small, and so in love with these experiences.

We started going on long road trips to tournaments up and down the east coast – to Melbourne and Mildura, Bendigo and Bundaberg. We couldn't afford to fly, so we took Dad's latest Ford – either the silver Falcon or the purple Fiesta or the orange Mondeo – down the highway, finding cheap places to stay along the way, like the Lismore Caravan Park and the Gosford Inn Motel. I got to control the radio, and always put my three favourite songs on repeat. Dad indulged my taste, letting me play 'Hey Jude' by The Beatles, 'Evie' by Stevie Wright and 'Rock the Boat' by The Hues Corporation on an endless loop from home to Parramatta or Wollongong or Albury and back.

I was the tomboy in our family of daughters, the son Dad never had or never wanted, and I grew up in real time alongside him on the road. I didn't realise it, but I was learning independence in increments, picking up some new life hack with each stop, about how to clean and pack and take care of myself. I was also getting instructions from Mum on how I needed to look after Dad while we were on the road.

One time we flew to Perth and stayed in a little cabin. I couldn't recall the name of the sauce we used in our stir-fry at home, so I walked up and down the aisles at Woolworths and finally bought a jar of honey and a jar of sweet chilli sauce, which I stirred into our meat and veggies that night. Dad smiled as he ate the syrupy dish, and I called Mum from our tiny room, proud of the recipe I'd invented.

It was all an exciting adventure, this strange sporting life. I didn't have a lot of friends to miss, and that was partly due to my personality. I had great friends – I just didn't need a lot of them. I enjoyed being independent, even as a child. I've always been confident and happy doing what I want, even on my own. 'This is what I'm doing,' I would say to my mates at school. 'If you don't want to do it too, that's fine, but this is the way I'm going.' I didn't experience girl dramas, in part because my friends tended to be boys, or older kids, or adults. It's actually easier to be yourself, I've found, when you spend time with people already notably different from you – similarities sometimes lead to more clashes than differences.

I was also spending less time at school anyway. I used to love classwork, and found it easy. I was dux of Grade 8, and my parents expected me to immerse myself in my assignments. On Mum's side of the family, that was simply the rule: you go to school, and then to uni, and then into the workforce. My skipping a few weeks here and there never sat well with her.

Mum was wary of the risks of me aiming at a career in professional tennis. 'It's so hard – you don't know if you're going to make it,' she would say. 'You could make it and get injured. You could make it but only to the fringes, and then struggle. You need something to fall back on.' And yet she also understood that I would never make it as a tennis player – never really succeed – unless I put more into the sport than into my studies.

Once Mum and Dad were comfortable that we could balance my tennis and my education, Dad sat me down for a talk. I must have been 12 and we were in a car park in Gosford. It was 7 am, and I was eating Weet-Bix out of a plastic bowl. We were in the front seat of his car, ready for a day of matches, when he turned to me.

'Do you want to do this?' he asked.

'Do what?' I answered.

'Do you want to try to be a professional tennis player?'

'Yeah, why not? It's what I do.'

'Cool.'

'Cool.'

And that was that. By the time I was entering Grade 9, we had decided to try distance education. I would go to tennis in Brisbane, and my training days would be structured to fit my schoolwork in. I communicated with my teachers online and worked with the educator provided by Tennis Australia in our classroom at the academy. And I hated it. I passed easily but I didn't enjoy their version of school. Classes became an exercise in ticking boxes rather than exploring the world. My curiosity was sucked out of me and I lost any sense of investing in my own learning. I also began to see myself more as an athlete than as a child, and I wasn't ready for that.

Each year my parents and I revised our decisions about what I would learn and when. Would I just study core maths and

English? Would I try a TAFE course – maybe a Certificate IV in Strength and Conditioning? When we were travelling, I'd be sent assignments to complete, and although I was clever enough to do them, I was too time-poor to commit to them properly. I got a C+ in maths in Grade 9 and was devastated. It was the first C I'd ever got in my life, but I was 14 and teaching myself calculus from a textbook. In hindsight, I think a C was actually a good effort.

By the time I reached the senior years of high school, I was attending school maybe 25 days of the year and struggling to keep up. When I was in Year 11 and Ali was at university, I messaged her from a tournament in Kuching, Malaysia, looking for help with an assignment. She helped me in exchange for more than a few bottles of perfume. Ali always favoured Marc Jacobs Daisy Dream.

Sara did the same thing to save me in Year 12. Her typical thank-you price was a MIMCO handbag.

There is no way I would have passed without the help of my sisters. We still joke that my high school certificate should also have their names on it.

I didn't attend one day of school in my senior year. I didn't go to my graduation. Or to my formal. In fact, I often have to ask my mates which year we actually graduated.

Mum was somewhat placated when I found the time for a small-business course at TAFE, and because I read voraciously, at least a few books every week. And Dad was happy because he thought I was. I remember I sent him a text – *Yo Daddyo, we've made it* – when I entered the top 100 in the WTA rankings in March 2017, after I won my first WTA event. I had no idea how far I could go yet, but I knew it would only ever be as far as their support would let me reach. If I was sacrificing my education, they were sacrificing much more.

Back in 2011, Dad decided to keep a spreadsheet, itemising how much he and Mum were spending on my tennis. By the time I was 16 it was costing our family $65,000 a year. All of Mum's wage was being poured into travel and gear and tournaments. They would offset the crippling expense by taking in young tennis players visiting Brisbane, so that I could stay with other families when away on tour. Sponsors helped, too. HEAD came on board to give me racquets when I was only ten. Adidas took care of my apparel, and eventually FILA. But tennis is an expensive game. You can be among the top 100 players in the world and live from hand to mouth.

Our holidays were no longer languid affairs at Straddie. A family trip meant my sisters or Mum or Dad would come with me to wherever I was playing, having a 'tennis holiday' – although most of their days in these exotic locations were spent watching me playing or hanging around a tennis club. It wasn't much fun for them, and it started feeling that way to me, too.

Tennis Australia had asked if I wanted to be in their national squads when I was ten and 11 and 12. But Jim held me back until I was 13. Selection to join that stable of talent is something to be proud of, but it also means you have to do what Tennis Australia wants. If you want to pick and choose and play your own schedule – doing what you think is best for you – then you have to go it alone, without their funding or support. And that simply wasn't an option for us, so I had to do as I was told.

I went on my first overseas trip of any kind – to New Zealand – when I was only 13, playing matches in Auckland

and Wellington, and staying in hotels with older girls. We had a chaperone but I was used to being with Dad or Mum, the comforts of their sounds and smiles, and our little routines and rituals. I wanted to come home the moment I arrived in the land of the long white cloud.

Things were even worse later that year, when I was chosen to join a 'young stars' tour of Europe. The trip was to be seven weeks long, including five tournaments leading up to the world junior teams. I was younger than all the other kids, coming along as the backup player on the girls' team. Thanasi Kokkinakis was the backup player for the boys. Nick Kyrgios was the biggest name there.

We flew to Paris and I tried to be excited. One of the girls showed me how you could watch as many movies as you wanted on the plane, and suggested that I should watch *Taken*, starring Liam Neeson.

'What's it about?' I asked.

'These girls go to Paris,' she said, 'and they get kidnapped.'

'No. I'm not going to watch that movie'.

'Suit yourself.'

I curled up alone in the darkness, already sad and worried, and watched Disney shows to cheer myself up. Then we landed and I realised I hadn't packed well. I figured we were just going to play tennis, and I'd brought just one casual T-shirt, for instance. We did a training camp at Roland-Garros but I did not appreciate the significance of the stadium or its statues. Afterwards, I needed to wash the clay off my gear, but Mum warned me that the industrial washers and dryers at public laundromats might damage my clothes, so while the other kids got out and explored Paris, I sat in a laundromat carefully watching my clothes spin dry. I'm glad I listened to Mum, though, as Thanasi burnt a hole in his shorts, while Nick burnt a hole in his polo.

We took a bus to the Netherlands next and were billeted out with families. My hosts were the Van Poppelins. The girl I was going to be sharing a room with had to go home after a death in the family, and I didn't know anyone else. I was suddenly alone, staying in the top loft of this narrow Dutch home, too scared to venture downstairs and mingle with strangers.

The Van Poppelins were concerned, and called Mum. 'Ash goes to her room and won't come down,' they told her. 'She's so sad. What can we do?'

But there was nothing they could do. I was only a few months into my teenage years, by myself, growing up on the road. I called Sara one night when I had bad period pain, not knowing what to do. She told me to run a hot bath, put a towel in it, pull the plastic liner out of the bin and pop the hot towel inside – that would do as a heat pack. I ate my feelings and put on seven kilograms. I cried myself to sleep each night. And then each day I would play in the Windmill Cup, a tournament played on synthetic grass.

I won my first round, and in the second round drew the reigning junior European champion, and I beat her too. The other Aussies lost, and prepared to make their way to the next tournament.

'But,' I stammered to the organisers, 'you guys can't leave me here ...'

'It's okay,' they replied. 'You'll get a bus at the end of the tournament and join us at the next stop.'

'No, you can't leave me here!'

'We're sorry, but we have a schedule to keep.'

So I threw the next match, because I didn't want to stay on there alone. I lost 6-4, 6-4 – just close enough that it wouldn't look bad, and I could get on the bus with everyone else.

I was able to communicate with Mum and Dad over Skype – it was such a relief to hear their voices. They explained that they never would have sent me if they'd known it would be this way. Still, they couldn't afford to fly over to visit me, nor could they pay for an early flight home. I was stuck.

I still can't believe that was my first experience of the tennis tour. It sparked what became a fear of travel, and for the first time I suspected that tennis might not be all I imagined it would be.

When I think of that trip now, it just seems crazy. It's not something to which I would ever subject my child or niece or nephew. The thing I remember most clearly is standing on that court in the Netherlands, weeping every time I hit a winner and sighing with relief every time I hit the net or pushed the ball wide. My dreams of success were getting mixed up with a desire to fail – to get off the court, pack my bags and fly home, and never leave home again. That was when I knew I wasn't meant for this life.

Spit the Dummy

Being on the road isn't all bad – not with views like this. America has some stunning places to play tennis. Early in 2019 I'm in Asheville, North Carolina, playing a Fed Cup tie against the United States. With its leafy lamplit streets, Art Deco downtown, cafes inside brilliant bookshops and the purple haze above the ridgeline of the Great Smoky Mountains National Park, this is one of those little cities where you could imagine yourself living.

We win there, and I move on to the Indian Wells Masters, the tournament known as the 'fifth Grand Slam'. It's played on the other side of the country, a couple of hours southeast of Los Angeles in the Coachella Valley. Palm Springs is a strange mixture of desert cacti and terracotta-tiled haciendas – retirement villages for the rich and famous. I always feel as though this hardcourt tournament should suit me, but I've never quite mastered the conditions. To make it worse, I hurt my foot this time, badly.

A strain? Stress fractures? Turns out it's capsulitis – swelling near the metatarsals and tarsals. That just means the ball of the foot, but as an athlete you come to know all these terms intimately. You learn about the capricious frailties of the human body, and this entire baffling lexicon of physiology and movement. The diagnoses always sound professional, yet the remedies are often makeshift and improvised. This time, I get a kitchen knife and cut a chunk out of my tennis shoes, to relieve the pressure.

In the fourth round I find myself playing Elina Svitolina, knowing that if I win I'll be in the top ten players in the world. And I further find myself playing the way I want to play – the way Tyzz wants me to play – but not for long enough. Nothing about this match turns out right. I shouldn't lose the first set, but I do. I shouldn't win the second set, but I do. I shouldn't lose the third set, but I do. And then it's all over. It takes three hours and 12 minutes for us to finish the longest match of the WTA season so far, but ultimately I walk off Court 4 knowing I haven't been brave enough.

I haven't been assertive enough and I haven't fully committed, because I'm too scared. I need to be more bold and aggressive in coming forward. I can't let Elina – or anyone else – reset each point so easily. If you stand back, you give a great player a chance to equalise within any rally, and you're likely to do it again, and again, until it feels as though you have to win each point ten times over just to prevail. If you come *forward*, however, you put the onus on them. You make them pass you. You make them attack. You make them defend. You make them play.

It's such a small thing. Instead of standing a metre behind the baseline, it's standing *on* the baseline. From there, getting to the net is easier and quicker. From there, you feel more energy on the ball. From there, you have a better opportunity to be positive and aggressive. You can control the court.

It changes your body language, too, as well as your mindset. It's about standing on the precipice of something and not teetering on that edge but diving off it and down into the deep. To make turns safely and swiftly on the ski slope, you have to lean into them. To win a car race, you need to accelerate through the turns. To win a tennis match, you need to be aggressive with your intent every single time you step up to that line.

That's what Tyzz and I discuss afterwards, after I've had an ice bath to treat the bruises on my quads – from the racquet I've smashed into my skin in a stupid unnecessary rage. Tyzz talks to me in an outdoor dining area, the glow and crackle of flames in a cast-iron fire pit warming the cool air of the desert at night.

'Mate, it's not the tennis that's the issue,' he tells me. 'It's the way you're playing the tennis. Elina is not beating you – you're beating yourself.'

I know this, and I ask myself all the right questions. *When will you learn? When will you commit to your own decisions? When will you be brave enough to lose on your terms?* I'm not sure of the answer, but it's coming. I can feel it. I can sense that much.

I'm crisscrossing the continent now. I fly east once more,

4000 kilometres this time, heading to the Miami Open, hobbled but hopeful. I like it here too. I never have time to explore the hotels on South Beach or drink a cup of café cubano, but the heat and humidity remind me of home. The change of site from Key Biscayne to the Miami Dolphins stadium brings a fresh new court, a bright aqua and blue. When you get into the zone on a hot day, playing a tennis match can feel like swimming in soupy tropical waters, as you sprint and sweat and swot. It's challenging, and I like a challenge.

That's what I'm trying to embrace right now. I can't push off on my serve. If I chase down a point and slam on the brakes, it feels like a long needle is being inserted roughly into my foot. I test myself with my trainer, Mark Taylor, and he holds me back a little, worried I might end up in hospital on his watch. We've worked together for a couple of years now, and he gets a bit nervous about such things.

I call him 'Tubs' because that's the nickname of his namesake, the former Australian cricket captain. Tubs has no say in the matter, and he hates this. He's English, you see, so the idea of being referred to by the same silly moniker as a champion of the baggy green cap is somewhat infuriating. He prefers his old nickname – 'Beef' – which was given to him when he worked in British tennis, for the LTA. But he doesn't work there anymore. He began working for Tennis Australia in 2017, then he started travelling with me in 2018, so he'll just have to deal with my naming conventions. I let him dictate terms in other ways.

Tubs runs my strength sessions, from warm-up to activation, from squatting to hopping to bounding, from box jumps to Romanian deadlifts. He makes me do interval sprint work – 30 seconds flat out, 30 seconds rest – and increases my maximum speed enormously. He knows I don't like running, especially on the treadmill, and puts me on the watt bike instead, because I love riding with resistance. He talks constantly about training for injury prevention, but also power. Get strong, very strong. Tubs has been building up both in me for a while.

We met at the Queensland Tennis Centre, where the Brisbane International is held. He had only been in the country a few weeks. I learned his story and liked his story. He comes from Bury St Edmunds, a small town in Suffolk, and played many sports as a kid – tennis, soccer, rowing, rugby. He had the desire to turn professional in all of them but never quite got there. Sport was still his biggest passion and working in physical training was the next best thing, which meant stints in tennis and swimming. He moved down under when he was 31, with his girlfriend, Fiona, who is now his fiancée. The weather was a shock to the system, in a pleasing way. And the change of pace – after a decade in London – was just right too. He needed to be calmed down.

Tubs can be highly strung – notoriously so, in fact. I joke with him over this, actually. It was only a few months ago that I wandered down an aisle in Woolies and a pack of pink dummies caught my eye. I thought of how Tubs is so quick to anger – how he 'spits the dummy' over the slightest things – and I came up with a game. Well, maybe it's more a rule: if anyone in our group gets too worked up, and arks up, they have to wear the dummy, by attaching it to the lanyard holding their tournament accreditation. If you get aggressive? You wear the dummy. Crack the shits? Wear the dummy. It happens often, too.

Here's an example of how it works. We've just arrived here in Miami, and we're checking in to the Marriott. Tyzz's room isn't ready, and he's already tired and cranky, and he loses his temper at hotel reception. The rest of us have an impromptu vote: 'Dummy spit? Show of hands.' And it's settled.

Tyzz has actually melted down twice here in Florida, which is uncommon for him. The other time, we were meant to be heading back to the hotel after a day of play, and the girl handling ground transport told him he'd have to wait 45 minutes until the next shuttle bus. He lost it – and he got the dummy again. Overnight this time – it's a privilege.

But Tubs is different. He wears the pink dummy 90 per cent of the time, because he's so easily wound up. Sometimes he gets annoyed answering questions from strangers about the thing around his neck, and those little tantrums mean he has to wear it even longer. He suspects a conspiracy – because there is one. He might wander away from the steel travel coffee mug he takes everywhere with him, and we hide it. That's when Tubs grouches and grumbles. Hook, line and sinker – he gets the dummy.

We're in the gym one day doing advanced hamstring stretches – a high-level deceleration exercise – and I fake a torn hammy. After the session, I pretend I'm in excruciating pain all the way into the physio's room, and I bring them in on the joke too, asking for fake strapping and treatment. They're all in. Tubs is mortified that he's broken me in the middle of a season. ('You had one job, mate …') And then I come clean. He raises his voice and lets the expletives fly – and fair enough. But it's still a dummy spit. On reflection, I maybe went too far with this one, but it was still a bit of fun. Definitely worth it.

We work on our exercises together now in Miami, and I feel strong in his care. In my first match I destroy Dayana Yastremska, a Ukrainian teenager. I tape up my foot and feel no pain either against Sam Stosur. I don't enjoy beating her 6-0, 6-3, but at the net she shakes my hand, and shakes her head with a rueful grin – 'Mate, that was unbelievable' – and instantly makes me feel better. Kiki Bertens is next, and the match is physical and high quality – a genuine tug of war. One of the best we've played.

Tyzz has warned me that this is where my career is now headed: I'll be in more important matches against top ten players that are not going to be one-sided. 'They're always close,' he says, 'and very little determines the outcome.' I have to accept that Kiki will produce brilliant play, and Kiki has to accept my talents, too. I win 4-6, 6-3, 6-2, and find myself facing Petra again.

It's been raining all day, and our match becomes a tussle all night. I win through tactics and composure, and I look to Tyzz and point a finger at my temple: *I thought my way through this one. We're bloody tough.*

I meet Petra at the net, and she knows what the result means. 'Well done, Ash,' she tells me. 'There's no one more deserving of being in the top ten.'

It's the first time I've been in that group. I'm now ranked number 9. It's what I've always wanted.

I work my way calmly through aggressive Estonian baseliner Anett Kontaveit in the semi-final, and days later wake up ready for the final. I text Crowey: *It's a beautiful day.* And he replies: *What does that mean?* And it means nothing, other than that I feel calm and happy. Ready.

I'm playing Karolína Plíšková. The Czech is tall and rangy, and most would say better than me. She's a serve and first-strike specialist who only a year earlier was ranked number 1 in the world. She crushes the ball. Flat, hard, through the court. But I have a plan. I'm going to get on my bike, run all day and use the hot southern Florida sun against her. I'll be happy if I keep her out there all afternoon.

I win the first set in a tie-breaker, going ahead at 2-1 with a 14-stroke rally. Then I wear her down physically in the second set, making sure to deny her any easy points on serve. She breaks back only once.

I'm in complete control all day, and before I know it I'm holding a tall glass trophy and orange gold streamers are raining down upon me. I've won my fourth trophy, and the biggest of my career so far. It's what's known as a Premier Mandatory title – one of the top tour events. I sign autographs on photos and racquets and big novelty tennis balls. I talk to the media and then shower and rest, and finally I pose for photos in front of the fountains outside the Hard Rock Stadium.

I know I'm headed for Europe next, to the clay, but I'm not thinking about that right now. I write down goals at the start of every year. At least, I've started to do this recently. *What do I want to achieve this year?* Now I think back to my list.

I want to beat Simona. *Done.*

I want to beat Petra. *Done.*

I want to be top ten in the world. *Done.*

There's so much more to do.

I feel calm
and happy.
Ready.

Black Skin, Red Rocks

Growing up, I knew nothing of the Ngarigo people. Why would I? I was raised in suburban Brisbane, by white parents whose geographical ties were to north Queensland and pastoral England. What would I have in common with an Aboriginal nation from the south – an ancient High Country nation of people whose territory encompassed Jindabyne and Queanbeyan, Canberra and Kiandra, Thredbo and Mount Kosciuszko? Nothing, I would have thought. But I would have been wrong.

I only came to learn what I've learned because of Dad. His skin has that same touch of olive as mine. When he was little, he thought it was just a tan, just something he got from the long summers spent outdoors in Bowen, where the tomatoes and mangoes grow and the palms sway and the rocks in Horseshoe Bay are bleached by the sun. He was 13 when a cousin whispered the real reason to him: their family had Aboriginal ancestry. Black blood.

Dad asked his parents about this, and they told him a lie. The family had ties to New Zealand, they said, and the Māori warriors across the Tasman Sea. He raised it again later, wanting to know more, and they told him to drop it. He tried again, and this time was sent to his room. It was not a conversation his parents could have with him. To his parents, Aboriginal ancestry was something to be ashamed of and not something he should be curious about.

But Dad was determined, he went on his own journey learning what he could and doing his own research. He unearthed a name, Nancy, his great-grandmother. He pieced together her story, too: how she was married to a white man, and their mixed relationship saw them shunned in the town, booted to the margins of society.

Dad decided to do something more – to connect with her somehow. He didn't know why exactly or how, but he wanted his heritage confirmed. I think he wanted to understand himself, and his place in this country. He was 17 when he finally confirmed the truth of his family tree. Dad's uncle later found Nancy's grave and headstone on a local property up north, untended and covered in weeds.

Dad told my sisters and me the truth as soon as we were old enough to understand. Sara was 12, Ali ten. I was just seven.

I don't remember the news as being a revelation, or even a conversation. I was too little, I guess. It just was. No secrets.

Yet I feel as though I've always known I have Aboriginal ancestry. My favourite picture book growing up was *The Rainbow Serpent*, about the great snake Goorialla, and how in the Dreamtime he used his body to make mountains and gorges and creeks and rivers and a lily lagoon. I remember being transfixed by the tale, from the two brothers seeking shelter and walking into Goorialla's cavernous red mouth, to the men of the tribe finding him coiled and sleeping and cutting open his belly with quartz knives, freeing the brothers, who had now turned into a pair of beautiful rainbow lorikeets. Goorialla woke and raged, of course, and in his fury broke the mountain and threw pieces of it over the land, and all the people fled, and some of them transformed into their totems, brolgas and wombats and kangaroos. Do you remember how it ended? Goorialla disappeared into the sea, and the people who were left knew it was their duty to take care of all the animals – these living things who were once their brothers and sisters. I loved that book, because it was about how our country, creatures, people and plants are all part of the same ancient story.

I was aware of Aboriginal culture in this way, and yet I didn't know then it would change, shape and feed my life going forward.

For Dad, the process of confirming his daughters' ancestry was important. Together, we visited the Kambu Aboriginal and Torres Strait Islander Corporation for Health, a local health centre designed to provide streamlined access to GPs and optometrists and dentists, but also a hub for helping us to connect with Elders.

Dad helped compile our family history into a long book, an archived paper trail of birth certificates and marriage records. He stood in front of the Elders and spoke his truth, and they approved what they heard and read. Our names were recorded as members of the Ngarigo Nation. It was official. We are proud First Nations Australians.

What did all this change for me? At first, not a lot. Perhaps I noticed my world expanding a little bit at school. There were First Nations staff and support workers there who extended a continuous offer of additional help. They also taught us general lessons, about Aboriginal weapons and art and culture.

I came home from school one day with a little didgeridoo and showed Dad.

'That's nice,' he said, 'but you can't play it.'

'Bet I can,' I said.

'No, I mean you're not allowed to play it.'

'What do you mean?'

'Women aren't allowed to play didgeridoo.'

Those are the kinds of things that are only taught to you when you're part of the mob. I learned other things myself, researching online.

The Ngarigo people lived on elevated plateaux, from the Monaro Tablelands to the Bogong High Plains. They were known as 'the moth hunters', because in the warmer months, when the alpine flowers begin to carpet the valleys and mountain meadows, they would begin gathering great masses of bogong moths, and feast on them.

Early accounts describe them as people of the Australian High Country, coming down to the lowlands only for shelter, often sending word in advance through men carrying message

sticks to neighbours like the Wolgal and the Yaitmathang, the
Theddora and the Biduelli. They swam in waterholes, where
children played in the reeds and men threw boomerangs at
drinking birds. They roamed the hills and camped by night
and only went to sleep when the moon came out to watch
over them. Historians say they spoke a mixture of the adjacent
languages in the area, and often intermarried and intermingled,
and their country in that way became a kind of refuge for lost
souls, what some came to call 'broken men'.

Their women became famous for the sound of their 'snow
song', a tune invoked during corroboree and overheard by a
white explorer in 1834, who just couldn't shake the earworm.
He sketched out the words, then found some friends who could
transcribe the musical notes. It became the first piece of published
Australian sheet music. The song was only recently 'cleansed' by
Ngarigo Elders of its European flavour and restored to what it
might have sounded like back then, sung at altitude, under a
full moon, an incantation calling out to the stars for snowfall.

I liked these stories and facts. I liked the way the Ngarigo
medicine man is called Murrimalundra, a doctor who extracts
the evil substances placed inside sick men. They lived in the
most unique environment in Australia, and they knew all its
secrets and its science. They knew that mountain celery could
be made into a paste to treat urinary tract infections, and that
alpine baeckea could be made into an effective cough mixture.

There are notes from anthropologists about it all – even the
way a hunter would break down the body of a kangaroo,
the burru. The father gets the backbone, and the mother
its right leg. Thighs and shins and forelegs all have specific
owners. There were such ways for eating all animals, from the

bellet-bellet (lyrebird) to the berribong (emu) and the mumung (black snake).

The Ngarigo people were athletes, too. They played a game with a ball made of possum pelt – women and children running and catching and throwing. It sounds a lot like Marngrook, the precursor to Australian Rules football, the game I love. Few people speak the language now, but a glossary of words exists. A journalist once used that partial dictionary to describe my game. 'Her forehand is like malub, lightning,' he wrote. 'Her smash is like miribi, thunder – her backhand slice like djuran, running water. And she glides lightly on the court like a mugan, a ghost.' I liked the way that sounded.

But I didn't learn any of that until much later. As a kid, I found comfort in the discovery of our ancestry mostly because it helped me understand why I had darker skin and a squishy nose. I distinctly remember being told of my background, and considering the source of my appearance and thinking: *That's pretty cool.* Knowing that we were a little different from everyone else, that we were connected to more people throughout the nation – or at least connected more completely, or more deeply, or in some elemental way – gave me a sense of pride. I wanted to walk a little taller. It gave me such joy. That stands in contrast to the sadness I felt for Dad, whose parents could never admit it to themselves or others – who wanted to hide this thing that I wanted to share, and understand, reconcile and celebrate.

I began reading about the Dreamtime, and storytelling, and was completely enthralled by it all. But there was also something I appreciated that wasn't so much thought as *felt.* Whenever I come home from travelling, I immediately want to be in bare feet, on the grass, sitting in a park, my toes gripping rock or scratching in the dirt. It's what I've always done. I've always wanted to be outside, to feel the land underneath me. Maybe when I'm doing that I'm feeling a connection to my ancestors, and to the Ngarigo people and land, but also to Bowen, because that sunny spot just north of Airlie Beach and the Whitsundays and the Big Mango – that's my country too, even if the traditional owners in that part of Australia – the Birri and Jangga, Juru, Gia and Ngaro – are not my people.

*

At the Tokyo Olympics in 2021, in the Australian section of the village, there was a giant map of our country hung on a wall, onto which the First Nations athletes all placed a pin, noting where they were from. I didn't put mine in Ipswich or Bowen – I stuck it squarely on the border of Victoria and New South Wales, where the Ngarigo roamed. A single red pin to represent my tribe, my family. I've never been there but I'm from there.

It was an act of celebrating the group of First Nations athletes in Tokyo and acknowledging past First Nations Olympians. That's what First Nations Australians do, right? We consider all those who came before us – the light touch of the steps they took, and the big shoes we have to fill. We remember the darkness they faced and the stereotypes they rejected. And the achievements and accolades that will be forever remembered.

I think of Jardwajali man Johnny Mullagh, a member of the Aboriginal cricket team that toured England in 1868.

I think of Yurra Yurra man Bobby Kinnear, who won the Stawell Gift in 1883.

I think of high jumper Percy Hobson, a Gundabooka man, who won gold at the Commonwealth Games in Perth in 1962.

I think of Frank Reys, with his Djiribul heritage, who won the 1973 Melbourne Cup atop Gala Supreme.

We all remember with goosebumps when Cathy Freeman won gold at the Sydney Olympics in 2000.

*

I was 14 when I met Evonne Goolagong Cawley for the first time. I had just begun entering junior Grand Slams. My first was the Junior Australian Open in 2011. I was playing and then practising, and oblivious to the crowd. Evonne and her husband, Roger, came and watched me one afternoon, and after the session Dad introduced me. I remember her sandy linen clothes and long, curly hair, and her lovely big grin. I was withdrawn and hunched over, shy and retiring, wrapped up in a big black hoodie. Evonne said simply, 'I love the way you play,' and gave me a gigantic hug.

I knew who Evonne was, but I didn't know the significance of her life and career – so I started reading. I read about a little kid who grew up in a small New South Wales town called Barellan. A kid who taught herself to play using a racquet fashioned from a wooden board pulled from an old apple crate. Who found her way onto the most magical courts and came to be known as the 'Sunshine super girl'. Who took on the world and won, becoming a seven-time Grand Slam champion, although not without obstacle or incident.

Whenever a car came down their road, Evonne's mum would tell her to hide, lest the welfare man take her away. Evonne loved music and dancing to disco, and even after she won Wimbledon in 1971 and became a national figure, she remembered going out with friends in Brisbane and being turned away at the door because of the colour of her skin.

But she became an inspiration on and off the court – a person who values celebration and opportunity. After that first encounter, we met occasionally on the outdoor courts at Melbourne Park, or at other tournaments or functions or awards nights. I would visit the workshops and events she conducts through her foundation in Griffith and Rockhampton and Cairns. And she would reach out to me, to be involved in my life – to observe and enjoy and mentor, but never to push or compare, or even offer advice, unless I asked. It was like she wanted to share my journey, and share what she knew.

I've now left tennis behind me twice in my life, and both times Evonne immediately got in touch.

The first time with a text: *Great decision, Darl. Go wet a line.*

The second time with a phone call. 'You okay?' she asked.

'Yeah,' I replied. 'I'm great.'

'Beautiful.'

Evonne is the kind of person I aspire to be – someone who gives back, and can use her experiences and profile to encourage others to be their best. She lifts people up. Evonne isn't interested in using her voice or platform to dominate the conversation or drown others out or shout anyone down. She's never going to be the pin-up for anyone else's cause or a weapon in anyone's fight. I'm not interested in that either. I want to learn and listen and lend whatever help I can.

I've seen glimpses and tasted the faintest bitter edge of racism. I'd win a Deadly Award but get vilified online. I'd become a Tennis Australia First Nations Ambassador and then find some muppet calling my heritage into question. I've been lucky to have so many incredible role models who have paved a path for me to believe, as a First Nations woman, that I am capable of anything. Now I see it as my responsibility to guide First Nations youth and help create opportunities for them to go after their dreams.

I've dipped a toe in those waters now, only recently immersing myself in clinics in the Red Centre – at a tennis club in Alice Springs, and on a court made of the timeless scarlet sands by Uluru. It was part of the Racquets and Red Dust program. Its mission is to help create sustainable tennis pathways for First Nations people, prioritising positive health, education and social outcomes. I was there to promote that, but in all honesty it was seeing the kids smile as they tried something new that got me truly excited. And it was a journey I'd wanted to make for a long, long time. Too long.

I was acutely aware that I was invited, graciously welcomed to Country by the Anangu people. I didn't want to intrude or interrupt or be disrespectful, so I simply listened to our guides as they told stories and explained the significance of the place, the sacred side, the wall art – a historical snapshot of this monolith and what it has stood for over the millennia. It was so much bigger and better than I imagined. I wasn't expecting to stand there and instantaneously feel compelled by the force of stone – *I have to touch it*, I thought, *I need to* – or that its pull would be so powerful.

I've seen amazing places before, and reacted in all sorts of unexpected ways. I saw the Taj Mahal during a Junior Fed Cup tournament and was gobsmacked. I bought Mum an elephant made of the same marble. The Eiffel Tower, by contrast, always looked to me like a piece of twisted steel and little more. Notre Dame Cathedral took me back to my childhood, and animated dreams of *Beauty and the Beast*. I visited Lord's in 2019 for a cricket World Cup match between Australia and England, and remember taking a grateful deep breath when I was invited into the dressing-rooms. I stood on the famous balcony with Justin Langer as Aaron Finch made a century and Steve Smith obsessed over tennis, and the boys all signed a World Cup shirt for me. The 150th Open at the Old Course at St Andrews brought that same feeling out of me, as did walking in through the black wrought-iron gates of the All England Lawn Tennis and Croquet Club. You can't help but marvel at such moments as they're happening.

But that trip to Central Australia was the single most important journey I've ever made. They say Uluru is the heart of the nation. I'm not sure I really believed that until I saw it for myself, and stood in its shadow, feeling the thrum of something ancient inside me, coursing and thumping and echoing through time.

I want to learn and listen.

Bullrings and Baguettes

Jessica Pegula. I don't recognise the name. She's American, apparently. I've never seen this girl hit a ball, which makes it a tricky way to begin my 2019 French Open.

Usually a bit of unfamiliarity doesn't matter too much – I'm not one to study a lot of vision of my opponents anyway – but I still like to understand how they swing their racquet. People think elite athletes have impeccable vision and freakish reaction time – and often they do – but so much of that anticipation relies on a detailed understanding of the mechanics and geometry of the game. Often, you're not *seeing* the ball better so much as *reading* it better through repetition.

There was a study done on this once, using hitters from Major League Baseball. Home run kings Barry Bonds and Albert Pujols were lined up against champion softball pitcher Jennie Finch. It was during the 2004 All-Star Legends & Celebrity Softball Game, and Bonds and Pujols were expected to stare down this blonde girl from the Arizona Wildcats, their star pitcher, with ease. The big sluggers were expected to swing for the fences and send her packing. But she struck them both out. Not because she packed more heat than any big league fastball pitcher, but because she threw underarm, with that big windmill energy, and they simply weren't accustomed to it. They couldn't read her mechanics.

I'd like to be able to read Pegula's mechanics ahead of our match-up. And I do. I pick up the way she plays quickly enough. This has always been a strength of mine.

We play on Court 1, which is also known as the Bullring. It's a 1970s brutalist concrete structure with 3800 seats and thunderous acoustics. I've heard people say it's beautiful in its ugliness, and I understand why. It's not as big as the other courts, and that seems to be the point. It's an intimate colosseum – the noise from the stands cascades down upon you, building like an avalanche. And the fans experience that proximity too, hearing every frustrated sigh, and seeing the sheen of your sweat mixing with the deep-orange clay dust.

My encounter with Jess is scratchy – typical of the first match in a Grand Slam tournament, really. If you're seeing the ball like a watermelon and crushing everything in sight at this stage, it's almost not right. In a way, an up-and-down challenge is what you want first up: to experience a few nerves but then settle them enough to win. In this case 6-3, 6-3. I'm settled now, and ready to build.

Roland-Garros holds a strange importance for me. I was never the type of kid to sit in front of the TV watching tennis at 2 am, but I did once, in 2010. Sam Stosur was in the final, and I dragged my mattress out into the living room to watch every point. That was special.

A year later, I was there in person as a junior. I won in the first round – my first victory at a junior Grand Slam. I watched Casey Dellacqua play in a mixed doubles final with Scott Lipsky, too, and because I was still a breathless fangirl, Casey gave me her towel. Watching those professional matches live in Paris for the first time, I quickly understood that it takes a certain kind of physicality to prevail on clay, and I never had it – at least, I didn't in that first phase of my career. Maybe now might be different?

I try to see it that way and drink in my surrounds. I don't do a lot of sightseeing on tour, but in Paris I always try to explore a few little pockets, just by wandering. We're staying near Stade Jean-Bouin, the French Open practice facility in the 16th arrondissement, a cruisy walk from the stadium. The FIFA Women's World Cup is on too, and they're playing matches in front of bulging crowds at Parc des Princes, the home stadium of Paris Saint-Germain, just around the corner.

Roland-Garros is flanked by the Auteuil Hippodrome racetrack and the Bois de Boulogne, a sprawling public park, and restaurants selling crepes and champagne. Patrons arrive often by metro and enter the tournament through three heavy security checks, where police carrying machine guns are the norm. Once you're inside, you discover that the staff here are elegantly dressed, and the tournament site is so much smaller than at the other Slams.

Spectators smoke cigarettes everywhere but in the grandstands, where there's no drinking either. They say the crowds at Roland-Garros are more discerning than most, and you feel that, too. They're more aware of the crucial shifting moments and the subtlety of great shots. All Slams have their traditions. The one I love here is a ceremonial run, in which the ball kids all jog 400 metres down the broad avenue that connects Court Philippe Chatrier to Court Suzanne Lenglen, ready to start play for the day.

On this day, against Danielle Collins, I want to stamp my authority and make a statement – which is difficult when the 63 other girls left in the draw are trying to do the same thing. Collins fights me in the first set, an arm wrestle that I win 7-5, but I'm able to put my foot down and create more pressure in the second set, which I win 6-1.

Andrea Petkovic is the perfect challenge in the third round. I always feel guilty around Petko. She came back from a knee reconstruction in 2013, and when she played me in the Hopman Cup she did the knee again. I was just 16 then, but I remember her agony as the limb buckled. Today, I'm deferential, or at least respectful, but I also want to show her how far I've come in three years.

We play at the gorgeous, curved Court Suzanne Lenglen, and the late-afternoon sun is punishing. Shadows streak across the court as we move, and the ball is impossible to track in flight. I feel as though I'm swinging blind at times, but I find a way to control the match. Petko's not the most fluent player, in that her strokes often seem manufactured. They rely on her finding a set position and then grinding you down with robotic repetition. I throw in a few surprises and watch her short-circuit; I win 6-3, 6-1.

I'm ready to feel anxious now, because the fourth round is new to me here, and so I turn to those closest to me. In truth, I lean on them. If not now, then when? I know Garry is coming over soon, as are Jim, Dad and Mum. I Facetime with my sisters and my niece Lucy and nephew Oscar. I feel as relaxed as possible coming into my match against Sofia Kenin, who makes me uncomfortable. Her unpredictable patterns often take away my rhythm.

It's overcast and drizzling, and conditions are heavy. I hit almost a dozen unreturnable serves and aces to start the match. Ridiculous. Maybe that's why I lose myself tactically, temporarily forgetting that I can't keep the ball away from her racquet all day with untouchable winners. Maybe that's why we suddenly find ourselves with one set each: 6-3, 3-6.

That's when I take a moment to think. *Regardless of whether I win or lose this match it'll be a statement*, I think, *about how I approach the game and how I want to play.*

I streamroll her in the final set, 6-0, and walk off court ready to play in my first Grand Slam quarter-final.

Madison Keys is up next, and there's no forgetting her. Only two years ago at this event, she knocked me over in 55 minutes, using her power to bully and embarrass me right off the court. I barely had time to register what had happened.

I have to take her kick serve and first strike away from her. Her kick serve is a weapon, and when you take away a weapon you make a player feel as though they're competing with one arm tied behind their back. In the case of her hopper, I'll stand back and wait for the high bounce, and on every second serve I know I have to be clear in my decision-making. A big backhand middle to put her under time pressure, or a short backhand slice to bring her forward and low, into a position on the court that she doesn't like.

It's a hot day, and we play high-quality tennis. Tense. Consequential. I'm serving for the match when I'm certain I hear a familiar voice talking and laughing. *Who the fuck is that?* I end the match (6-3, 7-5) and wander off court, and it's this grinning guy with sunnies and a backwards hat. Dylan Alcott. We cruise down the tunnel together.

'Mate, two French Open semi-finalists,' he says. 'How good is this?'

Torrential rain has fallen intermittently during the tournament so far, which means the finals have to be played without any rest days. I don't mind this at all. Keep 'em coming. Routine, routine, routine.

The semi-final is a dark day for me. Our practice gets interrupted, cut short by ten minutes – and not even by rain but by the *threat* of rain. The court staff begin winding down the net while I'm still hitting ground strokes. I've never wanted to be a prima donna athlete, but I'm so routined – my process is like clockwork – that being denied the chance to finish my work has me fuming. *There are blue skies above!* I have steam coming out of my ears. But the truth is I'm petrified. Shit-scared, really.

I'm playing Amanda Anisimova. She's 17, new to the tour and already making a splash, knocking over top ten players and winning events. There are demons in my head now – *So much to lose, and no excuses* – but I start on fire and she falters from the first step. I sit down at the changeover well in front, 5-0, but I'm thinking, *This isn't quite right – I've done nothing to get here*. Famous last thoughts?

My moment of hubris is over, and she breaks me, and I panic. *What have I done?*

I begin to feel small, and want to feel smaller. I'd like to hide. My body language says it all. Crouch down. Cover up. I play loose tennis, dumb tennis, and breathe oxygen back into her game. When you take the first set from someone 6-0, you're punching them in the face, telling them: 'This is the standard you need to meet.' Instead, I let her back into the match. I give her belief. I doubt I think about tactics of any sort for 25 minutes. I am panicking. I don't know what to call it, but this is the opposite of a flow state.

Amanda wins one game. Then another. Then another. Then another. And another. And another. And then she wins that first set in a tie-break, and I'm stifling tears, looking to Tyzz for something, anything. He holds his posture tall, and lifts his hands. *Chest up, mate, chest up*. But the second set continues in this way. I quickly go down a double break, 0-3. I want to stand up and be proud of my game, proud of my team, but I'm drowning – quickly. And then it starts to rain …

Amanda's team tells her to get off the court, and she argues this point with the chair umpire, who for now is saying the match will continue. I almost want to walk over and shake some sense into her. *Are you crazy? What are you doing?* I think. *Are you not looking at your opponent?* I'm capitulating before her eyes. She has me on the ropes. I've won just one of the past 11 games, and I lack any semblance of belief. Until now. I have been gifted a moment to reset. To think. To make a change.

I realise I have a chance. Now I rediscover that single truth about tennis, which is not true of any other sport: until you lose that final match point, you can always win.

Sitting in a courtside chair as the raindrops fall, I feel Little Tyzz sitting on one of my shoulders and Little Crowey on the other. They're both telling me how hard we've worked, reminding me that I've come too far to make the wrong turn now. I can hear myself making up my mind: *I'm going to play the Australian way, and fight to the end. That's what Aussies do. That's what Ash Barty does. Whatever happens happens*, I think. *Fuck it – have a crack.*

I want to be cool and calm but I'm feeling this game now. I'm not detached from it in some professional sense. I'm in it, and my heart is pounding.

I surge and create and find a way to win a game, and again, and again, and again, and again, and again, and the second set (6-3) is mine – as is the momentum. It's ugly and it feels awful, but I scrap and fight to find a way. I'm more than back in this. I can't be stopped now, and almost before I can draw breath I've won the third set 6-3 and I'm standing at the net, leaning on the net, ready to collapse.

I feel as though I need to apologise to Amanda, and my team, even myself, for making everything feel so shitty and emotional. But there's some mongrel in me too, and the athlete and the competitor inside thinks only one thing: *If I can win a tennis match like that, I can win any tennis match.*

It's stunning, though, how quickly even the most hard-won confidence can ebb and flow and then ebb again. I don't really want to debrief but I sit with Tyzz in the lobby of our hotel that night, nodding at whatever encouraging things he says, sullenly thinking only: *I don't deserve this, I'm not worthy of being here, I'm not good enough. I'm into the final of a Slam without beating a top ten player.*

He shakes his head. 'It doesn't matter, because you've outlasted them,' he says. 'You can only beat whoever's on the other side of the net.'

He points out, too, that this moment is pivotal. I need to be present. I need to understand how far I've come. He forces me to remember my old habit of letting one bad point or game or moment turn a winning position into a losing one. He needs me to understand what I did out there today. An imperious 5-0 lead became a sickening 6-7, 0-3 deficit, but I made a decision to play on, whether out of pride or stubbornness or anger or fire. 'It's a decision,' he says, 'that will shape your career.'

Because I made that decision, I'm 24 hours away from playing a tennis match to win the French Open. If I hadn't made it, I'm back where I was a year ago, at Wimbledon 2018, losing in the third round against Kasatkina, with nothing to show for all my work and growth.

Tyzz sees me crying now, and slaps me on the leg. 'Mate, you're in a Grand Slam final tomorrow. No one can take that away from you.'

I speak to no one else that night, and sleep for 14 hours.

I wake up on the morning of the final and pull open the curtains. It looks like Miami out there, sapphire sky and the barest puff of cloud. And it's windy – I like the wind. I pick up my phone and there's a voicemail from Casey Dellacqua, and a photo of Lucy and Oscar in their *Toy Story* pyjamas. I'm a blubbering mess and call Crowey, who calms me down.

I have the same breakfast every day. You make it yourself in our accommodation, and my daily Parisian feast is two fried eggs on a half-baguette, with a few berries on the side. I head to the courts for a half-hour warm-up, and then with my crew – physios, manager, trainer, coach – head to the gym to wait for the completion of the men's semi-final between Novak Djokovic and Dominic Thiem.

The match goes into a fifth set, and to pass the time we play cricket. A foam roller for stumps, and another one for a bat. My opponent for the day – Markéta Vondroušová, a 19-year-old left-hander from Prague – sees us taking up the whole gym area, rotating as bowler or batter or wicketkeeper or silly mid-off, and she smiles. She finds her own quiet corner to prepare.

We're called to start the match and I grab my bag. I've promised myself I'll walk onto the court smiling, no matter how I feel. I'm escorted by a beautiful young girl, who speaks only a little English, and I hold her hand and tell her, 'Hey, we have to smile, both of us, but how good is this?'

Tactics seem more important than ever now, so what do you do against someone like Markéta? She hits a mean drop shot, and my counter-plan is simple: take that weapon away from her. Be disciplined – push the ball down the line and steal the net position. She's also good at locking me into my backhand corner, and the solution to that problem should come naturally: get on the front foot and find forehands. Feet, feet, feet. Find the intent.

I'm in the zone quickly, and I recognise this as what Crowey calls my A game. At the first change of ends, I laugh to myself. *Fuck off, B, not today*, I think. *I'm not going to that place.*

There's a quirky advertisement at the French Open, where a change of ends is punctuated by a little fizzing 'pfft!' sound. It's a promotion for Perrier and drags your attention to the big scoreboards. Usually that's the kind of thing that bothers me, but today I notice it every time and enjoy it. It takes my mind away for a moment, and then I'm back into the game, and the game is just as good.

Before I know it, I'm pushing Markéta deep into a corner, and she flicks a lob skyward. I approach it on the bounce – and my smash is shitful, but the margin for error is vast. The ball goes in and the match is all over: *Six-un! Six-trois!*

I don't know what to do – how should I celebrate? I don't think it through. I put my arms up, turn to my team and mouth, *What the fuck?*

Markéta is beautiful at the net. We shake the umpire's hand and everything goes numb – my legs, my shoulders. I can't hold my arms up. I crouch on the court. I thank the crowd but, put simply, my greatest thanks is that this two weeks is now over.

I'm handed the Coupe Suzanne Lenglen – and I lift it up and kiss it, because it's a Grand Slam trophy. Then the national anthem is playing and my knees begin to buckle. I walk down from the podium and see Rod Laver. I bumped into him earlier in the tournament – 'You can do it,' he'd said, to which I had replied, 'Oh, thanks, maybe not, but I'll give it a crack' – and now here we are, hugging on Centre Court. *Rocket knows my name!*

I'm into the showers now, and doing the drug testing, and then hours of media. Finally, we sit down together as a team and take turns sculling a Kronenbourg 1664 beer from the tiny replica trophy they give you as your own to keep. The perfect size for a stubby. We have dinner at a beautiful steak restaurant recommended by the tournament. The evening turns raucous, with bottles of Bordeaux and shots of tequila. Security guards have tailed us for the last 30 hours, sleeping in the hotel lobby, because that's the custom for the finalists and champions here. They can head home now. I can't believe I'm a Roland-Garros champion.

When we go back to the hotel I can't sleep, though, so I stay up texting and talking, replying to every WhatsApp and Instagram message, flicking through photos, reliving everything until the dawn. At last I snatch an hour of sleep, then I head straight back to the site.

In the champion's photo shoot I wear a pair of So Kate pumps, the classic black Louboutins named for Kate Moss, which I bought in Paris earlier in the week, having dragged Tyzz there in the rain after the second round. Finally, I put aside the racquet that hit the winning point, and send it home in the post. Later, I'll frame it with photos and present it to Jim in the car park of the West Brisbane Tennis Centre. Although he's not a crier, I know he will weep.

In the coming days, I replay the tournament in my mind – every pivotal point and stroke – and my mind keeps wandering back to when it was all over, on the side of the court, my shoes scratching at the clay underfoot. I'm sitting in my chair, waving Tyzz down from the stands, and it takes him an eternity but he finally gets there. Someone takes a photo of us in that moment, hugging, but they don't know what we're saying to one another.

'No one can take this away from us,' I tell him.

'No one can take this away from *you*,' he replies.

And then I say one final thing, which prompts a look from Tyzz that's equal parts plaintive, confused and confounded. It's a joke ... but it's not a joke.

'Mate,' I say, 'can I retire now?'

The Detroit of Belgium

For almost two years, I avoided long trips for tennis. My experience in Europe as a 13-year-old girl had been harrowing, and I dreaded the memory. I imagined my life – my future – lived entirely on the road. Sleeping in sterile, silent hotel rooms. Figuring out foreign food. Talking with family and friends through computer screens, always at strange hours. Trying to stay on task and on schedule, even though my chosen lifestyle was one of constant disruption.

Other players enjoy parts of this experience. They find it thrilling to be in a new city every week, playing on a new court, navigating a new challenge. I guess, in a way, you are seeing the world – but only from within your accommodation, or through the window of your transportation, or within the secure areas of vast athletic precincts, behind velvet ropes and secure doors and signs that say 'Players Only'. I felt no desire to live that way. And so I didn't join another major tour until I was 15.

Again, we went to Europe. I found myself in Belgium, in the city of Charleroi. You might imagine tennis players tour only the finest locations – Monaco, Zurich, London – but Charleroi was not one of these. It has a reputation, in fact, as the Detroit of Belgium – a city of abandoned buildings and crime, and not a place young foreigners should walk the streets alone at night. Many junior tournaments are played a long, long way off Broadway.

Only a year before, for instance, I'd played halfway around the world at Nonthaburi, in Thailand, and we had no ground transport, so we walked to and from our hotel. I remember vividly each teen girl tramping through the humid streets, dodging tuk-tuks with our heavy gear bags on our shoulders, and a racquet always in hand. We weren't practising swings as we walked: the racquets were to fend off the feral dogs that came bowling out of alleyways to nip at our legs.

After Charleroi came the clay-court swing, and it was tough. I liked seeing Paris, albeit fleetingly, and I won my first-round match at the Junior French Open, before losing in the second. I was playing well enough, I suppose, but struggling all the same. I was homesick, chronically so.

We went to England next, to a junior tournament in Roehampton – the home of Wimbledon Qualifying – and I remember the feelings spilling out of me. I wanted to call Dad but I couldn't. I wasn't brave enough to have the conversation with him, so I sent him a long, sad, meandering email.

They say good writing is like opening a vein and bleeding onto the page. That's what I did, sitting on the ground in the players' dining area, leaning against my bag, thumbing an opus into my phone, bleeding onto that little screen. The message was about my misery, but there was one thing I wanted to ask. I needed to start working with a different coach. I needed Jason Stoltenberg.

I first met Stolts in 2007, when I was 11. I was playing in the under-12 nationals, on the outer courts of Melbourne Park. He liked checking out the talent coming through, and that's what he was doing this particular day when a man walked up to him. 'My name is Robert Barty,' he said. 'Would you mind coming and watching my daughter play?'

Stolts warned Dad that it might not be the best idea. Tennis Australia (TA) – the body controlling the sport in this country – was complicated. And, at that time, Stolts was not part of the TA family. But Dad didn't care, so Stolts came and watched anyway. I won the tournament, and it stuck in his mind.

Fast-forward a few years, to the start of 2011, and the coaching set-up that I had wasn't right. Dad was worried about me, and looking for the best fit. Jim was busy running his centre in Richlands – and besides, he had never coached a player on the professional tour – but he chatted with Stolts one day at Melbourne Park. They hit it off from the start, having similar styles and philosophies, and Jim returned to my parents with a message: 'This is the guy.'

That was all Dad and Mum needed to hear – in fact, it was all they would hear on the matter – but it didn't go down well with TA, who didn't believe Stolts was the right option for me.

Dad and Mum knew they couldn't afford a coach without support from the national body, but they were so concerned for my welfare that they stuck to their guns. A starting point was agreed: Stolts would work with me on a trial basis through the grass-court season.

Now I desperately needed that trial to start, so I hit send on that email to Dad. Stolts was on a plane within a few days and worked with me in England – first at the tournament in Roehampton, and then at Junior Wimbledon. I was immediately happy, bubbly, overjoyed to have someone with me who I trusted. Stolts seemed at times like a younger version of Jim – one who had been on tour, played in Grand Slams and had already experienced everything I was going through. And the way he communicated just made sense to me.

When Stolts arrived, he told me that he'd played in the semi-finals at Wimbledon, back in 1996. I told him that was the year I was born – which he didn't like hearing. We at least agreed that 1996 was a good year. But there's an interesting perk of being in the 'Last 8' club at any Grand Slam event: you can forever go back to that event and get free tickets.

'Come on, then,' he said, as my eyes widened. 'Let's see what tickets we can get today.'

Not long after, we walked into the grandstand, tickets in hand. Our seats were right next to the royal box, behind the players' box, and the multiple Grand Slam champion Maria Sharapova was on court warming up. I forget who she was playing against – Anna Chakvetadze? Laura Robson? Klára

Zakopalová? – but it didn't matter. I was buzzing. Stolts knew I was only a year or two away from taking the leap to playing against these very players, but I was also still a child, still a fan, still a spectator. He knew I needed something to draw me in to the tournament, and experiencing Centre Court on a beautiful summer day was the perfect way to do that.

I confessed to him – 'I've had an average trip' – and it was only a few days before he got to see that up close. In my opening match in the girls' singles, I was scheduled to play Lucy Brown, an English wildcard. She was 18 and I was 15, so I had a right to be scared. But the pressure I put on myself was something else entirely. It was as if I could sense every eyeball trained on me. I remember standing on Court 4, before the game had even begun, trying to hide the tears that were welling up in my eyes.

Those stands might only hold a couple of hundred people, but they also sit right next to Court 3 and at the thoroughfare to Court 2, which are popular courts, so people were constantly moving through that space, looking on and leaning in. For me, there was too much foot traffic – too much noise and colour. Too much visibility. Too much attention. My main hope was not to embarrass myself. In spite of myself, I managed to win.

And I kept winning, through the likes of Filipino-German qualifier Katharina Lehnert and wiry Dutch hitter Indy de Vroome. I remember one match well, against someone who would one day become a constant rival: Madison Keys. She was in the top five juniors in the world at this point, but I had more than a hunch I could beat her. I told Stolts as much.

'I *know* she can't hit a forehand down the line – I saw it last week,' I said. 'She can't hit it. All I have to do is force her to hit that forehand down the line.'

On Court 9, at 4-4 in the third set, 30 all, I knew it was time to force her hand and give her that option. She might hit the winner, of course, but eight times out of ten she would miss. I put the ball where it needed to be, and she pulled the trigger. Missed by a country mile. Stolts just smiled and shook his head.

After winning five matches, I was into the final. This was different: it was played on Court 1, where the grandstand holds 7500 people, and it was full. I've never felt physically ill walking out on court before, but a wave of nausea swept over me. I was playing against a Russian lefty named Irina Khromacheva, and I wanted to vomit.

I walked down the tunnel into the arena, past all the pictures of former champions, and I tripped and stumbled on the carpet. It was only as I walked into the light and sound of the court that I realised … This. Is. So. Cool.

The travel and the isolation and the scrutiny of professional play will never be enjoyable, but even when that becomes a struggle, an athlete never feels so comfortable as they do on their turf, training and playing – refining and competing. In our darkest moments, the game itself is always a source of light. This is what we train for. This is why we work so damn hard.

I won the final 7-5, 7-6, ending it with a forehand cross-court winner and a tiny little fist-pump. I was handed the trophy and told to do a victory lap. I told them I couldn't, or wouldn't – I didn't want to. 'I can't walk a lap parading this trophy,' I said. 'My opponent is right there!' Glorying in my win was the very thing I'd been taught not to do in victory.

You have to do it, they whispered in my ear. You have to present the trophy, clap and walk slowly past the line of photographers.

With the trophy in my hands, I was uncomfortable. Everyone was looking at me, and I didn't like that. They asked me to kiss the trophy too – 'Go on! Do it! Give it a kiss!' – but again I couldn't, or wouldn't. 'But you have to!' I had promised myself I would only ever kiss a Grand Slam trophy, and nothing else. I kept my promise.

The media circus began immediately thereafter. Two hours of talking – not just at a press conference but in one-on-ones with local reporters and reporters from Australia and reporters from Russia, seasoned adults with notebooks and recorders and cameras, whereas I was still a child.

I had my first experience with a doping test, too. A chaperone walked into a bathroom with me, to watch me pee in a cup. I couldn't go, and the lady was unimpressed: 'You need to go,' she said. It took me four hours to produce a sample. It was all so confronting that already I was wishing I'd lost.

'There's one more thing,' Stolts told me. 'There's a winners' ball tonight and you have to go.'

I had already changed my flight home once and was booked to depart that night, and I wanted nothing to do with any victory ball. 'Sorry, I can't,' I replied. 'My flight home is waiting.'

He kept making the case: I had to go. The champions always go. An Australian boy, Luke Saville, had won the final of the boys' tournament, so I could go with him. The professional champions would be there: Novak Djokovic and Petra Kvitová. The event would be fun.

'I can't change this flight again,' I declared. 'I have to go home.'

That was when Dad called me, and when I answered I didn't give him the chance to speak. 'I can't go to this ball tonight,' I blurted out. 'I'm not changing my flight.'

'First of all, Ash, congratulations,' he said, warmly. 'And, darl, you have to go.'

'I can't go, and I'm not going,' I repeated. 'I've been away for six weeks. I'm coming home.'

I knew some people would love to go to such a ball. I thought about how they would love to get dressed up to the nines, and walk the famous purple carpet into a ballroom filled with the most elegant and interesting and important people in Britain, to sip champagne and rub shoulders with royalty. I suspected that others wouldn't see anything attractive about surrounding themselves with the pointless trappings of wealth and celebrity, but would grudgingly attend out of a sense of obligation or tradition. I did neither. It was the first time a champion has ever skipped the ball.

I went to take a shower instead, and calmed myself down, thinking only of home. I didn't have to go back to my hotel for my things, because I was already packed – I'd done that the day before. I caught a Wimbledon car alone to Heathrow, boarded my flight, curled up in my seat and slept the entire way home, wrapped in a blanket as well as a snug sense of exhaustion. I awoke from my cosy oblivion in Brisbane and stepped off the plane with bleary, emotional eyes.

There were cameras everywhere. They had been everywhere else already – to Dad's work at the State Library, and Mum's work at the hospital in Ipswich – and now they were here to get a photo of me hugging my family at arrivals. They were there to capture the moment – and 'capture' feels like the right word. They seized it, after all, stealing it from me and mine, encircling it and locking it up in film and making it their own. I just wanted to give Mum and Dad a hug.

Arriving home as a champion suddenly felt disappointing. My victory itself wasn't sullied or diminished, but the response to it revealed something to me that I hadn't seen before, a truth I didn't yet know. *This is not tennis*, I thought to myself. *This is something else.*

Stolts knew it too. He made a point of debriefing with Mum and Dad later, walking them through it all – my wonder at Centre Court, my stumbles and tears on Court 4, my resolute rejection of all ceremony after the win. He summed it up for them with a compliment and a warning.

'Ash could do brilliant things,' he told them. 'But it's gonna be tough. And we'll need to be very careful.'

Golf Greens and Grass Courts

After the glare of Roland-Garros and the attention of the 2019 French Open, I want out of Paris, and quickly. So I go to England, to the Belfry – a hotel resort and golf course just outside of Birmingham – in a place with a name that could only be British: the Royal Town of Sutton Coldfield. Although homely and low-key, it's a Ryder Cup course, and stunning – the perfect place to stop and take a breath over nine drizzly and chilly golf holes.

Tyzz was a good golfer in his day, but he hasn't beaten me yet and I make sure he remembers it. We both love golf, which in many ways offers the opposite to what tennis does. Golf is slow and quiet. You always have time to think. As frustrating as a slice or a hook or a shank or a duff can be, you're still essentially going for a walk in a beautifully manicured natural setting while trying your hand at a fixed and discrete skill: hitting a small white ball into a hole. There's an astonishing array of variables that go into any swing, and yet you have the control. You can be lucky or unlucky based on a bounce or a lie, but there's no opponent trying to make your life difficult. Your score rests only with you.

I like the similarities, too, including the scoring. In tennis, you can convince yourself that a break point or set point or match point is more important than any other point, but it's not. Every point has the same value. And the same is true of golf. Your 300-yard drive off the tee is as important as your two-inch putt. A stroke is a stroke. Nothing teaches you process over outcome like counting every hit, good and bad.

My parents have come across, and when they join us on the course it's the first time I've seen them. Mum's hug is just what I needed. Mum caddies for me and Dad caddies for Tyzz. While Mum and Dad stay with some family friends, Tyzz and I stay at the Belfry Resort. We catch up for breakfast some mornings, over the comfort of scrambled eggs and baked beans on toast, which I eat every day. But we've come here mainly so that I can rest – so we can see each other but also not see each other, and spend time exactly as we might do at home, always proximate but not always present.

I take recovery seriously. There's the golf game one day. A massage another day. After a couple of days, we move to the Crowne Plaza in Birmingham, and even with the change of scenery, we take a few extra days to recover. I don't go anywhere except for a morning walk to my preferred cafe, Faculty Coffee, where I buy and then refill a keep cup with a strong skinny latte.

I fall sick – sneezy and snotty – which is regulation for me after an emotional two-week tournament, and find myself drained, and so I sleep and sniff and snuggle up. I binge the Jason Bourne movies on Netflix. I snooze. I flip through a book while a Disney movie plays in the background – probably *Tarzan* – and I do the same the next day with a chick-flick instead – probably *Bride Wars* or some other piece of so-bad-it's-good pop culture. And I snooze some more.

I wish I could do this for another week. Hibernate. Reflect. Recuperate. This is the way I like to refresh, before my next challenge: another tilt at the English grass-court season.

Taking things slowly gives me a chance to consider what I've achieved in the last month. For the first time in a long time – probably the first time in my life – I'm actually glad I'm not in Australia. I can escape within this place completely, and soak in my own thoughts. And within a few days I'm joined by all the people who mean the most to me – not just Tyzz and my parents but Garry, Nikki, Crowey and Jim – and we enjoy the start of a soft UK summer together.

I play the Birmingham Classic – a beautiful and quiet tournament – and as comfortable as that is, I know I need a push to get my game going again. It takes only a moment for you to start questioning yourself. I'm here not so much to win as to freshen up and sharpen up. My draw is brutal, yet I feel great. I don't know how, but I'm refreshed.

First up is Donna Vekić, who knows two things really well – how to play on grass and how to derail your patterns – but I get through 6-3, 6-4. Jen Brady is a ripping girl but I want to make a statement, and 6-3, 6-1 definitely says something: *Yes, I've just had a great win. I may be tired but I'm not here to make up the numbers.*

I move through the draw with a mantra of acceptance – *There will be noise, I will be sore, but the process will prevail* – and it holds me in good stead. The week becomes a study in balance. We step onto the court, and we work. We step off the court, and we relax. Expend energy, preserve energy. Focus, drift. We do it against Venus Williams (6-4, 6-3) and then against Barbora Strýcová (6-4, 6-4), and this means something. All week I've known that if I win this tournament, I will be ranked as the number 1 player in the world, and now all I have to do is beat my current doubles partner, Julia Goerges.

Winning back-to-back tournaments is rare – I've never done it before – but we are back on grass, the number 1 ranking is on the line, and my loved ones are here enjoying it with me. Game on.

I love Jules. That's not true of all my opponents. There are girls I dislike playing, and girls I just plain dislike – mostly those who can't separate who they are on and off the court. You're about to play them and they won't look you in the eye or say hello. Or you beat them and they don't talk to you for a week. Some fall into a fury when you give them a lesson during practice, unable even to train with detachment. I want to wipe the floor with those girls. I keep track of them, too, in a little black book inside my mind. Jules is definitely not one of those girls.

I stay in the moment against her, playing each point and each ball on its merits, and the final score is 6-3, 7-5 in my favour.

I put a hand up to my mouth and over my face, because I'm laughing at the sheer absurdity of this moment. Numero uno! WTA World No. 1! I'm 23 years old, and the first Australian woman to top the singles rankings in 43 years. 'Holy shit,' I murmur to myself. 'This is real.'

I walk to the net, and Jules has one of those smiles that says she knows what this means to me. She says it with the way she hugs me, too, and with the beers we share in the lounge that afternoon.

Now my body shuts down. It's been noble, and put up with my pushing, but my limbs need rest, and that means I need to withdraw from the next tournament, in Eastbourne. I'll do it there in person, as that's where I'll be presented with the Chris Evert Trophy – named in honour of the woman who ruled the sport in 1975, when rankings were first computerised, and who went on to hold that perch for 260 weeks. It's a gorgeous piece of silverware: three metallic arms rising up and holding a tennis ball, encrusted with diamonds, one for each of the women who've reached the top. Mine is the 27th diamond, forever sparkling. I'm given a replica of this trophy, too, which today sits proudly in my parents' living room at home.

Wimbledon is next. That's the way the tour unfolds. There's always something next, something coming. Something for which to train and prepare. Something to dwell on and worry about. Something looming. Only this time I have a new identity, too. In the space of a few months I've gone from grappling with the notion that I'm a top ten player in the world, to being a Grand Slam champion, to being the World No. 1 and the top seed at Wimbledon – exactly 12 months after melting down (very publicly) in this exact setting.

Right now I don't feel pressure but I do sense *interest*. There's an unmistakable buzz all around me. Gentle questions and inquiries begin to feel like inquisitions. *Where are you going? What are you doing? Who are you playing?* I've never planned my assault on Wimbledon adequately – somehow I always arrive here a little drained and flustered, and that's when my demons come out on court. I'm determined now to ignore my exhaustion, and handle my shit. I try to plan accordingly.

I love the house we rent, ten minutes away from the venue. Some days I only need to take a backpack with me to work, meaning I can walk across to the courts while people throw frisbees to their dogs. Garry is a passionate fan of the English Premier League, and I like that he knows he can make the trip to Liverpool to see his beloved Reds at Anfield without me, and that this is not deserting me but giving me space to focus and relax and keep things calm.

I've always said that if I was to live anywhere else in the world but Brisbane, it would be London. Garry and I would probably struggle in the winter, but perhaps not. We could cosy up in front of the fireplace at the local Pig and Whistle on a biting British night in January, order a pint and their best Sunday roast, and turn our attention to the sport on four flatscreen TVs, as I do now, without being recognised. Yes, I could get used to this kind of peace.

But I have a tournament to play. I walk down the tunnel to Court 1 and there's a photo on the wall of me as the winner of Junior Wimbledon all those years ago. I don't want to look at it. I want to start this first-round match against Saisai Zheng, who I know will be switched on from the outset, and she doesn't disappoint. I want her to challenge me. I don't want to go through the motions. Let me sink my teeth into the tournament straightaway. I'm solid, though not flawless – 6-4, 6-2 – and walk off court thinking, *Yep, I found a way.*

Problem-solving my way to victory like this sometimes seems a far better way to win than munching the ball flush in the centre of the racquet. I like winning ugly, imperfectly – by *thinking* my way through. Excellence is exhilarating but strategy is more satisfying.

It's like the difference between winning as a drag racer and winning as a rally driver. One is physical and the other cerebral. With the latter, it's all about the choices you make. When the tricky moments come, sometimes you have to stick to what you know works, keeping faith that your ability will prevail. Other times, you have to see what your opponent is giving back to you, and recognise the need for change, and alter your plan. Knowing when to stick and when to switch – that's the challenge. It's gratifying to get things right.

In my second-round match, against Alison Van Uytvanck, I stick to our game plan better than I have for a long time. I dissect her tactics well and win 6-1, 6-3, and keep my feet firmly on the ground. I try to be a no-bullshit personality on tour. My reputation here is important to me. Respect is important to me – that I give more than I receive. I come to the net and shake her hand – 'Well played today' – and I look her in the eye. She shakes my hand – 'Thanks for the lesson, mate' – and gives me a grin. Sometimes that's all there is in a tennis match, and all there needs to be.

In the third round I play British hopeful Harriet Dart, and I feel terrible. This is my singles Centre Court debut, and I want to try to use my experience, even though we are both nervous and intimidated by the atmosphere. From the outset it's important that I make Harriet feel uncomfortable and assert my authority. Although my legs are like lead, I serve exceptionally well, with speed and shape and control, and the first set is over quickly, 6-1. Soon I'm 4-1 in front in the second set, but I'm serving loosely now and facing a break. I play five unbelievable points and end up winning 6-1.

I'm unflustered, and measured. Three months earlier, I'd probably have started to overthink things and lost that service game. I would have got tired and grumpy, and begun noticing things I shouldn't. Like the fact that I'm playing on Centre Court, in front of British royals, and my opponent has a home crowd behind her. But today I've squashed all of those thoughts and stuck to my process. I didn't even look at the royal box, because I didn't want to know who was there. I walked off the court in under an hour.

I know this all sounds so serious, and it has to be at times. But just as often it has to be the opposite.

I'm sitting in the cafe overlooking the courts and I just don't want to do press. They have plenty to ask but I have nothing to say. I know I'm going to walk into the interview room and that I'm going to spit out the same answers I always do, changing only the name of my opponent. I need to break the monotony.

Crowey has an idea – something he's done with AFL players and some of the leaders at Cricket Australia. 'You take a line from a movie or a TV show or a song,' he tells me, 'and you have to find a way to get it into the press conference. Come up with a quote that's meaningful to you and, the first chance you get, shoehorn it into your answer.'

I like this idea. *Lighten up or tighten up.* The child in me decides that Disney should be our theme for the tournament. I know every movie back to front anyway. Should be easy, right?

In my first presser, I talk about the opening match, against Zheng. 'We kind of came into it thinking like, Hakuna Matata, just relax and go at it,' I said. ('Hakuna Matata' means 'no worries' – or so says the song in one of my favourite Disney movies, *The Lion King*.)

After the second round, I'm asked about my family, and I opt for the words of Buzz Lightyear in another childhood favourite flick, *Toy Story*: 'I chat to my niece, and over and over she just tells me, "You can go to infinity and beyond."'

Following my straight-sets win in the third round, I'm asked about shot selection, and I use a lyric from 'Under the Sea', an Oscar-winning song in the animated classic *The Little Mermaid*: 'I think sometimes I look at a shot, I play a shot, I think, "The seaweed is always greener in someone else's lake."'

I coerce Tyzz into playing the game too. He's about to do a side-by-side interview with me, and in advance I give him the quote: 'You've got to work "You've got a friend in me" from *Toy Story* into an answer.' The first question he gets makes his task too easy, so I steal it from him. I want him to squirm and struggle to get the reference into his answer. Sure enough, he butchers a response, but he gets the job done: 'Ash, you know,' he says, while I smirk, 'you've got a friend in me.'

I'm playing Alison Riske next. I remember losing to her in the very first tournament of my return to tennis in 2016 after a break. I came off court that day three years ago and told Tyzz exactly how she plays. 'This girl gets better when her back is against the wall, when she's under the pump,' I'd said then.

'When she's down a set, down a break, Ali gets better.' Today, I'll need to stick to my plan.

And I do at first, winning the opening set 6-3. But I feel myself fatiguing in mind before body. It's been a long month, and now I'm redlining again – panicking as I try to stay afloat. In the second set I have a chance to break her, but she hits a running cross-court winner. In that one moment – when I'm still ahead by one set, in a position of scoreboard strength – I tell myself a sad truth. *I don't have it in me today*, I think. *I don't have the strength and the fuel in the tank to keep pushing here.*

It's strange what one point does to me in this moment. Strange because of the way I feel about points in tennis. *In tennis, remember, you can convince yourself that a break point or set point or match point is more important than any other point, but it's not. Every point has the same value.* As much as I know that's true, and as much as I'm comfortably in front in this contest, I guess I also know that she isn't going away.

In the end, Riske overruns me. I go back to bad behaviours. I don't want to hear from my team. I don't want the support they're trying to give. I'm working each day on my mindset but I haven't completely outgrown those old habits. All I can do is stop them from taking over too often. The wolves of Wimbledon are always going to howl. Today, again, I feed the wrong wolf. Two steps back …

Tears of exhaustion wet my cheeks in the locker room immediately after, and Donna Kelso, the WTA supervisor, comes in and gives me a hug, which makes me cry even more. She's a motherly presence, and if you can't let it all go when a mother figure is holding you in her arms, when can you?

Being on the road is getting harder with every trip. Leaving my home in Brisbane, I kiss the kids on the head – Affie and Chino, my pair of Maltese cross shih tzu brothers – and I hand them each a treat and bolt out the door before they've inhaled their snack, because I'm a mess even before I reach the airport.

I fly and practise and play and recover, and I keep doing it again and again in one city followed by another and another, and sometimes it brings me joy and other times it brings me low. All I can do is appreciate the opportunities I have and recognise that, if it all ended tomorrow, I would be fine with that. Not everything has a perfect Disney ending.

That reminds of what I say in my final presser at Wimbledon in 2019. My parting shot for the media is an ode to another old favourite film, *Annie*.

'I didn't win a tennis match. It's not the end of the world,' I say. 'It's a game. I love playing the game. I do everything in my power to try and win every single tennis match, but that's not always the case. Today, it's disappointing. Give me an hour or so, we'll be all good … The sun's still going to come up tomorrow.'

Chicken Wire and the Riot Act

Training with Stolts was so much fun. He knew to allow me to work on the slice and the chip and the drop shot. We would do drills where he would ask me to hit a different shot on every ball, to be spontaneous and build on the variety I had already developed. He never wanted to stifle my creativity. For Stolts, it wasn't about teaching me how to play tennis – it was about letting me know that it was safe to play the way I liked to play, and that he was okay with it. 'Let's never hit the same ball twice in a row,' he suggested. 'Let's have some fun.'

He kept the sessions short, too, or at least never too long or tedious. Quality over quantity. But he also nudged me, and corrected my faults and flaws. At 15, I wasn't moving my feet nearly enough. A tennis player needs to be soft and precise, always moving, rarely planted, acting before reacting. I wasn't doing that. I was standing still but I was getting away with it – my talent was allowing me to win matches while basically staying stationary. If I wanted to get even better, Stolts said, I needed to be on my toes more, thinking with the balls of my feet – comprehending the flow of the game through my body instead of my mind, through physical instinct instead of mental calculation. Good habits, he called it – I should start to build the good habits.

Partly, this was his philosophy for teaching tennis. But that didn't mean he would coach every player in this way. Stolts got to know me – and Dad, and Mum, and Jim – and learned what would work based on who I was, not just how I hit the ball.

It's not that way with all coaches. Often, the teacher expects the student to be in lockstep with their preferred and proven program, forcing each player into the same stream, one size forced to fit all. But have you heard the phrase 'Consistency is overrated'? It means you need to treat every athlete as an individual, tailoring what you're doing to them and maximising what they can bring. Stolts had me working on variety not simply because he believed in that *style*, but because he believed that style was inherently *mine*. If I were a six-footer with long limbs, launching missiles over the net, using nothing but long-levered power from the baseline to overwhelm my opponents, the drills he set might have been different. But that wasn't me. Stolts taught me to use my strengths and build the rest of my game around them, because that's how he learned, too.

Jason Stoltenberg grew up in the country, in northern New South Wales, on a vast property an hour from the town of Narrabri, north of Tamworth and south of Tenterfield. The sign on the way into the little agricultural village boasts that it is 'Australia's greatest sporting town', in large part because Stolts and a few others – swimmer Nira Windeatt, league player Jamie Lyon and rugby player Chris Latham – were born or started their careers there.

Stolts grew up playing cricket, tennis, golf and rugby league. He was eight when he picked up a racquet to compete in a tennis day being held in town, and he won, so his family decided to build a court on a paddock near their house on the 2000-acre farming property that his father managed. Stolts told me about the space where he learned to play; I'd love to have seen it. His dad took a little patch of land, scraped and flattened the earth, smoothing the dirt and rock down nice and level. He laid down taut strings for lines, and between two posts ran a reel of chicken wire for a net. Stolts would come home from school in the afternoon and play.

He left home at 14 and stayed with a family in Sydney, living with future Australian doubles champion Todd Woodbridge. Stolts went to the Australian Institute of Sport (AIS) in Canberra next, as part of a strong squad. And he was exposed to formal coaching there for the first time. He was lucky to find a succession of coaches who allowed him to play his game and find his own way, tutoring him with subtle tweaks and positive experiences. He developed his own feel for tennis, and it shaped the way he learned – and would one day teach.

He became a damn good player, too. In 1987, he won the boys' singles title at the Australian Open, and was the number 1 ranked junior player in the world. He turned professional later that year and made it as far as the semi-final at Wimbledon in 1996. His career-high ranking was 19, and he stayed in the top 100 for more than a decade, living in Orlando for much of that time. He married former Czech player Andrea Strnadová, had two kids, retired in 2001 and moved home to Australia.

Stolts' first job in coaching was Lleyton Hewitt, who had just become number 1 in the world and was at the peak of his powers. They had 18 months together, during which time Lleyton won Wimbledon. Stolts loved encouraging talent, finding ways to coax and cajole the very best out of people, then refining their rough edges en route to glory, but it came at a cost. Stolts once told me that during the first year he coached Lleyton, he was with him on the road for 41 weeks, and it forced him to ask a question: 'Am I going to be a father or a coach?'

I love that he asked that question of himself. Ultimately, he found a way to do both. Leaving behind the all-consuming global tour, he began working in local development. He coached juniors from a court in his backyard in Templestowe, in northeastern Melbourne, working each day with 15-year-old boys, nurturing their skills, whether they played lefty or righty, flat or with spin.

I began working with him at 15 too, the week before Junior Wimbledon, and then I moved by myself to Melbourne, to live in an apartment in South Yarra – so I could eat and sleep and train and play under his guidance. It was winter, and I'd never felt so cold or alone. I didn't know how to dress for the southerly winds coming up from the Antarctic, biting through my flimsy jackets and right to the bone. Coming from Brisbane, and playing a game that chases summer and the warm sun, I didn't know it could stay so grey and grim and wet and wild for so long. I would leave for training in the morning before first light, and come home to an empty apartment after dark.

I had no idea how to live. Mum had prepared a binder with all my favourite family recipes, which I attempted to learn one by one – from spaghetti bolognese to beef stir-fry with fried rice – and even step-by-step instructions on how to prepare a simple chicken wrap. I wanted it to taste just like it did at home.

It was also the first time I'd ever gone into a hard, professional training block. I ate up the work. I enjoyed the sense that I was doing something at the highest level – being tested and challenged, getting home tired and waking up sore, and doing it all again the next day, and the day after that, building endurance and resilience and belief.

Stolts was my coach but also my drill sergeant – my new big brother and another father figure. He was assessing my tennis but also my mood and motivation. He was trying his best to truly *see* me, but I was a 15-year-old girl: he could study me all he wanted, but I was already adept at internalising my worries and hiding my fears – keeping quiet and carrying on.

Emotionally, I was brittle. But in other ways I was hardening up, building my body and making it susceptible to stress. Walking lunges. Lateral jumps. Running with resistance. Planking with resistance. Weights. Boxing. Sprinting from side to side on the court, and tipping my racquet head down like a batter touching the crease between runs. Stolts organised for me to hit with men who were playing pennant tennis – guys who knew how to hit monster forehands that would test out a teenage girl, but who would also not get rattled if they lost a

few points to her too. I came out of that block a better tennis
player, yet still fragile.

Stolts, Dad and I went to the United States, where I was ranked
the number 2 junior in the world. In a warm-up tournament
before the US Open, I lost my first-round clash to a Canadian
wildcard, and I cried. 'It's alright,' said Stolts, somewhat confused.
'We've just trained for six weeks. It'll take time.'

At the US Open itself, I found a way to win some tough
matches in tough conditions. I felt adaptable, and Stolts was
able to see that and praise that and teach me that this was what
growth looked like. I made it to the semi-finals but lost, and
again I wept. My explanation sounds ridiculous now, but I
cried and cried and tried to explain why. 'I've failed,' I said.
'I didn't win.' I was like a six-year-old, still needing to be told
that I couldn't win all the time.

Stolts was worried. He could sense my struggles. People
looking in from the outside must have thought I was flying – I
was winning matches, with a coach I liked, my dad with me
on tour, playing in perfect conditions – but Stolts knew better.
On the way home we stopped in Los Angeles and received a
phone call from Tennis Australia. They wanted me to divert my
return flight and head south instead, to play in the Junior Fed
Cup in Mexico.

Stolts didn't want me to play; he knew I was exhausted and
drained. He got on the phone to TA and told them I shouldn't
be going.

Of course, I had no idea this was happening. Stolts did his
best to protect me from drama like that. But that buffer also led
to confusion. I was still in Los Angeles, enjoying a day off, and
when I was called and asked to represent my country in San

Luis Potosí, I said yes and got on a plane immediately. I didn't know enough about the discussions going on around me, and I just wanted to do everything I could to please everyone. I was always aware, too, that if my financial assistance was withdrawn, my career would be done. No matter how often Dad and Mum said everything would be fine, I knew my family couldn't afford for me to go it alone.

Part of me knew there were perceptions to manage, too. I was now 'Junior Wimbledon champion Ash Barty', and the last thing I wanted was to be known as a privileged and precious player, too big for her boots. I felt I had to play, because I knew how it would be made to look if I didn't.

And so I flew south by myself, to join two girls who were older than me, whom I didn't really know or have a relationship with. I didn't play in the qualifiers either – they just put me straight into the finals team, which I didn't like. I've never liked the idea of jumping the queue or taking the place of someone who has made the effort and ticked the right boxes.

We were escorted to and from the airport by a full complement of military police, all carrying automatic weapons. We stayed in a compound with 12-foot-high fences, fringed with steel stakes, and weren't allowed to leave. The American team didn't even come – they were too worried about drug cartel violence.

At least on court I could put the whirlwind aside, knowing that I was there for a purpose. I won, and we won as a team, taking out the Junior Fed Cup for the first time in years. Immediately after, I felt as though I had done the right thing: the next time I was pressured to play in a tournament I wasn't prepared for, I could point to this – at least in my mind – and say no with a clear conscience. And that's exactly what happened the following year, actually, in Barcelona. People tried to persuade me, but I had earned the right to take care of my welfare.

I flew home afterwards, but the very thought of going back into training for a summer series of tournaments and travel made me miserable. I told Stolts I didn't want to play anymore. At least, that's how it came out. He remembers this moment as 'the first time Ash quit tennis' – the time no one else recalls. In truth, I just needed to step away for a while, but I didn't have any idea how to do that.

How do you ask for a little rest? Are you even allowed? Can you take a breath? I needed a break, but what came out of my mouth was something else, something that sounded more – as if I were all in or all out.

'I can't play tennis,' I said. 'And I'm not going to. I'm done.'

Let's have some fun.

Mortgages and Monkey Bars

It's late 2019. I'm the French Open champion and world number 1, but I don't reach the quarter-finals at Wimbledon, and I flounder in the American hardcourt summer too. This is no cause for panic, but a conversation is required.

I fly home and ease back into myself the way I always do, waking in my own bed, walking my dogs and making my own coffee. That's a ritual for me. I have a La Marzocco Linea Mini coffee machine, white with timber features. I love taking my time making my coffee, with local Merlo beans. I like to fret and fuss over the extraction and the timing, searching for strong latte perfection.

But today I drink a blend made by someone else, the barista at Cheeky Monkey, a cafe in Swan Street, Richmond, an inner-eastern enclave of Melbourne. I've flown south and find myself sitting opposite Tyzz and Crowey, having the chat this moment demands – this moment in which I'm doubting myself again.

I question my success. I put an asterisk next to every accomplishment. I'm listening to too many pundits, and they have a clear message: *You're winning, but you haven't had to beat Simona Halep or Karolína Plíšková. You're looking good but you haven't had to knock over Naomi Osaka or Serena Williams.* I begin to feel it, too.

They're right, I think. *I haven't played anyone in the top 20.*

Crowey takes the emotion out of the moment and turns straight to logic, making the pragmatic point I need to hear. In the early days, when I wasn't seeded, he says, I would meet top players earlier in the draw. That's the way the system works: give an advantage to the higher-ranked players so they could plough through the field en route to tougher opposition in the finals. Now I'm the seeded one, so I'm bound to come up against lower-ranked players.

Tyzz says it doesn't even matter. Not even a little bit. What matters isn't how I play in the big moments against the top players, but how I play against everyone at every tournament.

First, it's an attitudinal issue. 'This is about having an even keel,' Tyzz tells me. 'It's about not being so affected by the ups and the downs, and instead enjoying everything in between.'

Second, if I feel as though I'm losing to lower-ranked players and only rising to meet the challenge against stiff competition, then there's an issue of respect Tyzz wants me to address. 'You have to *earn the right* to play the top players by fighting your way into the finals, and you do that by absolutely respecting everyone you face,' he says. 'They are all equal. There are no easy matches.'

Now I'm feeling embarrassed, as if I'm back at the West Brisbane Tennis Centre being reprimanded by Jim, and reminded that I'm not better than anyone else, even if I can hit the single slice backhand and twirl my racquet on my finger like a gunslinger. I shouldn't feel entitled to quarters, or semis, or finals. I have to approach every match and every opponent as a challenge, because they are. The WTA ranking system, after all, is incredibly volatile. It's like a game of snakes and ladders. One or two big results can see you slide or climb a few dozen spots in a moment.

Basically, the message Tyzz and Crowey give me is that it's okay to lose to the 47th-ranked player because, shit, they're the 47th-best tennis player in the entire damn world! They have talent and drive, and they're not here to roll over for me.

I head to Asia with this firmly in mind, and by happenstance find myself trading blows with the very best. I do well in Wuhan and lose in the semi-finals to Aryna Sabalenka (ranked 9). I continue that form in Beijing and lose in the final to Naomi Osaka (ranked 3). I move on to Shenzhen, excited to play in the novel WTA Finals series, a contest pitting the elite against the elite, searching for the best of the best players of 2019. I love the degree of difficulty, from the calibre of the competitors to the conditions.

A quirk that those who only watch the game every Wimbledon or Australian Open might not know is that each tournament uses different tennis balls. They might look the same but they do not feel that way. The players need to adjust to the chosen manufacturer for every tournament.

Wimbledon uses Slazenger balls, and has done since 1902, in the longest partnership in sports equipment history. Over the two-week tournament, some 54,000 balls are used there. The Australian Open uses Dunlop balls. The French Open and the US Open both use Wilson balls, although the French clay-court ball is vastly different from the American hardcourt ball. The US Open ball is as light as paper, floating unpredictably through the air, taking off quickly but drifting late, like a badminton shuttlecock.

As well, there are so many variables in how the ball will react. The weather has a major impact, as does the length of rallies and games, and even the court surface can make an enormous difference. The same ball will play completely differently on a rough, gritty hard court as opposed to a slick, shiny hard court.

The technology and data available to players and coaches is fascinating but I don't do a deep dive into such things. I prefer to research with my feel and my racquet. Quickly adapting and learning how I will need to adjust. And I know that the balls they use in Shenzhen – made by HEAD – are denser than others. They're heavier, and the rubber stays harder for longer, and they don't suit my game. I like a ball that's receptive and reactive to spin, that I can grab and direct, lifting it up and turning it over with racquet-head speed, hoping for rotation and torque.

But that's not on my mind right now. Right now I'm in big-game mode, as I'm through to the final against Elina Svitolina – the worst head-to-head match-up of my career. She's beaten me the past five times we've played. She's a scrapper and fighter who always moves well and always competes. She doesn't have a game with big weapons, but she really owns the game she has. Basically, she doesn't miss. Ever. Her strategy is simple: make balls. The more balls she hits, the more opportunities she gives me to miss, and then it becomes a game of patience. Do I wait her out? Do I take a risk? *When* do I take a risk?

Now? Yes? No? Shit. I shouldn't have taken that risk.

The Shenzhen court is purple, which is strange but I enjoy it all the same. It's dark in this makeshift stadium. The lights are lowered but the playing surface is bright and there's a gigantic screen dominating one end of the arena. It doesn't feel like a stadium so much as a podium. It's as if the whole purpose of the structure is to focus on the court alone and not the seats or the stands. It's a stage, and I walk onto it through a puffing smoke machine.

Elina is the reigning champion, and this court suits her. A purpose-built, timber-base court, laid over a basketball court. It's low and slow, so she can run all day, and that means she can force me to hit and hit until I get reckless. Tactically, I do want to be aggressive and I do want to come to the net, but I know I need to be balanced, too.

My body is sore today but my backhand is fluent and strong. My serve is assertive and creative. It takes time to find her breaking point, and even that is hard to discern. Elina doesn't roll over for anyone, but she does show me a slight crack –

a break here or there – and then it's up to me to hold my nerve. It's a mature and clinical win – 6-4, 6-3. I celebrate with my team and give Tyzz a hug, and say to him with a smile, 'No one beats Ash Barty six times in a row.' The WTA Finals is arguably the most significant title outside of the Grand Slams. I am pretty damn proud of my week and the way I finished the season as the WTA Year-End World No. 1.

The winner's cheque – A$6.4 million – is more prize money than has been awarded to any player at any tournament ever, male or female. The tax bill will be massive, of course, but I've never wanted to hide anything. Tax havens are popular on the professional tennis circuit, with players making their homes – on paper at least – in places like the Bahamas or Bermuda, Switzerland or Dubai, Monte Carlo or Mallorca, Florida or Texas, where they pay little to no tax on their winnings. But I've never wanted to be worried when the tax man calls. Ever since day one, I've told my accountants: 'An audit should never be a concern.' I'm risk-averse.

I'm also a homebody who has never seen herself living anywhere but Australia. It's not an option, and people know that about me. I've begun winning large purses now, though, and plenty of people have tried to convince me otherwise – but how much money do you need? A cut of steak can only taste so good.

Right now, I'm thinking of a new home. My dream home. My forever home and – I hope – family home. And it's liberating to know that I can afford to buy exactly what I want. I know what I want, too. I want two storeys and a big stone fireplace and a butler's pantry. I want a floor and a bed. I settle on building a new place high on a hill, adjacent to a golf course 15 minutes from Mum and Dad, with a pool and a gym and grassy lawns and a big garage and an outdoor area to entertain my nearest and dearest.

Money has never been my motivation for playing, of course. I play for the love of the game, for the thrill of the fight, for the reward of a challenge met, and for the people who support me. When I stepped away from tennis as a teenager, I remember coming back to the game. No one knew I was planning my return, although Dad had an inkling when ten boxes of HEAD tennis balls were delivered home.

I was scared to tell him, in fact, because he had given up so much for me – for a career I'd already abandoned once. I remember walking into his room one evening, petrified to break the news. I don't remember what I said, but he remembers.

'I'm going back,' I told him, 'but do you know what I want out of tennis, Dad? I never want Sara or Ali or you or Mum to ever have to worry about money again.'

My parents had every right to resent my tennis obsession, as it derailed years of family plans, but they were only ever encouraging. My sisters had every right to be jealous of the way all attention was diverted to my hobby, but they were the first ones to bake me a #1 cake. Now I want to repay them all.

Ali is a primary school teacher, taking classes for preps and Grade 1s at a small independent First Nations school. Sara is a nurse and midwife and lactation consultant at a private hospital in Ipswich. Mum and Dad both have good jobs too, but the home they raised me in isn't yet fully their own.

I don't know how long it will take for any of them to pay off their mortgages, so I do it for them. I drown out their protests – 'It's too much' and 'You can't' – because isn't this the point of money? To make life easier and more comfortable for those you love, so that they can live out their dreams? It is the best money I've ever spent. Well, that and the monkey bar set I buy for the kids for Christmas – and which I give to them a month early, because I'm soft as butter.

I need
to be
balanced.

Wildcards and Weight Gain

I had needed a break and taken one – I'd quit after Mexico but come back again after a fortnight. I felt ready to play, and as though I'd proved a point. Having won Junior Wimbledon and then helped anchor a Junior Fed Cup victory, I also felt as though I had credits – as though I'd worked hard and shown grit for my country. I had given myself to tennis, and I hoped tennis might give me something in return. Perhaps I could control this thing at least a little more than I'd been letting it control me.

In late 2011 I did another training block with Stolts in Melbourne, so I'd be ready for the long national tournament circuit to unfold. Earlier in 2011, when I was just 14, I had won the under-16s national championship. That felt like an eternity ago. By early 2012 I was still only 15, but now I was playing in the under-18s at nationals. I won that, too. Apparently, that made me the only person in Australian history to have won the national title in under-12s, under-14s, under-16s and under-18s by the age of 15. When I heard that, I could feel that old familiar pressure building once more.

Next, I was entered into the wildcard playoffs for the 2012 Australian Open. It's a pre-tournament tournament, where 16 Aussies who sit outside the top 100 compete for one wildcard spot in the Grand Slam event. The playoffs are divided first into pools: mine was affectionately nicknamed 'the pool of death'. Aren't they always?

In my first match I faced Casey Dellacqua. The woman who would later become my dear friend was 26 at the time, a full 11 years older than me, and even though she was managing injuries, she was experienced and at a great place in her career. She had a spot in the singles draw of the Australian Open in her sights, but I belted her. She was pissed, but I went on to win our pool, and then I continued winning my way through to the final, where I beat Olivia Rogowska in the biggest match of my young professional career. And that was that: I had earned a place in the main draw of my first ever Grand Slam event.

In the first round I drew Anna Tatishvili, a journeyman Georgian player who mightn't spark many memories for most, but who was among the top 50 players in the world at that time. Can you imagine being ranked that highly at what you do? Can you imagine being among the best 50 lawyers or accountants or builders or teachers in the world? To me, as a 15-year-old tennis player, it was unfathomable to think I might reach those heights one day. Yet there are so many almost anonymous but utterly elite players in Grand Slam tournaments every year, toiling away on the outer courts in relative obscurity. You notice these things when you swim in these waters – and even more so when you're on the receiving end of their low-key greatness. Anna Tatishvili dispatched me with ease.

I had at least been part of the main competition, as a young and still slightly built teenager, and my ability was clearly growing. Emboldened by that, I took my first tentative steps out of junior competition and into professional play, albeit at the lower level.

Everyday tennis fans know the names of the four majors. They might also know the next biggest WTA tournaments after that, like Indian Wells and Miami. They perhaps know a few other stops on the calendar, like Rome and Madrid. But they likely have little knowledge of the ITF Women's Circuit that lies beneath, in which you can play for US$15,000 in Monastir, Tunisia, or for US$25,000 in Chiang Rai, Thailand, or for US$60,000 in Braşov, Romania.

In early 2012, I sought out tournaments that were much closer to home. The first was at Homebush, in Sydney – an event that I entered through the qualifiers and went on to win. I won another a week later, on grass in the mallee heat of Mildura, in northwestern Victoria. I compiled a singles record that season of 34 wins and just four losses across nine tournaments. Stolts tried his best to keep my progress steady, but I kept on winning and my improvement kept accelerating.

I wasn't being overworked, either – I simply got better through natural, incremental growth.

The pressure began throbbing again, too. I feared failure: *What if I don't achieve these things that people think I should?* But I also feared success: *What if I do well enough that this lonely way of living becomes my life?* I was trapped in the game – this sport, this industry of winning – cornered by my own ability.

I began entering slightly higher-level competitions, and found some success there too. My team wanted me to pace myself but the wildcard entries and offers kept coming, and before I knew it I was in the main draw at the French Open and at Wimbledon, too. I lost to Petra Kvitová and Roberta Vinci, respectively, but both were seeded and seasoned players, while I was still a girl.

I also started playing doubles and began winning there, too, taking home the Nottingham Challenge in the lead-up to Wimbledon, and then, near the end of the year, teaming up with Casey to take out an event on carpet, the Dunlop World Challenge in Toyota, Japan. It was my biggest win so far, and yet also only the start of something.

In 2013, Casey and I began crashing our way into doubles finals all over the calendar. I was only 16 when we made the final of the 2013 Australian Open, the first Aussie duo to reach the women's doubles final since Evonne Goolagong Cawley and Helen Gourlay in 1977. We made the final at Wimbledon and the US Open, too. We won the Birmingham Classic on grass and the Internationaux de Strasbourg on clay. But doubles wasn't the reason I played – singles was – and in singles I was struggling at the higher level.

In a way, our doubles success masked this issue, but also made it worse. In the pairs format – with an experienced teammate to guide me and share in the pain of a loss – I was supported and shielded, but the prominence we won together on the court left me overexposed off it. Our victories in doubles drew my name out into the open more and more, which was fine when I had a friend there beside me – but in singles, when the wins weren't coming and the toned bodies of the ruthless professional women on tour took me apart, I was suddenly alone with my losses. My opponents were too strong and severe and I was too weak and callow. I left matches haemorrhaging points and streaming tears and drained of all confidence.

I wasn't by myself during this time. Stolts was there. Casey was always nearby. Jim was never more than a phone call away. You would think having that safety net would have lightened my load, but I felt only *burdened*, as though I were responsible for their happiness as much as my own. It's one of those strange things about an individual sport that a team athlete rarely has to consider: that the livelihood and reputation of other people rests immediately on what you do. How you perform directly affects the careers of those who've taken you on as a job. They've followed you to Surbiton and Tbilisi, Wichita and Gurugram, and suddenly you realise that their standing in the game and future in the industry rides on your results.

I was 16, too. I wasn't exactly a child anymore. All my life I'd been told I was a prodigy: 'You're gonna be the next big thing' and 'You'll be world number one someday.' And I had started to believe it. That scared me – what were all those people who put me on a pedestal going to think if I failed?

'Watch this girl,' they used to say within earshot, 'she's going places.' And the people listening would sagely nod and murmur their own endorsements. 'Nothing surer,' they would confirm. 'She's the next Martina Hingis.' But Martina Hingis won the Australian Open when she was 16 years and 117 days old, the age I reached halfway through 2013.

I knew I wasn't being fair on myself – I couldn't seriously expect to perform as well as the youngest Grand Slam winner in the history of tennis. That's not a standard anyone should force themselves to meet. But it didn't matter how logically I looked at things, or how I rationalised my career so far. Put simply, I felt like a failure.

I didn't know how to name these issues either, or understand the way they were breaking my mood and spirit, although I did know a little bit about depression, through my dad, who has suffered from this through his life. I could always tell the difference between those times when Dad was taking his medication and when he was taking a break from them. I knew he had found his right balance, with the help of my Aunty Robyn, an extraordinary general practitioner. Dad had overcome the stigma around mental health enough to have the tough conversations and regulate his life, in order to be the happiest version of himself for his girls. Now I wondered if perhaps I needed to do the same thing.

I was at an ITF event in Birmingham, Alabama, when I took action. I was sitting on a grassy hill above a green clay court in a beautiful southern country club when I fired off a Facebook message: *Aunty Rob – are you available to chat?* I almost hoped she wouldn't reply, but she did, when I was back in my hotel room. She wanted to know more, and so I told her, crying as I typed. I didn't know how to articulate what I was feeling. *I just know I'm sad*, I wrote. *And I don't know why.*

That was the start of my therapy. That was the way I inched into treatment. It was my way of being brave enough, not face to face (yet) or by phone (yet), but by brief direct messages and long emails and texts. I trusted Aunty Rob, loved her, and she helped me unravel my situation, looking at the when and the what and the why, with questions that were light and warm and inquisitive.

She helped me recognise the way my demeanour would plummet in the weeks approaching any tour, as I counted down the days before the departure I so dreaded. We tried different options, different medications, different conversations, and eventually we found the right blend and I started to feel more stable. My emotions began to level out, giving me a sense of contented calm each day. I began opening up and talking more to my family and friends about how I was feeling – the people I knew I could lean on, but was never courageous enough to. Aunty Robyn helped me understand why I was feeling the way I was.

I don't have to do what I'm doing, I began to think. *I have a choice.*

But identifying your problems isn't the same thing as eliminating them. Looking at the sky and seeing the storm won't stop you getting drenched. I was still a kid, far too emotionally immature to handle the cauldron of elite global competition while living this nomadic life. I had enough issues just being a girl in the world.

I had massive insecurities about my body, which developed, as they often do for girls, when I was around 13, maybe even younger. When I was away from home on tour, I had no awareness or routine for play, and therefore no normal routine for meals, so I over-ate. I didn't know how to navigate different foods in France or Belgium or the Netherlands, where the traditional breakfasts were bread and pastry, and the most non-threatening dishes are always desserts. I would put on weight by comfort eating, too, burying my sadness or boredom in food at night before going to bed. Do you know how many different flavours there are in the Milka chocolate range? More than you can imagine.

And when I wasn't putting on useless kilograms through the middle of my frame, I had to contend with functional weight gain elsewhere. I'm not built like other girls – I'm built like an athlete. So I would train and play and eat and sleep and my quadriceps would explode. You need that strength as a tennis player because you rely on your legs for every single shot. Every part of your movement is driven by the power in your legs and the strength of your core. I would do drills to strengthen my forearms and upper body, but watch with melancholy as my shoulders grew more rounded and defined. I hated the way the training showed.

I couldn't celebrate being unique because I was too worried about being seen to be different – not just by the public but by those around me. When I was 15 and won that wildcard entry into the Australian Open, I remember talking to people about the thrill of it all, but I never mentioned the terror.

I didn't tell anyone what I felt like sharing a locker room with women who had trained their entire lives to be lean and long and strong – athletically gifted and aesthetically beautiful goddesses from South America and Eastern Europe. I didn't tell anyone about how they would walk around without a towel on and I wouldn't know where to look, only that I didn't want anyone seeing me so exposed. I got changed in a shower cubicle each day.

By the time 2014 rolled around and I was 17 years old, none of that discomfort or unease or modesty or confusion had been shaken. I was still a girl, still trying to figure out what I wanted, still unwilling to jump in with both feet. Naturally, that was the year fate decided that my first-round match at the Australian Open would be played against the great Serena Williams.

I've never felt so intimidated. We stood on the court in Rod Laver Arena and I felt as though I was beaten before the match even began. In truth, I knew my Australian Open was over the day her name was drawn against me. She wore her ponytail up – I remember the way it magnified her presence – and turned her shoulders over and over during the warm-up, a picture of perfect prowling menace. I went into that match hoping to last an hour, but the 6-2, 6-1 rout took all of 57 minutes. Again, I experienced that feeling of failure.

Looking back, I just wish I had been more courageous in that match. I wish I had given myself a chance. I wish I had fought. Scrapped. Maybe even believed.

I wish I'd known that bravery isn't always something you're born with: it can also be something you learn, little by little, through sheer survival. It can be something you recognise in yourself much later, too, after you've travelled to scary places and faced fierce competitors, after you've texted a family doctor and asked for help, after you've looked at yourself in the mirror and begun to see what everyone else sees.

I wish I knew then what I know now.

Commanding Attention, Consuming Oxygen

After my WTA final win, I fly immediately from Shenzhen to Australia, although not for the long rest I need. You might think a Grand Slam victory plus the number 1 ranking in the world would be enough for me in 2019, but I have unfinished business in the form of the Fed Cup.

Later it'll be known as the Billie Jean King Cup, but from 1963 through to 2019, it's the Fed Cup – and it offers the singular chance for women to play tennis as a team, nation against nation. Australia last won it in 1974; since then we've been runners-up a heartbreaking eight times. Now we've made it into the final for the first time in 26 years. And we're playing on our home court in Perth, meaning we have a great chance to win the trophy back.

I want this one badly. It's right at the top of the list of goals that I penned back on New Year's Eve. We're playing against France, who are well balanced and well drilled. Perhaps most importantly, they have the motivation of a recent defeat in the 2016 final. They're tough. We're tough too, though, and we'll have a roaring home crowd at our back.

Women's sport in Australia feels different now: it's commanding attention and consuming oxygen. I can tell that we're a prime-time attraction in this moment – one of a series of moments that suggests something special is rising.

Sam Kerr has just signed a new deal with English Premier League club Chelsea, making her the world's most expensive female footballer; according to many judges, she's the world's best player, too. Hannah Green has come from the stars to win the PGA Championship, our first female golfer to win a major since Karrie Webb in 2006. Almost a million people tuned in on TV to watch the Super Netball final. Only a few months earlier, in South Australia, the crowd held their breath as Crows star Erin Phillips collapsed on the Adelaide Oval, her knee buckling under her during the AFLW Grand Final between Adelaide and Carlton. The 53,034 people watching it live was a record for a women's sporting event in Australia. Only a few months later, that figure will be comfortably surpassed when 86,174 fans flock to the Melbourne Cricket Ground to watch the 2020 Women's T20 World Cup final between Australia and India, which the Aussies will win, the team dancing on stage with Katy Perry afterwards. A shift is underway.

The setting in Western Australia is perfection, too: ticket sales are going wild, with a capacity crowd of 13,109 expected for both days of the two-day event at RAC Arena, not far from Kings Park and the Swan River – a record for a Fed Cup contest in this country. But all their cheering and goodwill and support can't do it for us. Our captain, Alicia Molik, makes that clear from the outset. Mol is not stern but she sure is serious, and staunch. I love the way she goes about it. I love her, really.

She first learned who I was when I was only 11. I was playing in the national clay-court juniors at the Glen Iris Valley Tennis Club in the leafy eastern suburbs of Melbourne. She was in her mid-20s, playing professionally and living in a share house in South Yarra. 'You have to get down here and see this girl,' her coach had told her. 'A Queensland junior. Ashleigh Barty. You need to take a look.'

The Glen Iris club is tiered, and I was playing on one of the lower-level courts. I had no idea she was there, and barely remember the game, but Mol tells me she saw a short girl using every tool in the kit – topspin, slice, drop shots, lobs – in the space of a few minutes. I had hands, she says later, and touch. There's a difference between smashing a tennis ball hard and playing hard tennis.

We didn't actually meet until I was 15, and even then it was only fleeting. Mol had been watching me practise before Junior Wimbledon, just standing at the side of the court, one Aussie observing another. She saw the same skill set she had seen before, only by then it was more developed. She said hello to me, and looked me in the eye. I smiled and immediately looked down at my shuffling feet. I had manners but also nerves.

Mol became connected to my world in 2013, when she had just been made Fed Cup captain, leading a team featuring Sam Stosur, Jarmila Gajdošová and Casey Dellacqua. I was only 15 and well outside the top 100, but Mol told me I had been picked for the way I was playing – not for my ranking, or my age. Having played doubles with Casey helped me feel like I was part of the team.

We stayed in Lake Como that week and travelled across the border to compete against Switzerland in the beautiful town of Chiasso, carrying our passports to and from the courts each day. I was still only finding my feet but Mol was already seemingly a diplomat. I remember she thanked our hosts at an official dinner, not with some brief and self-deprecating mumble of a speech, but delivering her message of heartfelt appreciation in fluent Italian. *Grazie mille!* I couldn't imagine being that kind of leader.

I practised with Sam one day for a couple of hours, and in the end we worked our way through a practice set. Sam was number 4 in the world at the time, but as the practice session went on, Mol could see me posing some problems for Sammy, even on her preferred clay surface, causing headaches by using a heavy forehand and a chip backhand and a kick serve. Sam went to her after that practice with a question about me: 'Does she always play like that?' I used to wonder why Mol told me about that later. She says it was because she knew my court craft was strong but my confidence was weak.

Mol is from Adelaide, and grew up playing tennis in Henley Beach for a tiny centre called Seaside Tennis Club. She never chased the idea of a professional career, but she got better quickly and was picked in state teams, and by 18 found herself representing Australia. Her first WTA title came in Tasmania at age 22. In 2004 she proudly won a bronze medal at the Athens Olympics, and stood on the dais alongside absolute giants in Amélie Mauresmo and Justine Henin. She had surprised herself when she entered the top 100. She surprised herself even more when she made the top 50. Entering the top 25 was a shock. But she truly surpassed her own expectations in 2005 when she was ranked eighth in the world.

She had her own trials, too. At the tail end of that same year, she suffered middle ear damage: vestibular neuronitis. A doctor gave it to her straight: 'You should think about another career.' But tennis had become a part of her by then. It happens. The outlandish training demands become ordinary, routine, while the exquisite physical mastery of the game and all its quirks become motor memory. Sometimes, when you put the racquet down after holding it for so long, you feel it in your hands when it isn't there, like a phantom limb. Mol was out of the game for over a year – through no fault of her own – at the peak of her career.

The uncertainty and the isolation ate away at her. She retired at 27 and came back. Then she retired again at 30 but stayed retired this time, with marriage and kids on the cards, and the daily frustration of a bad elbow injury meaning she could no longer put herself through the battering daily serve regimen she needed to tread that fine line between failure and success.

A year later, Mol put her hat in the ring to become Australia's Fed Cup team captain. She'd always found tennis to be an insular sport, except for those times when she got the chance to play for something greater. Giving that experience to others suddenly felt like her duty.

During her final Fed Cup tie as a player, Mol had been left out of the team, but went along to practice anyway – dejected, and with her pride stung, but knowing she had to be there to help the team. That's the kind of devotion she brings. She also had a working knowledge of the team, and she knew that would be an advantage. She saw a chance to build a new future using the present as a base, mixing fresh ideas with institutional knowledge. She could lead like no other.

In Perth, in our Fed Cup final against France, she is a rock for someone like Ajla Tomljanović, who is making her team debut. Ajla is 26, and comes to the side via a long and rocky road. Born in Croatia, she got Australian permanent residency in 2014 but couldn't represent the green and gold until she became a citizen in 2018. Always a promising prospect, she suffered a shoulder injury, then a hip injury, then another shoulder injury. Now she is finally fit.

We all understand what it means to her to play for Australia at last. In the locker room, I ask Mol if I can lead the huddle, as I have done in every tie this year, and I look Ajla in the eye. 'Ajla, we are so proud to have you in our team, so genuinely happy for you. We know how badly you want this,' I say. 'I can't think of anyone more perfect to be kicking off a final for us.'

The build-up is perhaps too much for Ajla, or maybe Kristina Mladenovic is just too good, but either way it's over in an hour, the powerful Frenchwoman winning 6-1, 6-1. Those kinds of results happen sometimes. Immediately after, I square the ledger by playing perhaps the most perfect tennis of my life, thumping one of my best friends from the tour, Caroline Garcia, 6-0, 6-0. I sleep soundly on that Saturday night.

The next morning I open the play. I know I have one more big effort in me, one more day for my season. I have my chance to beat Mladenovic, but I don't take my opportunity. The match drags on and draws out, and the feeling of a true Fed Cup tie burns: it becomes a war of attrition. I'm grimacing at every change of ends as the 32 doubles and 69 singles matches I've played this season catch up with me.

'I've got concrete in my legs,' I tell Mol. 'They're so heavy.'

'I know, mate. I know your legs are heavy. I know you feel horrible,' Mol says. 'But you've got this.'

I want to stand up in this moment. I want to block it all out and be a leader. I want to win this title for our nation. For my teammates and for Mol. I know I can, too. I remember playing Fed Cup doubles earlier that year in Asheville, North Carolina, with Priscilla Hon. We were trying to serve out the set against the Americans and she walked up to me pleading, 'I can't hit it, I can't lift my arm, I can't hit a forehand.'

I remember being steely in that moment. 'No,' I demanded. 'You can. You absolutely can. You and me, Pri. Let's go.' And she got it done.

But that isn't happening for me now. All the encouragement and all the self-talk and all the demands I place on myself aren't changing a thing. In my mind, I'm convinced and committed, but my poor body is in complete denial. It's as simple and as devastating as that. I try firing up, breaking back in the third set and doing a running fist-pump and screaming into the sky. I've never had to force the energy in this way, but I do, but it proves an illusion. The match is a two-and-a-half-hour epic – 2-6, 6-4, 7-6 (1) – but I'm the loser.

I walk into the gym, broken, and slump on the treadmill in tears. Mol has crouched down on the treadmill next to me and I look at her through red eyes. 'I'm sorry! I'm sorry! *I'm so sorry!*' I offer up. 'If I could give back the French Open to win that match, I would.'

Mol bursts into tears now too, and gives me a hug. She wanted this just as badly as I did. It's only then that we realise Ajla is warming up for her singles challenge against Pauline Parmentier. I needed to let it all out, but not in that setting – not in a way that might affect someone else and their preparation. Athletes are strange beasts ... who knows what might unhinge their mindset?

Shit, I think. *What have I done?*

But Mol resets and Ajla shrugs it off, and they walk out together and they get it done. Ajla walks back into the rooms 92 long minutes later with a 6-4, 7-5 victory that keeps us alive, and she walks straight over to me. 'I knew you always wanted this,' she says, 'but I didn't realise you wanted it that much.' Seeing me so distraught wasn't a hindrance, she tells me; on the contrary, it fired her up and sent her chasing the win.

We go to doubles now, a deciding rubber, with me and Sam Stosur facing Garcia and Mladenovic, and I don't know exactly what happens or why, but we don't quite gel on court. And we don't use our voices enough to compensate. We get a few unlucky points against us, and no lucky ones back. We find no momentum. Nothing clicks. And it begins to feel as though it wasn't meant to be.

We chase and lunge and try, but the French girls cruise to a 6-4, 6-3 win in the match – and a 3-2 victory in the Fed Cup. The crown is lost again. I try to absorb it all, standing on court throughout the ceremony, doing my best to stifle the sobbing, but I'm a crier, and this moment is worthy of weeping over.

We celebrate and mourn together at the Westin Hotel afterwards – something that people who play team sports get to do regularly, but which we only enjoy rarely. And because the final is being played at home, we all have our families and friends there. Mum and Dad are there. Sara is there too, with Lucy, who was able to walk out onto the court with me at one point. Her smiling face as we entered the arena remains one of my favourite photos. And then we fly home to Brisbane, where Ali is waiting because she's about to give birth.

Now, at the end of an enormous year, I spend six hours going through all of my suitcases – washing and ironing and folding – because that's what I do when I get home. I can't ever let my cases sit. I open them up and hide Christmas gifts that I've bought in cupboards. I put socks in drawers and shirts on hangers. I put every belonging away in its right place, knowing that I'm now in mine. It's therapy after all the turmoil.

That night, Ali gives birth to baby Olivia, and I go to the hospital the next morning and give my new niece a cuddle. When I look at the first photo I take with Liv, I cannot believe how tired I appear. I'm a shell of myself, stretched and pale and desiccated. But I'm also about to get stronger, hearty and hale, because I'm around the people I love and cocooned in the place I love. I'm finally home.

Big, Ugly Tears

Something was building. It was the middle of winter in 2014, and I found my mood careering all over the emotional spectrum. I would be hypersensitive and then numb, disciplined and then lazy, delirious and then despondent. Mainly, though, I think I was wistful, regretfully longing for the normal life I always thought I could live in parallel to my abnormal profession – a life that was now clearly out of reach.

In one of the cooler months down in Melbourne, I flew north to a family gathering – one of those big get-togethers where aunts and uncles and cousins slowly multiplied throughout the afternoon and evening, until there were dozens of us enjoying one another's company.

It made me imagine children of my own, and I could see how those little creatures might one day join the extended Barty brood. I pictured holidays on Straddie where they would learn to fish, just as I had done. I could teach them how to tuck little bags of worms into their togs and how to balance while holding a rod on the rocks by the shoreline. I could tell them stories about the fishing charter I went on for my 16th birthday, when I caught a 16-kilogram amberjack. I could show them my favourite place to wander there – the Gorge Walk along elevated boards to Point Lookout – and watch as they tasted twin-scoop waffle cones from the Oceanic Gelati & Coffee Bar. I could ground them – and myself – in the fixed and fleeting reality of what was once an idyllic but ordinary life.

Instead, I was spiralling through a different universe entirely, like some alien child. What teenager travels the world alone for a living, sleeping in an interstate apartment, making her own meals and exercising daily in some cold, faraway city? I remember I was training one day in Melbourne, as part of a long block of frigid days in which my racquet began to feel like an unwanted extension of myself, and I was suddenly fed up. That makes me sound defiant, but in reality I sat crying alone on the changing room floor at the National Tennis Centre. I knew I was done in that moment. I made up my mind to quit, but I didn't yet have the courage to let it be known.

Instead, I texted Stolts. *I can't train tomorrow*, I wrote. *I feel sick.*

In truth, I just wanted to go to the 18th birthday of a mate, so I flew to Queensland and did exactly that. It might seem nonsensical now, but I felt as though missing that party would have been awful in some irreconcilable way. It was as though this one drunken shindig for a bunch of teenage mates had become symbolic of all the normalcy I'd given up – and I refused to do that any longer. Out on the town in Brisbane, I immediately felt like I could breathe again.

After a few too many drinks, my decision crystallised. *Professional tennis is not for me*, I thought. *I want to sever this tie. I want to do something different.*

Days later, back in Melbourne, I asked Stolts if we could talk. We sat on a couch in a large open area on the third floor of the National Tennis Centre, where there's a cafe and floor-to-ceiling glass overlooking the practice courts. It's a busy public thoroughfare within this place where professional players roam and the bureaucracy of the sport is headquartered.

I looked up at him with a tremble in my lip, but I couldn't hold his eye. 'I think I want to stop,' I whispered. 'I can't do this anymore.'

Stolts was silent but looked right into my eyes, offering a gentle, encouraging look. He said nothing, but if his expression could have spoken it would have warmly said two words: *Go on*.

'I'm not enjoying it,' I continued. 'I need to step away ... and stop playing.'

He wasn't surprised or upset. He didn't offer alternatives or seek details. He just nodded and smiled. 'Ash, I know,' he said. 'I get it. And it's okay.'

I looked back at him, eyes wet, and now it was my turn to wordlessly implore him to continue. *Go on*.

'It's no problem,' Stolts continued. 'It's fine. You need to disconnect. It's the right thing to do.'

He sat next to me and put his arm around me, and with that I had a big, ugly cry, gulping and gasping, and the weight of the world slipped from my shoulders.

'I'm proud of you,' he said. 'I'm proud of your decision.'

I decided later that I wanted to play one last tournament: the US Open in September 2014. But this wasn't a victory lap or a farewell or a final taste – I simply didn't want to let Casey down in the doubles. I decided to make it a three-week trip, so I could have fun and enjoy New York. I was now 18, and I came through the qualifying rounds to earn a place in a main draw for the first time without needing a wildcard.

I didn't quite know how to tell everyone else in my circle, but none of them were surprised. It was clear to them all already that I was suffering from depression. I'd been quiet for weeks, speaking to almost no one. That's unlike me: when I'm comfortable, I'm the clown of the family. I guess I was nervous, and too scared to jump right into the deep, dark water.

I made my family aware one by one, on the phone or in person, tearing the bandaid off slowly. I couldn't bring myself to tell Mum and Dad until they dropped me off at the airport. My last words before saying goodbye: 'This is going to be my last tournament.'

I played terribly, of course. There were no flashes of brilliance to make me reconsider. There was no cinematic moment in which I played a point and hit a ball square in the middle and heard that rich sound of something struck perfectly and decided that I couldn't give up this game I knew so well and loved so much. There was no long dogfight rally where I scrapped and growled and convinced myself that my competitive fire was still burning. There wasn't even a shared look between me and my doubles partner, from which I might have concluded that life is better on the court with my mates than sitting at home wondering what might have been.

I lost my first-round singles match to Barbora Záhlavová-Strýcová 6-1, 6-3, and Casey and I lost our first-round doubles match to Gabriela Dabrowski and Alicja Rosolska 6-2, 6-3. Comprehensive losses, without drama or desire. The end could not have been more perfunctory.

Straight sets. Both times. Going, going, gone. I headed to John F. Kennedy International Airport and boarded a plane with no job, a high school certificate and no idea what I was going to do with my life. I flew home smiling, as if drifting on a cloud.

*

And then … normal programming resumed. A regular teenage life. I lived back at home with Mum and Dad, helping Mum in the garden and taking out the bins every Thursday. I began hanging out with my mates on weekends, doing things that for so long I hadn't been able to, like frequenting my favourite watering hole. I liked the 'RE' – the Royal Exchange – a dive bar in Toowong off the banks of the Brisbane River, where a basic spirit with Coke cost three bucks a glass. I watched Test matches at the Gabba. I went camping in the Scenic Rim, outside the city. I wasn't bored but I wasn't stimulated, and that was actually ideal. For a while.

Cricket found me in 2015. The Women's Big Bash League (WBBL) was about to start, with the aim of becoming a major domestic women's sporting competition. I knew the physio of the Australian women's cricket team and she gave me a call. 'They're looking for a few different athletes,' she said. 'Would you be keen?'

Cricket was, in a way, my first sporting love – the game I watched more than any other. When I was a nine-year-old girl in 2005, I didn't stay up overnight watching Justine Henin win the French Open – I stayed up watching Shane Warne play the cricket of his life in a losing Ashes series.

But I had never played cricket, other than in the backyard and the driveway. I'd never owned my own bat, or worn pads. And yet I found myself at cricket training one Saturday morning at Allan Border Field in Albion, ready to practise with the Queensland state team. I didn't know what to take, so I slung a Country Road bag over my shoulder with a water bottle and some sunscreen inside.

It's strange how the nerves can build up inside you in settings such as this. I arrived for little more than a loose warm-up – I was mainly a spectator, there to watch and listen and learn – but it might as well have been the first day of school. I had never seen women's cricket up close before, and I marvelled at the players' skill level. The technique was sound, they bowled faster than I imagined was possible, and the way they could use the willow to crush those deliveries – wow.

Then it was my turn to have a net, and I faced up to an automated bowling machine. Andy Richards, the head coach, chucked me a bat and some pads from his kit bag. He asked about a helmet. 'Nah, mate, I think I'll be okay,' I said. I'd never worn one in my life – never needed to. With all the girls watching on, I punched a hard cover drive off my first delivery and felt the ball rocket off the centre of the bat. I missed a few, too, but I had fun, bringing my own skills to the drills, like throwing and catching and moving laterally. It was all over in 90 minutes.

I'd thought it was a meaningless casual session, but found out later that I'd actually been auditioning for a spot with the WBBL club Brisbane Heat. And they wanted me.

Delissa Kimmince was the captain at the time, and she took me under her wing, quickly making it clear that no one was fazed by my tennis career. 'Are you gonna keep bringing that Country Road thing,' she asked me the following week, 'or get yourself an actual cricket bag?'

In little ways like this, my new teammates gave me a hard time, razzing me and heckling me, and I gave it right back to them. I loved it. I fitted in without having to change myself at all, and was soon doing three sessions a week, as well as playing locally for the Western Suburbs District Cricket Club on weekends.

Mum came along to watch my very first grassroots game – an intraclub practice game before our season started. Australian spinner Jess Jonassen – one of the best bowlers in the world – was at the other end of the pitch. She crept in to bowl and knocked me over for a duck. Mum had come along to support me, and had watched with glassy-eyed boredom as I stood in the field all day – only to see me go out first delivery when I finally got my chance with the bat. A day's worth of work undone with a single bad stroke.

I did better next game, scoring 63 runs off 60 balls and taking two wickets bowling gentle (very gentle) offies, and then I settled in for a full summer season, averaging around 42 runs per innings. I played well. I'll never forget the first century I made, at our home ground in Graceville. I called Dad immediately after coming off the field – 'Dad, I made a century!' – and he laughed down the phone line. 'You're an idiot,' he said, 'but I love you.'

I spotted Mum on the drive home, while she was out walking the dogs. 'Mum!' I screamed from the car window, 'I made a hundred!' – and she nearly fell over I gave her such a start.

I enjoyed playing for the Westies, and never more so than in our Grand Final. I was our top scorer that day with 37 runs, but I couldn't have cared less about my performance so much as the new sensations that came with winning as part of a group. I remember being roasted in the sun and then cracking open cool beers in the sheds, celebrating together with cans of XXXX in hand and thinking, *How good is this?*

By now I had signed on with the Brisbane Heat for the inaugural season of the Women's Big Bash League, and I was lucky enough to play in the first ever WBBL match. I made 39 off 27 balls in our game against the Melbourne Stars, as domestic women's cricket was televised for the first time. There was real excitement building among the girls who had waited so long for rightful recognition on the national stage.

I remember the way they approached the sport with such love for each other. I loved that element of the game. I loved the fact that even if I lost – failing dismally as an individual – the team could still win.

And yet, in another way, I didn't like that at all. I missed the accountability – the sense that my errors are my errors, my decisions are my decisions, and they have consequences for me. I missed the one-on-one competition of tennis, and the fact that the result was always within my control.

I could still see that up close most weeks, too, because I didn't give the game away entirely. I began coaching tennis with Jim, in fact, back at the beautiful old West Brisbane Tennis Centre, under the jacarandas and poincianas and between all those factories and warehouses.

Jim was happy to have me, because I was happy to do everything, working mornings and afternoons and nights across all five courts. I would take charge of junior fixture competitions, teaching little kids how to score the game. I did group lessons for promising teenagers. I did private lessons for little old ladies playing socially. Jim had a school tennis program, and would send me out to Graceville State School at 7.30 am, St Joseph's Primary School at 10 am, Sherwood State School at 1.30 pm and Corinda State School at 4 pm.

Jim joked with me about how he'd given me the boring jobs he didn't want to do. He was open with me about his scheme – he hoped I would grow tired of coaching and realise I was made to play, but I loved it all. I mean, I'd get frustrated if I was trying to explain the difference in grips or the rules for the games and a few little clowns wouldn't listen, but otherwise I did what was needed with a grin. I cleaned the pergola, I strung racquets, I swept courts – I considered cutting the grass with his ride-on mower.

I even tolerated Jim's tongue-in-cheek taunts about cricket, and the way he'd get into my ear after I'd spent an entire weekend baking in the field before losing my wicket cheaply. 'That must have been fun,' he would say, smirking. 'Compare that to playing Serena Williams at the Australian Open.' And, slowly but surely, without even realising it was happening, I found myself with a nagging itch.

Part of me knew that I had left tennis without ever fully investing in it. Sure, I had felt the monotony of the travel, the isolation of the tour and the pressure of expectation, but I had also never committed to giving the game my all. Whether from fear or desperation – or from the sense I was playing tennis on everyone's terms but my own – I had always held something back.

Now I felt simultaneously guilty and curious – not about how many tournaments I might have won, but where tennis might have taken me. *Maybe*, I thought, *I owe it to myself to find out.*

I had
always held
something
back.

Lovely Complete Strangers

The year 2020 begins, and with it comes the claustrophobia, and I think of what Tyzz always tells me when there's too much sound and fury around me. 'When you're on the court, this is your bubble,' he likes to say. 'This is where no one can touch you. This is where you can do your thing.' Really, it's our thing – we do it together. But he narrows my focus and gives me independence.

Normally that helps me right the ship, but not this time. My bubble has shrunk. The pre-season – that blessed annual chance to escape and isolate – has shrunk, too, the languid stretch of summer days suddenly contracting. Ten days. We had just ten days of 'off-season' after our Fed Cup final and suddenly we were back at it.

Lunch with a sponsor. A photo shoot. An interview. Things I can only do when I am at home, in Australia. And that is rare during the season. I enjoy reconnecting with my extended team because I know how fortunate I am to have such great sponsors and to work with such authentic people. We've built great relationships over the years. To the people involved, each commitment might seem like a minor drain on my time and energy, but the cumulative effect of such appointments is huge. It takes hold by increments, each interruption requiring a degree of preparation and debriefing, meaning I can't really relax – not fully, anyway.

The tennis arrives right on cue, but for me it feels too early, as though I've missed my chance to take any meaningful time off. I'm coming off a big year, yet rather than reset and refresh and recharge, I've charged right on through, and the trappings of my new-found fame are closing in, even at home.

I play the Brisbane International and line up against Jen Brady, who has improved out of sight during the pre-season. I practised with her earlier in the week and felt it in her strike. I know she will be at the pointy end of tournaments by the end of this season. I don't yet know that she will end up beating Sharapova, Svitolina, Vondroušová, Garbiñe Muguruza and Angelique Kerber, but I know she's good enough to beat me right now – and she does.

I'm usually good for a first-up loss to start the year. I always feel rusty, and never sharp enough to compete with the best.

Playing a tournament while sleeping in my own bed always felt super strange. Ordinarily that doesn't matter to me, but I can sense the public judging this loss, and it grates. I can explain in the media that Jen is rising fast – perhaps much faster than they know – but to them it's not really about the Yank winning as much as the Aussie losing.

I try to shake it off but the feeling drags and nags. For one of the few times in my career, I call on Jim for help. I want him out at my next session with my hitting partner. 'I need you on court with me. Tomorrow,' I tell him. 'I need you to watch.'

I'm angry and apprehensive, and I try to explain the tension. 'I know how harsh the Australian public can be,' I say. 'I feel like there's this hope that some Aussie is finally going to win the Open, but I'm so far off it. I'm going to get pummelled.'

As I go through a simple but intense session with Tyzz, Jim watches from the side of the court, studying my shot making and assessing my stance. He knows he's not here to intervene or mess with my technique or my form, so his message is one of simple and familiar reassurance. 'Mate, you just need to hit balls,' he says. 'You need to loosen up and trust yourself. The tennis is still there.'

He's right, but I go to South Australia for the Adelaide International and I'm still tight, and my world constricts a little more. The players' hotel there is the InterContinental, a short walk across the bridge over Karrawirra Parri from the Adelaide Oval. I usually love this quiet spot, but not right now. All I want to do is check in to my room, but the lobby is loud and full – and then someone spots me.

A woman comes over to say hello, to tell me how much she enjoys watching me play, to ask for a selfie – and it's fine, really, it's fine. Happens all the time. Only now something is different. All eyes are upon me. It's a curious thing when the entire collective stare of a room is on you. I once heard a footballer describe being a star athlete in public as like being an animal in the zoo. And if you reach a certain point of success, you're not just one of the monkeys or the tapirs or the tree frogs – you become the lion, the attraction everyone stops to see.

They're sure stopping now. They're literally stopping me, in fact. It's as if one person saying hello to me gives the next person permission to do so as well, and the next one after that. The more I smile politely, the more time I share, and the more readily I pose for a photo, the more people wait for their own turn for an encounter. Good manners creates this gravitational pull, until I realise I need to wrench myself away or I'll be there listening all day long.

I love what you do.

My daughter loves you.

My son loves you.

My mum loves you.

I go to fetch a coffee from a cafe I like, and I'm stopped six times during the two-minute walk. I go to the shops to get some snacks and I'm stopped going down every single aisle. I turn a corner and people who have already spotted me stand waiting, smiling, expectant. And they're lovely people. Lovely complete strangers. Complete strangers who know the names of my parents and sisters and dogs. Strangers who want a hug, and I don't know what to do because this is scary, and weird.

'I'm sorry,' I stammer, 'but I don't know who you are.' It sounds rude saying it to them.

I go back to my hotel room and sit alone, trying to navigate my frustration. I send my sister Sara a text message and she tries to call me, and I don't answer, so she texts me immediately: *Answer my call, bitch – don't you screen me!* I call her back and cry to her about this moment of panic and dread. 'We're only in the second week of the year and I can't handle this,' I say. 'This is not me. This is not what I want.'

The night before my first match, Crowey calls me. 'So, okay, how are you feeling?' he asks.

It all spills out. I'm suffocated and confused. I cry to him, naturally, and he explains that I don't have to feel threatened by anonymous well-wishers, but can instead be thankful for their kindness. Rather than being stand-offish or feeling forced to communicate, I can choose to be appreciative. Smile and lean on a new spoken mantra: 'Thank you so much for your kindness – I really appreciate it.' And then I can turn and leave, because I have to – because if I ask a question of my own or linger too long on one of theirs, I'll end up giving too much of myself away. I don't want to resent any fan, but I don't want to get stuck with them either.

I cry to Tyzz, too, and he puts it all in context. 'You've connected with these people. They feel like they know you,' he says. 'But you're going to have to understand that, when you're competing in Australia, other people will need to help you. *I'll* need to help you. We'll need to get your gear for you, and grab your coffee, and go to the shops. You just have to accept that – right now, at least – you cannot do those things. You just can't.'

It's a delicate week, but one I learn from, match by match. The first round is steamy and I lose the first set to Anastasia

Pavlyuchenkova, but I scrap and fight to find my nerve to break back and win. Next I play Markéta Vondroušová and I begin to feel more relaxed, and the win comes easily.

My semi-final, against Danielle Collins, ebbs and flows. At one point I look up at the supporters who've been crowding me this past week, and I decide they're going to help me – and so in the third-set tie-break I do something I've never done: I look up at them as they cheer like crazy and I urge them to amp it up – 'C'mon, a little bit more!' They get louder and I can see it annoying Danielle, and I have more fun with it as I charge to the line. Even after match point, I wind up my arm and fist-pump for the celebrating crowd. *If you can't beat 'em, have them join you.*

I beat Dayana Yastremska next, and for the first time ever I have won a WTA final in Australia – third time's a charm. I glance around the arena on what feels like one of the most important days of my career, and I begin to see how this new life might function.

The people in this crowd make me wonder about that separation professional athletes strive to find, between who we are and what people think of us – the psyche versus the story. They're two separate entities, of course – the person and the persona – but they're both real. They overlap, compete and sometimes coalesce.

Someone once wrote that one of the primary characteristics of a boxer is lying, in that the sport requires you to systematically cultivate a double personality: 'the self in society, the self in the ring'. I can see why that's necessary in combat sport, but as the crowds who stopped me in the street now sit in the stands cheering, and as I encourage their applause and lean into this moment, I begin to realise that it's true of tennis too.

Maybe I can do this, I think. *Maybe this is my reality, and maybe I can handle it. Maybe I can harness this army of lovely complete strangers. Maybe I can be me.*

*

The quick turnaround between the Adelaide International and the Australian Open, in Melbourne, is what I need. Adelaide is like any city – if you spend too long there, the stimulus of the new fades and the allure grows stale, and all you can think about is how much time you're spending away from home. The quick transition from one place to the next helps me avoid getting too distracted or hyped up about the approaching Grand Slam on home soil. There's no time to sit and think – and that's a good thing.

The first few sessions of January 2020 are played indoors, with the roof closed for rain. On the subsequent days it's hot and hazy and windy, and the sky turns crimson and grey. It's a portent of something much bigger, happening not far away. The east coast is burning, in a string of fire fronts that will define this as Australia's Black Summer, razing 19 million hectares of land and claiming 34 lives.

I watch with my team, and understand the seriousness and scale of the destruction. I read in the newspaper that as many as a billion animals have died. I've seen images of cattle carcasses cooked against farm fencing, of colourful native birds now blackened and washed ashore. I've watched footage of koalas drinking water from bottles, a sign that their dehydration is about to kill them. In such moments I feel small about what I do, almost embarrassed to be playing a game for a living amid so much loss.

I'm torn in these instances, too. I want to lend a hand in any way that I can, but I have to stop and think. Do I give money to a worthy cause publicly, drawing attention to the issue so that others with means might follow my lead? Or do I recognise that the country is in mourning, and simply do what I can to help without letting the world know that a tennis player is donating cash to a cause? It's not about me, I decide, so I quietly make a charitable contribution to the Red Cross and the RSPCA. And then I turn myself to the task at hand.

I feel great coming into this Australian Open. Lesia Tsurenko is a match-up I hate, pairing an awkward style with challenging patterns, so I'm more than thrilled to win, even though it takes me three sets. Polona Hercog, on the other hand, is a match-up I love. She's a big server who takes the game on, meaning cheap points are on offer if you play with discipline, which I do. My opponent in the third round, Elena Rybakina, is young, raw and has been running hot, and I'm unfamiliar with her – which is why I'm so pleased to take her down quickly. I've wanted to make a statement at some point in this tournament – 'This is the level you're going to need to play to compete with me' – and I do exactly that.

Alison Riske knocked me out of Wimbledon only the year before, and is often underrated, but I want to approach her as if she's any other opponent. This is not personal. This is not about redemption. Nor is it a grudge match. She's won three tough matches to get this far in this tournament, and players are not given enough credit for what that represents. It's easy to put all of that out of my mind, though, because the conditions are tough. The end-to-end wind is brutal, like playing inside a fan-forced oven, and I find myself trapped by it at times, as Ali pushes me further and further behind the baseline, hitting flat balls with difficult depth. To find a way to win against her in three sets might not seem significant from the outside, but it's hugely meaningful to me.

Petra Kvitová is my quarter-final opponent, and I brilliantly execute my plan against her, ignoring the noise. I feel as though I'm meeting every challenge and manoeuvring around every obstacle – winning through with tactics and patience more than skill or passion. Finally, I feel like I've broken through at my home Slam.

The attention goes to a completely new level in the semi-finals, as I'm told I'm the first Australian woman to make the final four at Melbourne Park since Wendy Turnbull in 1984. I speak to a woman who would know about that kind of pressure, my friend Evonne Goolagong Cawley, and her message is consistent and warm: 'Keep having fun. I'm proud of you. I love watching you play.'

I'm playing against the young Russian-born American Sofia Kenin, and recognise that I've never quite felt comfortable against her. She is unpredictable, in a way that almost seems designed to confuse and confound. She makes wild errors in one game and paints her own lines in the next. She hits with discipline to the point you feel trapped, and then plays the most aggressive shots to obscure parts of the court.

It's 40 degrees but feels much hotter on court – I love playing in this weather. I have two set points in the first set, and one set point in the second set, but I take none of them. I'm passive – way too passive when it matters most. Kenin plays the big points better today, summoning the courage I can't quite find. I'm too caught up in the struggle, focusing on the fact that this is ugly tennis, when actually I need to step up and play the beautiful game. Sometimes that happens. I lose a tough encounter – 7-6 (8-6), 7-5 – and my heart is bruised. Badly.

When I walk into the press conference, I have my newborn niece with me. This is not the first time I've taken a niece to a press conference: Lucy joined me at a Fed Cup tie in Brisbane early in 2019. My newest niece is just 12 weeks old and wearing a pink onesie.

'Her name is Olivia – she's telling you that right now,' I say to the reporters. 'I mean, perspective is a beautiful thing. Life is a beautiful thing. She brought a smile to my face as soon as I walked off the court. I got to give her a hug. It's all good. It's all good.'

I leave Melbourne and lick my wounds, have a few beers and try to congratulate myself on making it into the semi-finals. I have a whole year ahead of me, and I feel as though I'm coping well – or at least working my way through the issues and meeting the continuous obligations my career has become.

Five days later, a friend texts me: *It's bullshit, mate, don't worry about it.*

Worry about what? I reply.

Did you not see the comments?

What comments?

I don't sit on social media, or follow news about myself, but now I see. People are turning against my moment with Olivia in that final press conference. I'm livid, straightaway. I want to retaliate, right now. It feels like an attack on my family. My values.

I know every journalist in that room and they know me. They know I don't bullshit, and that I've never avoided a press conference. If they were too scared to ask a tough question because a gurgling three-month-old girl was sitting on my lap, that's on them, not me. I chat to my team, and their view is that if I say something, the 'issue' will only grow. I trust them, so I say nothing and focus on what's next.

I choose to dwell on better moments, too, like the night immediately after that press conference. I was out with Crowey and he handed me his phone. His old friend Cathy Freeman had watched me play that night – the first time she'd seen me live. I tried thanking her, and telling her what she meant to me, but it all came out as a blubber and bawl, and me babbling about wanting to be just like her.

'Oh, bub, just keep being you,' Cathy told me. 'It will happen. Just keep believing.'

ABCD

There's a story people tell about me, about my comeback to tennis after a teenage hiatus, and it gets a little more muddled with every telling. The short version is that Casey Dellacqua, my best mate and doubles partner, brought me back to tennis with a casual hit one day – 15 January 2016, to be specific – on the back courts of the Sydney International.

It's true, at least in a basic sense. But it's also important to know that Case wasn't necessarily trying to get me back into the sport at all. In fact, she was easing herself back into tennis, having gone through her own much harder stint on the sidelines than my voluntary leave of absence. She was overcoming an awful injury, and trying to make her way in that delicate recovery – taking one of many laborious steps she has climbed in a gritty career. And I'll always help a mate.

I should zoom back first, though, to when Case and I met. I was just 13, little more than a scared kid, and she was 24, an already fierce competitor on court, and someone known for extracting every bit of her potential. I texted her at the time to ask if she would play doubles with me at the Brisbane International, as a wildcard entry. It was a risk for Case, yet she took a chance on me. I was just a kid and she was already a well-established doubles player, building her brand in singles and entering her prime. She took the gamble, though, and we clicked from the get-go.

She loved my tennis. She told me that I had the athleticism and the shot-making, but what impressed her more was my court sense – that spatial awareness that allows you to cover the right parts of the playing surface, and the capacity to understand the decisions that determine why you win or lose. It's lazy and reductive to describe strategy within sport as being like chess, but tennis is definitely as much about the choices you make – the shots you take and the places you run – as it is about the skills you develop and the fitness you build. Talent and hard work are a big part of the equation, but no bigger than the moves you make. Case could always see that.

She took the time to learn my story, too, and she loved it. I loved hers just as much. Case had never really been a top junior. She had to fight her way through. We were different in that way, but in other ways she was exactly like me. She grew up in Perth, far removed from the southeastern centre of tennis in this country, and she moved to the Australian Institute of Sport in Melbourne – also alone – when she was 16. She struggled with that just as I had, with being away from family but also with the pressures of being a young woman and a national-level athlete. The next few years were a struggle for her, as they had been for me, but she reached the top 100 by the time she was 20.

When I met her, Case had been through a lot of what I was yet to experience. I think I could sense that about her – a certain worldliness and stoicism. It was one of the things that drew me to her most. She was a decade older yet made me feel like a peer, a friend – someone I was going to have fun with on court. She's the most childlike, caring, fun-loving person ever. As I was introduced to the tour, Case became my sister, my mum, my *person* when we were on the road. I had found a mate for life, but also someone with whom I enjoyed stunning early success.

We became a perfect partnership. Our games complemented each other's. Case gave me the belief and permission on court to go nuts – to be creative and have fun. She plays on first court, on the deuce side, and has one of the best cross-court backhands in the game – particularly her return – while I love to hit my forehand inside out, and chip around with a backhand slice. So her strengths covered my weaknesses, and vice versa, and we became a deadly lefty-righty combination.

ABCD. Ash. Barty. Casey. Dellacqua.

The doubles competition often gets passed over in assessments of tennis. When we consider the annals of the sport, how many of the great players flash through our minds – Björn Borg, Steffi Graf, Ivan Lendl, Serena Williams, Rod Laver, Chris Evert,

Pete Sampras, Evonne Goolagong Cawley and so many more. But do our minds ever turn to the pairs? Martina Navratilova and Pam Shriver won 21 major doubles titles – 21! – including the 'Golden Slam' in 1984, but do we even recall that they competed together for so long? And what of those doubles specialists, such as the Bryan brothers, Bob and Mike, who never competed highly in singles but have together won more doubles titles than any other pair. How many exactly? One hundred and twelve!

It's true that Australians might have a little more familiarity with doubles than most, given the partnership of Todd Woodbridge and Mark Woodforde – the Woodies – who won 11 majors together, along with a gold medal at the 1996 Olympic Games in Atlanta. But overall, it's often dismissed or even forgotten.

That was fine with me at the time I was playing with Case. I didn't want any attention anyway, but it could easily have come for me in 2013, when we made three of the four Grand Slam finals in doubles. Then I retired, of course, but she kept playing and succeeding. Case completely redefined herself in singles and had a career-best season in 2014. She continued to be successful with other players in doubles, too, making more Slam finals and winning big tournaments.

That's what she was doing in October 2015, playing doubles with Yaroslava Shvedova at the China Open. In a tournament halfway around the world, which few people back home would have been watching anyway, she turned to get up for a smash but tripped and fell and hit her head on the hard court. Case doesn't remember the final minutes of the match at all, but was told later that she walked off the court and vomited immediately, complained of severe headaches, then woke up in a Beijing hospital.

She had suffered a horrific concussion, one that left her with debilitating ongoing symptoms. She couldn't walk in the light. Headaches were a constant companion. Normally she was outgoing and bubbly; now a quiet anxiety began to boil inside her. Case didn't want to talk to anyone or go anywhere or do anything. She tried to get back on court but couldn't find her equilibrium or coordination or clarity. She never played another singles match, and thought she would never play again at all.

That's where her life was at in early 2016. And me? I was about to head to Adelaide for a cricket game. That was when she texted me.

Yo bra when do u get in? Is it tomorrow or Thursday? Are u bringing ur racquets?

Yo tomorrow! 10 am I think I land. Yeah I'll bring a couple of racquets down, chuck them in with my cricket kit. Gotta bring it all down with me 🙄

Yah cool mate. I will come & get u from airport just text me when u land & I'll meet u in the pick-up spot. Would you be keen for a hit tomorrow arvie & then watch a bit of tennis at Homebush? Excited to see ya!!

Oh, you're a legend. Yeah, I'll have a bash. Not sure if it'll be any good 😂😂 *I'll come out for sure, no worries.*

Haha, don't worry, I'm only a few hits in so I'm rusty. We can just have a quick light fun around bash 😆 *yah cool* ✌️

We walked into Homebush together while the Sydney International was being played. We picked a quiet time to go out on one of the courts, later in the afternoon, when no one was around. I'd like to say something built inside me over the course of our cruisy session, as if each little hit and movement drove me deeper back into my groove, but it wasn't gradual at all. Straightaway, first hit, first ball – straight out of the middle.

Ohhh, I felt. *I've missed this.*

It was the slice backhand that got me: hook, line and sinker. We hit some more and had a few laughs and screwed around, and I realised I'd forgotten how much I loved doing that together. We were both self-conscious, of course. *Is Case making a comeback? Am I? Or are we just two friends hitting balls to one another?* All I could think about was how much joy I felt. As much as I'd seen all the old ladies and juniors at the West Brisbane Tennis Centre smiling throughout their lessons, I'd forgotten how much the game could make me smile too.

And I'd forgotten how easy it is to fall into a rhythm with the person on the other side of the net, whether it's your coach or hitting partner or opponent. Have you ever not seen a friend in ages – maybe months or even years have gone by without contact – and you're nervous about seeing them again, and all those nerves are completely irrelevant because you slide back into your relationship as though you'd never stopped talking in the first place? In the fading afternoon light that day, with the last of the sunset casting across the court, tennis suddenly felt like that – like I was slipping seamlessly back into a conversation with a close friend.

Naturally, it helped that it was Case. I needed her. She needed me. We needed each other, and we needed the game that had brought us together. We hit and hit and I messed up a few but went through the whole repertoire, and we sweated and laughed and stretched.

What the hell am I doing out here, in the back of beyond? I wondered. *Why are we not on court together, playing in this tournament?*

We went back to Case's for a BBQ and a beer, and that evening I called Stolts. My decision was made. I think when he saw his phone ring, he knew exactly what the call was about. I went home to Brisbane ready to return to the game.

When I told my family, they simply nodded as though they'd seen this coming. Jim definitely knew, after we met and chatted for hours in the tennis club pergola in Springfield, where I hit my first ever tennis ball. He had been to Europe on holiday, so we talked about Spain and Portugal and France. I was still playing cricket, so we talked about runs and spinners and slips. We talked about the lessons and tournaments at the West Brisbane Tennis Centre. But mainly we talked about how to plan my return.

'Jimbo, I reckon this is what I'm meant to do,' I told him.

He agreed, with no fuss and no 'told you so' smart-arsery either – just a nod and a wink. He had a few ideas about what Ash Barty 2.0 might look like: how I would need to embrace everything and make this second phase of my career utterly my own. Choose my own team. Choose my own tournaments. Book my own flights. Make decisions for myself. If it doesn't work out, then it ends on my terms and no one else's. I wanted that accountability.

'This time around, do it your way,' he said. 'Do it *all* your way. Keep the ball in your court.'

Laying Low, in Limbo

It's early March 2020, and we arrive at Indian Wells on the Saturday before the BNP Paribas Open is due to start. We stay at the Miramonte Resort & Spa, not far from Joshua Tree National Park and in the shadow of the Santa Rosa mountains, and although the quaint boutique hotel is famed for its wellness treatments – including gemstone facials and eucalyptus-infused steam rooms – we're here on business.

That's a pity in a way, because it's a gorgeous spot, and the crowds here seem to delight in the atmosphere – not least the celebrities who flock to the tournament, from the worlds of entertainment (Ben Stiller and Will Ferrell), sport (Mike Tyson and Wayne Gretzky), business (Larry Ellison and Bill Gates), not to mention music (Gwen Stefani) and fashion (Anna Wintour). I never really notice them while I'm on court, but I see snaps of them from the paparazzi later. I begin to feel a little like one of them myself as I submit to a parade of promotional photo shoots for the WTA and HEAD and FILA.

I'm waiting for the qualifying playing schedule to come out so we can confirm our practice times, and the girls from the tour are bouncing messages around on WhatsApp, wondering why we don't yet know who's playing when. There are whispers, too – none confirmed – that the tournament might not be staged at all. Surely not? We've only just got here. This thing called Covid-19 is worrying, but isn't it on the other side of the world? There's only one case in the entire Coachella Valley.

Soon word comes through and it's official: Indian Wells is cancelled. We'll have to wait and see what happens with our next stop, the Miami Open. There are no crowds here yet anyway – not a soul throughout the venue – and certainly no comedians or actors or fashionistas or tech entrepreneurs. I do a photo shoot in the morning and play golf in the afternoon. I walk past a Corona beer tent and take a photo, taking the mickey out of the moment. I have no idea what's coming. None of us do.

We're told we can stay and train while we wait and see whether we'll be heading to Florida or not. The practice courts are full because there's little else to do, and because we're professional athletes, we're addicted to our preparation. But at the same time, we're practising and preparing as we usually would, while wondering aloud: 'What are we practising for anyway?'

I have a long, hard session with Croatian Donna Vekić, and I feel sharp and strong. I tell Tyzz it's one of the best sessions I've ever had. I'm ready to go. Primed to pounce.

Donna is on the WTA Player Council, and after our practice she picks up her phone. 'Oh my God, the men have just cancelled the ATP Tour for six weeks,' she tells me. 'They're doing their player meeting right now.'

The World Health Organization has just declared a global health pandemic, and Donna rushes off to a meeting while I pack up my gear and wonder what will happen next. I do the maths in my head. If the girls do what the boys are doing and eliminate the next month and a half of tennis, that will take us to the middle of the European swing.

I go shopping with my team at the outlet malls to take my mind off things. A few of the Aussie boys are booking flights home, and I know I should do the same – my travel agent can book them for me right now – but we still don't know what the girls' tour will be doing. I can't confirm any change until we know for sure. I head out for a couple of hours anyway, and when I get back I learn that President Donald Trump has closed the borders to Europe, and a two-week quarantine system is about to be established in Australia. Funny how you can pop out for lunch and some window-shopping at Kate Spade and Tommy Hilfiger, Ray-Ban and Disney, only to get back and find that the world has changed.

The team gets back to Australia by any means necessary, which it turns out means different classes – premium economy and business – and different destinations, Brisbane and Melbourne and Sydney. Each ticket is now at least $5000 more expensive than it was five hours earlier, but I arrive home in Brisbane, via Melbourne, having beaten the timeline to quarantine. We isolate at home for a fortnight anyway, laying low, in limbo.

This is the beginning of information overload, where one case becomes ten cases becomes 100 cases, and news starts emerging about where and how all this started. People point the finger at Wuhan, in China. I was there in October, and I remember how one of the girls flew home to Australia and thought she had Ross River fever – but maybe she really had something else.

Many members of my extended family have a medical background, including diagnostic technicians, nurses and doctors. Being actively involved in the medical world, the Bartys have a swift understanding of how bad this is and might yet become. We're not naturally sceptical, either. In times of uncertainty, we have always relied on what we know, which is study and science – the only information worth assessing. And when you're done assessing risk, you assess priorities. Hitting tennis balls comes last.

People seem to understand this quickly, too. Tennis isn't football or rugby or soccer or gridiron or basketball. There is no sense of setting up a domestic bubble in which we all can live and ply our trade, because we come from all over the world and play all over the world. Tennis is an international sport in the way that golf or athletics or swimming is international. The tour as we know it is not going to happen.

The tournament organisers at Roland-Garros have other ideas, finding a two-week window and deciding the French Open will go ahead. The tournament director, Guy Forget, phones me, asking if, as world number 1 and defending champion, I'll play. He says it's an important time for the tennis world to unite, and that we shouldn't be fighting with one another for calendar spots to play tournaments.

I think again of the risks and my priorities, and I feel that playing would be inappropriate. I tell him that I honestly don't know when I'll consider playing again.

The WTA tour is still unsure of the current circumstances and the calendar, but it seems the French Open is the only confirmed tournament.

Wimbledon is cancelled – a dagger to my heart. The Asian swing is cancelled – one of my best hunting grounds. I can't sleep. I'm tossing and turning and responding at all hours to messages from the girls. I have multiple Zoom calls with Simona Halep in Romania and WTA CEO Steve Simon in Florida, not to find answers – because I know there are none – but to share the uncertainty with someone else. I chat to Kiki Bertens and she's worried because cases are spiking in the Netherlands. Petra Kvitová says she's experiencing the same thing in the Czech Republic. Jo Konta is concerned over case numbers in the United Kingdom.

I'm one of the first players to announce I won't be competing at the US Open either, and it's challenging at first because I wonder if I'll be the only one. I'm making the decision for the right reasons, so it really shouldn't matter to me if anyone else makes the same call, but I'm relieved when others – including top seeds Bianca Andreescu and Simona Halep and Elina Svitolina – pull out as well. The vaccine rollout hasn't even begun. The tour – if you can even call it that – doesn't exactly seem unprofessional or makeshift, but to me it looks too improvised and compromised. There are more than a few who believe the risks are too great.

Even if I wanted to play, I'd have to get an exemption to travel out of Australia, with no guarantee I could get back in. I don't care about making that sacrifice and putting in that effort and then losing in a first-round match, but I do care if I go through it all and contract the coronavirus and bring it back home and infect someone else. I do care if one of the team of people professionally bound to me follows me abroad chasing trophies and gets sick. Tyzz would come with me – of course – but he had pneumonia only 15 months ago. Could I forgive myself if he caught this disease? The answer is no. And once that decision is made, I sleep soundly.

The US Open goes ahead in early September, and I watch nothing except a few games of the final, a high-quality contest between Victoria Azarenka and Naomi Osaka. It seems so eerie as they attack one another inside an empty Arthur Ashe Stadium, and this three-set epic, won by Osaka, is an amazing match that nobody sees live.

The sound is the strangest thing. Usually, the noise inside Arthur Ashe has a way of spiralling at the top and swirling down upon you like you're at the bottom of an aural vortex, but the only thing you can hear now is the girls on court, and a smattering of other players allowed in suites. There's one other noise, too. When the subway trains pass by Arthur Ashe, you can sometimes hear them, even with a crowd in full voice. Now, when there's no crowd at all, the squeal of carriage wheels on steel rails is ear-splitting. I listen out my window instead, and smile at the warbling of a magpie.

A few weeks later and the weather is appalling in Paris. I flick the telly on to the French Open and see raindrops streaming down the camera lens. The tournament has been moved from May to September, so the weather is unusually inhospitable. I watch for a few minutes – Ajla Tomljanović playing Maria Sakkari, then Victoria (Vika) Azarenka playing Danka Kovinić – and I know I've made the right decision not to play: my chronic arm injury would have blown up in those conditions. I can tell from Ajla's body language in the muddy clay that she's freezing cold and frustrated.

I don't have to wonder how Vika feels, because she walks off the court after three games, fuming. 'We are sitting ducks,' she tells reporters. 'It's too cold. It's eight degrees. I live in Florida.'

I'm on the couch in Brisbane, sipping from a glass of red wine. I wake up the dogs and take them for a walk, and then I train in the afternoon. It's 24 degrees. I've made the right decision.

*

My pre-season begins early, in October, and Tyzz comes north from Melbourne to be with me, which means submitting himself to two weeks of quarantine at Howard Springs, near Darwin, in order to cross the state borders. It's the first time we've seen each other since March, when we frantically departed Indian Wells.

We work on my backhand a little, and I feel light, and energised to be at home. I play golf three days a week – every Wednesday, Saturday and Sunday in the club competition. Without really noticing, I get my handicap down from 11 to three. One day I'd like to play off scratch, but I have no desire to turn my hobby into anything serious. I enjoy the game no matter what my handicap is.

The AFL season is coming to a close, and it's nice to see it up close for once. Australian Rules football is a winter sport – a confusing but beautiful mixture of soccer and rugby, gridiron and Gaelic football, hurling and handball – and so is played throughout the northern hemisphere summer, which is the time of year I'm always on tour.

I barrack for the Richmond Tigers, and they've created a dynasty these past few years, which I've missed almost entirely. In 2017, they won the premiership after a 37-year drought, and I was in Wuhan. In 2019, they won again, and again I was in Wuhan. In 2020, they've a chance to win once more – a third flag in four years – and because Covid has ravaged the southern states, it's been decided that the Grand Final will be played in Brisbane. If the Tigers can win through to the decider, I'll be able to watch them from my hometown stadium, the Gabba. And that's exactly what happens.

I can't wait to see them play. I know them so well – and one player in particular, club captain Trent Cotchin. We met more than a decade ago, when I had just won Junior Wimbledon. That title opened doors for me, and one of the best was to the gymnasium at Richmond's home ground, Punt Road Oval, in Melbourne, where I was able to watch footy training and meet Cotch. He's a veteran player now, but back then he was a young leader of an old and storied club – one with a grand history but a restless, impatient and mighty supporter base. Back then, I knew none of the pressures he was under.

I did know that he liked tennis. He grew up with it in suburban Reservoir, a hardscrabble suburb north of Melbourne. His parents played at the local Cranross Tennis Club – his dad on Thursday nights and his mum on Saturday afternoons – and he used to hit balls at a wall and occasionally over a net. But I learned all that later, when Cotch started coming to watch me play, sitting in the stands at Melbourne Park each scorching summer during the Australian Open, after putting in a long, hard day of pre-season footy training.

We ran together sometimes, too. The former high-performance manager at the Tigers, Matt Hornsby, had worked with me and Stolts, and so we all got together, along with Bachar Houli – a Richmond half-back flanker and the first devout Muslim to play AFL – and we did laps of 'The Tan', a famous running trail around the Botanical Gardens by the Yarra River. Cotch and I had coffees together, too, reflecting on the fact we were both really just kids, both barely scratching the surface of what we could do, both seemingly answerable to gargantuan and dormant supporter bases. He didn't give me advice, but I took comfort in knowing that the struggle was common to us both.

I think he thought of me like a little sister. He texted me from time to time, and I found that invaluable. When you lose a hard match as a professional athlete – when everything has gone to shit and you're feeling most alone – people tend to think you don't want to hear from anyone, and sometimes that's true. But Cotch always seemed to know when that silence was lonely, and when to reach out.

He became a family friend, someone who would have me over for dinner with his daughters, Harper and Mackenzie, and son, Parker, and wife, Brooke. I came to know that he was always watching me, and only ever a phone call away. Cotch works with Crowey too, and has done for longer than me. When I had questions about letting this unknown 'mindset coach' into my life, it was Cotch's endorsement that nudged me over the line. 'I wouldn't be half the person I am today without him,' he told me.

Now Richmond have won their Preliminary Final against Port Adelaide, and they're flying back to play in the Grand Final in Brisbane. Cotch texts me one afternoon: *Peggy is going to call you.* He means Peggy O'Neal, president of the club. I don't know what this call is about, but in her beautiful West Virginia drawl she quickly explains. 'If the Tigers win,' she says, 'we'd like you to present the 2020 AFL Premiership Cup to Cotch.'

I can't believe this opportunity is falling my way. The serendipity – of my team playing in my state in the year I decide to stay home from the tail end of the WTA tour – seems too good to be true. And then they win the bloody thing, and soon enough I'm on the dais, handing the cup to Cotch and his coach, Damien Hardwick, and shimmering black and gold confetti is raining down on the playing surface around us.

A couple of weeks earlier, I'd been to a Richmond game and was captured by the TV cameras cheering. A gif of me fist-pumping with one hand and holding a plastic cup of beer in the other went viral. It made me shake my head and laugh. The photo of me presenting the cup to my club is the one that counts.

Cotch calls me later, but I'm on the road with Garry, heading home. He asks if we want to drive south to the resort where the boys are celebrating, to grab a beer with the AFL Premiers, but I can only imagine where the party will go when a professional football team wins a flag and releases all valves after a pressure-cooker season.

'No chance,' I say, as we roll through the suburban darkness towards home. 'I don't know what you guys are going to get up to, but it'll probably last for the next week. Have one for me, and go for your life.'

*

I arrive in Melbourne on 3 January 2021 to prepare for the Australian Open. The international players are in one bubble, descending upon Melbourne Park, while the Aussie-based players are in another bubble. There are about 15 of us, all training at a local private school, Xavier College.

It feels convivial and a little odd, like an under-12s training camp. An already strange Australian summer has become even weirder, and in an attempt to find something that feels closer to a normal, well-managed pre-season, I separate myself a little. I'm not antisocial but I want my training to be as specific as possible – I want to do what I need to do, hitting when I want, how I want, for as long as I want, rather than getting sucked into a shared boot camp mentality simply because we're thrust together. Priorities over proximity.

It pays dividends, too. I roar into the new year, first knocking over Garbiñe Muguruza in a tight title victory at the Yarra Valley Classic. It's been almost a year since I last played competitive matches but it feels like I never stopped.

Next the Open begins, and I find my feet better than ever, destroying Danka Kovinić 6-0, 6-0, despite hurting my leg in the warm-up. I play Daria Gavrilova next, and although I'm in total control, I lose trust in what I'm doing, breathe belief into Dasha and almost lose. What a shitshow.

Tyzz wants to catch up and debrief. 'Righto,' I say, 'but we've got four minutes to talk about this. After that, we're not talking about it anymore.' Short, sharp, talk it through and move on.

I play my way through Ekaterina Alexandrova and Shelby Rogers and find myself in the quarter-finals, against Karolína

Muchová, and it's bizarre. I do nothing, yet she can't hit the ball into the court, and loses the first set 6-1. I'm quickly up a break in the second set, too, and see that she's struggling physically. This has been my plan. I've asked to play during the day, knowing today would be 35 degrees, because I know she's coming off the European winter, and that's never an easy transition.

It's writ large in her every movement. She walks slowly, and tries to get to the back of the court where the shade can be found. She isn't playing a physical game, and instead tries to end points quickly. She calls for her trainer to do a three-minute evaluation, which is normal. They start taking her blood pressure, apply heatstroke treatment with ice bags, which again is pretty normal. She's feeling it. I don't need to change a thing.

But then the confusion emerges. She goes off court and I look to the umpire to understand what's happening, and he waves as if to say he doesn't really know. I asked the umpire, 'Is she done?'

'No, they haven't started the medical timeout yet,' he says.

'What are you talking about?' I ask. 'They went off the court minutes ago.'

The break stretches to beyond ten minutes, in which my momentum is interrupted. What's more, I'm standing out here in the heat while she's sitting in an air-conditioned space, hydrating and icing and cooling down.

Finally Muchová comes back, and I know I need to maintain my focus in these first few points. I need her to know how hard it's going to be. She still looks dazed and confused. I'm almost waiting for her to pull the pin as she rolls through the motions. And then …

Childhood

1 A very young me in 1997, eating a biscuit. Mum tells me that Digestives were my favourites.

2 Sara, Ali and me in the living room of our childhood home (where our parents still live), showing off our handmade togs. Mum and Dad couldn't always afford to buy clothes for all of us, so Mum was often busy sewing away, creating matching outfits we could wear.

Childhood

3 With my cousin Josh, pushing little carts on the 'bumpy road' outside my house. He and I were the closest in age and spent a lot of time playing together.

4 Me with Sara and Ali, enjoying raspberry ice blocks out the front of our home. The red brick façade hasn't changed much since this photo was taken, in 1998. Behind us is the garage roller door that hid my first tennis court.

5 Mum, Dad, my sisters and me on the verandah at my aunty and uncle's house in Toowoomba, where we would visit for Easter weekend. We got such a kick out of seeing the chickens they had on the property.

6 Standing in the kitchen in Toowoomba during a family holiday over Easter. I loved these trips, spending time with our extended family at their home.

7 Grade 2 school photo. I loved learning at school and met some of my best friends during my early years at Woodcrest State College. To this day, they are still some of my favourite mates and fondest memories.

Early Sports

1 On Court 3 at West Brisbane Tennis Centre, 2003, after I won one of my first trophies – the photo the entire world has seen time and time again.

2 Met West Trials in Home Hill, north Queensland. Hugging one of the organisers after making my first Queensland State Team, age ten. Vanette Tobin (at left) helped direct and organise the Regional and State Trials for years. Ebony Panoho was my regular doubles partner for Regional and State competitions.

Sean Dempsey / PA Images via Getty Images

Tim Marsden / Newspix

Junior Wimbledon

1 With my trophy on Court 1 of the All England Lawn Tennis and Croquet Club, after defeating Irina Khromacheva in the final of the Wimbledon Girls' Singles, London, 3 July 2011. A moment that changed my life and career forever.

2 Back in Brisbane, a few days after winning Junior Wimbledon. The moment I saw Mum and Dad for the first time at the airport was plastered all over the news – it wasn't a very private reunion.

3 Seeing Evonne for the first time after I won Junior Wimbledon. At the Queensland Tennis Centre, Tennyson, July 2011. It was the start of an important friendship, and I will be forever grateful to Evonne for her guidance and support during my life and career.

Taking a Break

1 Playing a forehand at the 2014 US Open versus Barbora Strýcová, New York, 26 August 2014. This was the last tournament I played before taking a sabbatical. My decision had already been made and I was ready for what came next.

2 My Women's National Cricket League debut, playing for Queensland Fire during the 2015/2016 summer, Railways Oval in Adelaide. Celebrating the wicket of Alex Price with Jess Jonassen and captain Delissa Kimmince.

3 Batting for Brisbane Heat, my first runs in the inaugural Women's Big Bash League season, Junction Oval in Melbourne, 5 December 2015. I went on to make 39 runs off 27 balls in that innings against the Melbourne Stars.

Streeter Lecka / Getty Images

James Elsby / Cricket Australia via Getty Images

Representing Australia

1 Casey and me celebrating our doubles win during the Fed Cup tie v Ukraine, in Canberra, 11 February 2018. It was the win that clinched the tournament 3-2 for Australia, and was also Casey's last professional match.

2 Hugging Alicia Molik, my captain, after defeating Aryna Sabalenka to give Australia a 2-1 lead in our Fed Cup semi-final tie against Belarus, in Brisbane, 21 April 2019. Mol is an exceptional leader, and she had the ability to bring out the best in me when playing for Australia.

3 With my niece Lucy, before my match against Kristina Mladenovic, Fed Cup Final v France, in Perth, 9 November 2019. I will never forget Lucy's smile when she heard the roar of the crowd as we entered the arena – a favourite memory of what turned out to be a heartbreaking day.

4 On the podium with John Peers, celebrating our bronze medal win at the 2020 Olympic Games in Tokyo – one of the proudest moments in my entire career. John and I have also played mixed doubles together at the Australian Open, Wimbledon and the US Open – there was no one else I wanted to partner with for the Olympics.

WTA Tour

1 Winning my first WTA tour event, Kuala Lumpur, 5 March 2017 – a moment to be cherished when I learned I had broken into the Top 100. An incredible week capped off by winning the doubles with Casey as well.

2 Taking a selfie with fans after my semi-final win, defeating Julia Goerges, in Zhuhai, 3 November 2018. It was the biggest final of my career at that stage, and I finished the year ranked number 15 in the world.

3 Playing a backhand during my second consecutive Sydney International final, 12 January 2019. It was a match in which I had chances but my opponent, Petra Kvitová, stood up in the big moments to take victory and win the title.

1

2

3

4 Shaking hands with Elina Svitolina after our marathon fourth-round match, which lasted 3 hours 12 minutes. Indian Wells, 12 March 2019. Had I won that match, I would have ranked as a World Top 10 singles player. This was one of my toughest defeats, and what I learned from that match gave me the courage to trust myself more – and play a more aggressive brand of tennis.

5 The moment right after defeating good friend Julia Goerges to win the Birmingham Classic, 23 June 2019. I instantly turned to my team, having realised I had just become the WTA World No. 1 singles player – a moment made even more special because Mum, Dad and Jim had flown from Australia to be there for the tournament.

6 Celebrating after defeating Elina Svitolina for the first time and winning the WTA Finals, Shenzhen, 3 November 2019. Usually, I am not one to celebrate after winning a match, but this shows how much that moment meant to me.

7 Holding the Billie Jean King Trophy after winning the WTA Finals in Shenzhen. This was one of the biggest wins of my career and I remember playing some of my best tennis during that event. An incredible week was made extra special by finishing as the WTA Year-End World No. 1 for the first time.

8 Third time's the charm! After winning my first WTA event on Australian soil at the Adelaide International, 18 January 2020. Having lost in the final in Sydney the two previous years, it was amazing to finally win at home. Sharing the moment with physio Adam Schuhmacher, Tyzz and Garry.

9 Hitting a forehand at the Hard Rock Stadium in my win against Bianca Andreescu in the final of the Miami Open, 3 April 2021. It was the first time I'd successfully defended a title – having had my No. 1 ranking questioned earlier in the week, it felt like a statement match and statement week.

7

Clive Brunskill / Getty Images

ADELAIDE 8

Mark Brake / Getty Images

9

French Open

1 Sliding into a defensive slice backhand during my quarter-final match against Madison Keys on Court Suzanne Lenglen, Paris, 6 June 2019. It was the first time I had broken through to make a Grand Slam semi-final.

2 Taking a moment to soak in my maiden Grand Slam victory during the on-court ceremony on Court Philippe Chatrier, 8 June 2019. I played one of the best matches of my career and savoured every moment when accepting the Coupe Suzanne Lenglen.

3 One tradition at the French Open is that both singles finalists are accompanied by two personal security guards in the lead-up to their match. Here, I'm heading back to the hotel the evening after winning my semi-final, with my security detail riding on motorbikes – it felt bizarre having two men shadowing my every move. The night before the final, one guard stayed awake in the hotel lobby and the other kept an eye on my hotel room door. I'm not sure they enjoyed our post-match celebrations following the final, though.

Doubles Partners

1 The first WTA doubles title that Casey and I won together, Birmingham Classic, 18 June 2013. An amazing moment for us to share and the catalyst for an event that became a very happy hunting ground for me during my career.

2 Celebrating winning the doubles title with partner Victoria (Vika) Azarenka at the Internazionali BNL d'Italia, Rome, 19 May 2019. Playing with Vika through the 2019 season was the start of a great relationship, and I loved the energy and focus that she brought to every match.

3 Holding the Rogers Cup doubles trophy with partner Demi Schuurs, Montreal, 12 August 2018. Demi and I were great mates off the court and paired together twice during the 2018 season – both times we won the title.

Ben Hoskins / Getty Images

Paolo Bruno / Getty Images

Getty Images

4 Finally – a Grand Slam doubles title! Kissing the US Open women's doubles trophy with Coco Vandeweghe, New York, 10 September 2018. We saved multiple match points in the final and eventually won 3-6, 7-6 (7-2), 7-6 (8-6). Having lost five other Slam doubles finals, this was a moment to celebrate.

5 My last doubles match ever. Fist-bumping Storm Sanders during the final of the Adelaide International, 9 January 2022. Winning a doubles title on Australian soil was something I'd always wanted to accomplish and sharing that moment with Storm was amazing. Having played together in juniors, trained together and lived together, it felt like the perfect way to finish my doubles career with her.

6 Having Casey courtside during my Australian Open final was the best thing I could have asked for. She was the first person I was able to hug (and kiss) after winning my third Grand Slam title. It felt like a full-circle moment for both of us. Rod Laver Arena, 29 January 2022.

Wimbledon

1 Playing my first-round match on Court 12 against Stefanie Vögele, Wimbledon, 3 July 2018. Having felt confident going into the 2018 Championship, it turned out to be the toughest fortnight of my career and the tournament when I hit rock bottom.

2 My Centre Court singles debut, playing against Harriet Dart, 6 July 2019. It was also the first tournament I played as World No. 1. Ultimately, it was another disappointing Wimbledon, but the experience of playing a Brit on the most iconic court in the world was something I will always cherish.

3 The moment it started to sink in – I was the 2021 Wimbledon Ladies' Singles Champion.

4

5

4 Box celebration. Celebrating the moment that *we* became the winner of the 2021 Ladies' Singles Championship. My favourite photo of my amazing, caring and loyal team.

5 Kissing the most iconic trophy in our sport: the Venus Rosewater Dish. It was such an elegant on-court ceremony – emotional and filled with tradition – that included the trophy being presented by Kate Middleton, then Duchess of Cambridge. I'll always remember the moment I took a quick glance at my team and they beamed with pride.

6 The best team in the world. Without the love and support of Matt, Garry, Tyzz and Mel, I never would have achieved my biggest dream. Celebrating our 2021 Wimbledon journey.

6

Australian Open

1 Posing with my 2012 Australian Open Main Draw Accreditation after winning the AO wildcard playoff, 11 December 2011. It was exciting and scary to know that at just 15 years old I would be making my Grand Slam singles debut the following month.

2 Shaking hands with Serena Williams after our first-round match on Rod Laver Arena, 13 January 2014. An enormous occasion that I wish I could have enjoyed and embraced more.

3 First round at the 2017 Australian Open, 16 January 2017. Enjoying my first AO singles win, defeating Annika Beck on a brutally hot day on Hisense Arena.

4 Fourth round v Maria Sharapova, Rod Laver Arena, 20 January 2019 – one of my most favourite matches of my career. This is the moment I went to 5-3 in the third set, yelling 'C'mon, mate' to my team.

Malcolm Fairclough / Getty Images

Cameron Spencer / Getty Images

Mark Kolbe / Getty Images

Robert Prange / Getty Images

5

Quinn Rooney / Getty Images

6

5 My fourth-round match against Amanda Anisimova, Rod Laver Arena, 23 January 2022. The slice backhand became my biggest weapon during my career and the one shot I loved to use tactically to make my opponents uncomfortable. During this match against Amanda, my slice drove her crazy.

6 Celebrating becoming the Australian Open Champion, 29 January 2022. Having played some of my career-best tennis during the tournament, being presented the Daphne Akhurst Memorial Cup by Evonne Goolagong Cawley was one of my most cherished memories. It made this kiss even more special.

7 An incredible moment sharing my Australian Open victory with Cathy Freeman and Evonne just moments after I walked off court. My mentors, my mates and, most importantly, my sisters.

Scott Barbour / Tennis Australia

7

Teamwork

1 My first coach, Jim Joyce. Taking a moment to celebrate winning the under-14s Clay Court Nationals at George Adler Tennis Centre, Ipswich, 5 April 2010. Jim created my game and built me into the player that I always wanted to be. I will be forever grateful for the 21 years we spent together on the tennis court.

2 With Jason Stoltenberg, after I won the under-12s National Hardcourt Championships at Melbourne Park, 21 December 2008. This was the week my dad approached Stolts and asked if he would watch me play. From the first time we spoke, I knew Stolts would bring out the best in me. He was always honest, kind and passionate – the perfect person to guide the beginning of my young career.

3 My favourite photo from the journey of a lifetime. Looking at my coach, Craig Tyzzer, after winning the 2021 Wimbledon Ladies' Singles Championship, 10 July 2021. Tyzz was the person that challenged me, pushed me and drove me to be the best I could be. He was also the first to wrap his arms around me, listen to my tears and make me laugh. I will be forever in debt to him for his love, effort and professionalism.

4 Indian Wells, 13 March 2019. Enjoying a round of golf with my team after a tough loss to Elina Svitolina. It became a tradition for us to always fit in a round of golf in Indian Wells before we moved to the next tournament. We always played in the same teams: Team Tiny (Adam and me) against the Big Boys (Tubs and Tyzz). (L–R: my trainer, Mark 'Tubs' Taylor, physio Adam Schuhmacher, Tyzz and me)

5 Team Barty's Backyard Cricket Team. Our last few days of a *big* pre-season celebrated with a presentation of personalised cricket caps, Pat Rafter Arena, Brisbane, 23 December 2020. We enjoyed presenting Tubs, our Englishman, with his first Australian cricket blazer. (L–R: Tyzz, Tubs, me and Adam)

6 Accepting the Chris Evert Trophy with Adam and Tyzz, Shenzhen, 2 November 2019. This was the day I officially became the WTA Year-End World No. 1.

Teamwork

7 My team. My family. The people that have dedicated so much time and energy into my life and career. The 2022 Australian Open final was the first time in my professional career that they were all together to see me play live. (L–R: Nikki, Tyzz, Ali, Mum, me, Garry, Sara, Dad and Crowey)

8 Celebrating my 2022 Australian Open win with my three tennis father figures: Jim, Stolts and Tyzz. Having the three of them gather together for a beer was a special moment.

9 With Ben Mathias and Molly Picklum, a future talent in surfing who Ben manages, at the 2022 Rip Curl Pro, Bells Beach. I've always loved watching and supporting Australia's surfers and I enjoyed sitting on the other side of the ropes that day at Bells.

7

8

9

Training

1 Shadowing a backhand swing with a medicine ball while working through a movement session. Often we would use medicine balls to practise certain footwork patterning and during warm-ups – particularly when changing surfaces during the season.

2 Catching a cricket ball in a small cone during a warm-up session in Adelaide. We would throw balls at targets and also launch a ball across the field, needing to move quickly to try and catch it in a cone.

3 Warming up for my quarter-final match against Karolína Muchová, playing a game of 'piggy in the middle' with our own little spin on it, Melbourne, 17 February 2021. It was practical movement mixed in with some childlike fun – and we were always super competitive. (L–R: Tubs, Adam, me, Garry and Tyzz)

4 Using a small soccer ball to warm up with Tubs before practice sessions and matches at the Australian Open 2022 became part of our daily routine. We continually changed the game and rules to keep it stimulating.

Sporting Legends

1 Evonne Goolagong Cawley. My dear friend and mentor. I wish I'd had the opportunity to experience playing against her and watch her dance around the court. Evonne overcame enormous challenges in her life and career, which continues to inspire a nation and paved the path for so many.

2 Pat Rafter. From when I was young, Pat has always supported my journey and shared his knowledge and experience. Pictured in Noosa after a training camp with him. Throughout my career, he was always open and honest. I love picking his brain.

3 Stefanie Graf. An icon of our sport – I was lucky enough to spend some time with her in Las Vegas in 2010. She is incredibly kind-hearted, strong and passionate. Without a doubt, she has the most damaging slice backhand I have ever seen in our game. An inspiration.

1

2

3

4 Rod Laver. In my opinion, Rod is the greatest to ever play the game of tennis. Style, grace and athleticism. He changed the way our beautiful sport is played. He takes the time to engage and connect with people in a way not many can. I am grateful to have so many amazing memories with Rocket.

5 Steph Gilmore. Authentic, laid-back, competitive and, without a doubt, the best I've ever seen surf a wave. Steph is the Queen of the Kids and has inspired so many young surfers to explore curiosity and to unapologetically be themselves. I love this girl.

6 Trent Cotchin. A true leader, a champion and someone who will always support, love and encourage. Cotch inspires me to be more kind, to dream bigger and be brave. He continually helps me to grow into the best version of myself. I am so grateful to be able to call him my mate. Pictured presenting him with the 2020 AFL Premiership Cup at the Gabba.

My Game

1 The serve. In my opinion, it is the single most important shot in tennis and it is also the only shot when you have full control. As a kid and throughout my career, I would practise my serve endlessly. It held me in good stead even though I wasn't the tallest girl out there. I turned both my first serve and second serve into a weapon – and opponents knew that.

2 The slice backhand. My favourite shot to hit and a skill that I loved developing over my journey. It was the one shot that I felt separated me from other players on tour.

3 The double-handed backhand. It was the shot in my game that I was never 100 per cent comfortable with. Over time, it became less of a weakness, and I learned how to use it to bring the ball back to my strengths.

4 Forehand. The most damaging shot in my game. I structured my game around finding forehands and hurting my opponent with this shot. I loved hitting forehands in different ways with pace, spin, angle, depth. When I was hitting my forehand well, I felt in control.

1

Scott Barbour / Tennis Australia

2

Andy Cheung / Getty Images

3

Paul Crock / AFP via Getty Images

4

Cameron Spencer / Getty Images

Supporters

1 The original Barty Party sign! Two of my best mates, Lyndel and Tania, debuting the Barty Party sign at the 2017 Australian Open. I didn't know they were coming so prepared. They continued to travel with the sign whenever they came to watch me play.

2 Signing autographs for some young fans at the Australian Open in 2017.

3 The Vegemite Barty Army at the Australian Open in 2018.

4 Walking onto Margaret Court Arena straight after my 2022 Australian Open win. It was surreal to see so many patriotic fans who had watched the match outside the stadium. The support from the Australian crowd is something I've always been grateful for.

First Nations Community

1 Chatting with kids at a tennis clinic with Evonne in Cairns, 2019.

2 Group photo with the kids from Bentley Park College after our clinic in 2019.

3 Tiwi Islands, 2018. The first time picking up a tennis racquet for these youngsters!

4 Evonne sharing her story with school students. She's holding her first racquet, which was made out of a wooden apple crate. I love the way she completely captivates the room when she speaks to students.

Chris Hyde / Getty Images

1

Chris Hyde / Getty Images

2

Glenn Campbell / Tennis Australia

3

4

5

5 Group photo after a tennis clinic, Cairns, 2020.

6 Celebrating the 2022 Australian Open title after our Racquets and Red Dust program in the heart of our nation, Uluru. The most picturesque tennis court I've ever played on.

7 Learning how to play tennis and rally, Uluru, 2022. This was the first time most of the kids had ever picked up a racquet. It didn't take long for us to be having mini rallies. One of the most fulfilling experiences of my entire life.

6

7

Passions

1 North Stradbroke Island, 2004. Happy with my shortfin pike and finger spot bream after a fishing afternoon with my uncles. My cousin Nick is trying to get a look in at the pike!

2 Kicking the footy at Xavier College, warming up for a practice session in the lead-up to the 2021 Australian Open. A Grand Slam can be a stressful environment, so my team always tried to keep training sessions fun and light.

3 The most nerve-racking wedge shot of my life, trying to do a 60-metre shot onto a floating green in front of Tiger Woods, Ernie Els, Adam Scott, Cam Smith, Xander Schauffele and Justin Thomas – just to name a few. Presidents Cup, Melbourne, November 2019.

Vince Caligiuri / Tennis Australia

4 Always finding time to play a game of cricket. This game was played in the players' physio area at Wimbledon just moments before we warmed up for the final, 10 July 2021.

5 The Wolfpack: Origi, Chino and Affie.

6 A relaxed afternoon in my swinging egg chair with Chino and Affie.

Family

1 Dad, me and Mum at the Queensland Tennis Centre. I was doing a sponsor photoshoot and pulled them in for a photo.

2 Girls' weekend away. Me, Mum, Sara, Ali, Lucy and Olivia, on the Sunshine Coast. The first time all six of us had gone away together for a quiet weekend.

3 Oscar and me, April 2022. It was awesome to escape on holidays and spend some time with my family after announcing my retirement.

4 Being silly Aunty Ash – showing Oscar, Olivia and Lucy the Australian Open's Daphne Akhurst Memorial Cup. The kids thought it was pretty cool.

Nic Morley

5 With Garry in Rome. We both love to explore on a day off. The Colosseum is one of our favourite landmarks.

6 Garry and me, on our wedding day in 2022.

1 A full-circle moment for me. Taking Lucy, Oscar and Olivia to West Brisbane Tennis Centre for a tennis lesson. Here we are on Court 4, where it all began for me more than 20 years ago. It was the most amazing experience seeing the kids play on the same court that made me fall in love with the game of tennis. Not long after this photo, Jim and I rolled down the net for the last time.

2 My retirement press conference, with Tyzz by my side, 24 March 2022. A difficult but exciting day.

3 Reading the Little Ash books to Lucy and some of her friends. I loved reading as a kid, and I hope these books will encourage a love of reading in children.

Jono Searle / AAP Image

Muchová takes a couple of risks and slaps a few balls, but she hangs in there physically. I wonder where this is coming from, and I think back to that medical break, and the whole series of events shakes me. I'm up by a set and a break, yet instead of feeling imperious I feel vulnerable, like I have everything to lose. My racquet speed and ball speed drop, and I'm utterly distracted.

Why didn't she pull the pin? I think. *How is she still out here? How did she get that treatment for so long within the rules? Was that timeout even legal?* I look to Tyzz, and he sees me staring, eyes wide open. *What the fuck am I doing?* I want my expression to say. *And what the fuck do I do now?*

I return to my old ways, blaming instead of going back to basics. I'm still in front but I'm steaming and melting now, consumed by self-sabotage. I lose, and come off court and look at myself in the change room mirror. *That's two years in a row you've walked off the court with regret,* I think, staring into my own eyes. *Two years in a row you've completely fucked yourself over.*

This is also the moment I recognise what the Australian Open means to me. In seeing myself in ruins, I see how big this goal has become. I understand now that the dream of winning here is bigger than I've ever wanted to admit. I believe in all those high-performance platitudes about sticking to process and finding intrinsic motivation – it's the journey, not the destination, all that stuff – but it's okay to recognise a desire for reward, too. Not every achievement has to be intangible. It's okay to want to hold that trophy, as I do.

The whole match is dissected for days, and it's unedifying. The media tries to bait me into criticising Muchová, but I don't need to add to the vitriol. The timeout is described by one journalist as 'legally fine but ethically icky', and by another as something that 'seems legit, but doesn't sit well when it pivots a match on a dime'. I don't give the commentary any oxygen, because I'm the one who lost the match. Not my opponent. Not the rules.

Do I wish that never happened? Of course. Does it change how I sleep tonight? Yes, but only for one night. I speak to Cotch sometimes about moments like this. He's been in similar situations and seen me face other tough times. He tends to send messages that go like this: *It was a tennis match. You lost. Get over it. No big deal. I love you, mate.*

It's good to know people like him, who've been there and can comprehend how useless and helpless you sometimes feel. Right now, I feel judged. *She's thrown it away. She's screwed it up. She's choked.* Cotch knows how easy it is to hear those voices, so he replaces them with the affirmations he's found in football. One of them is 'You haven't been buried, you've been planted', but my favourite is his personal mantra: 'Your greatest growth comes from your darkest times.'

In this dark time, he sends me a long text, explaining how he was able to watch me play until late in the second set, when I was faltering. So he didn't see the collapse, but he read about it later.

Ash, I know nothing will really help, nor change anything, as you have all the answers, and you know it doesn't change the incredible human you are and the impact you're having on others. I'm proud of your continued growth! I'm grateful to watch and learn from you on how to be a special and authentic human being! Love you, mate! Chat to you soon 🖤

I want to
do what I
need to do.

Faster, Flatter

You need to reward yourself once in a while, and my big gift to myself when Case and I made the doubles final at Wimbledon was a brand-new car: a jet-black Ford Focus, which I named Frankie. I was only 17 at the time, so I drove him out of the dealership with my L-plate in the back window.

A couple of years later, in February 2016 – with my L-plates replaced by P-plates – I took Frankie on a road trip, driving him down the coast through Byron Bay and Coffs Harbour and Taree, Newcastle and Sydney and Albury, headed for

Melbourne. Specifically, I was headed for the headquarters of Tennis Australia, to chat with CEO Craig Tiley about resuming my career and starting from scratch, utterly unranked.

That meeting led to one of the great cosmic moments of my life – part happenstance, part sliding doors, part serendipity – because before I could get in to see the TA boss, I spied a guy sitting at his desk looking not particularly busy. His name was Craig Tyzzer.

I had worked briefly with Tyzz back in 2012 and 2013. Stolts had asked him to come on a couple of different trips to give me some tactical instruction. I remembered that his analysis and coaching was always practical, grounded in reality and never tied to emotion. He had a way of breaking down opponents and helping me walk around inside their weaknesses.

I played a memorable match in Prague against a Russian girl back then, and I was absolutely roping the ball into the corners, but she ran like a whippet and hit everything back, unperturbed by the way I was stretching her. I kept waiting for her to tire or falter, and then I got angry when she refused to buckle. Tyzz broke me out of that with the simplest few words on the sidelines.

'You just need to hit ten good balls up the middle,' he said. 'Just rally with this girl.'

I must have looked at him like he was an idiot, so he stepped me through his thought process. Two days prior, he said, he had seen this girl training. She was coached by her father, who couldn't really hit well, so he just stood in the middle of the court rifling fast and unpredictable balls into corners. The way I was playing might have beaten most girls, but it was exactly what this girl wanted, because all she had ever been trained to do was chase rabbits down burrows.

'Just hit ten balls up the middle,' Tyzz repeated. 'Just rally with her.'

I did as he said, and she fell completely apart – she was not prepared to play with any rhythm or strategy. When I gave her no pace, she had no idea how to generate her own. When I offered her the whole court to hit, she became paralysed by choice. Without the angles I had been giving her, she had nothing anchoring her to the court, so she missed short and long and wide, and soon folded.

Simple, yet effective.

Tyzz came to this kind of acumen via the scenic route. I reckon the path of the journeyman often leads to that happy marriage of quizzical and critical thinking.

He grew up in Oak Park, a housing development area north of Melbourne, near Essendon Airport. He played footy and cricket growing up, and tennis came into his life later, when the local council built some tennis courts virtually in his backyard, along the Moonee Ponds Creek. The whole family played, and the whole family was good.

Eventually, Tyzz played on the tour, for a few years anyway. He was the same age as John Fitzgerald, and played against him. He struggled to maintain a presence on tour, though, because of a lack of funding. He also badly injured his shoulder, and tried to grimace through the pain of a calcified supraspinatus tendon, but it became a choice between an operation and rest. He couldn't really afford to do either, although it wasn't uncommon to skip both in the 1970s anyway. That was an era in which injury prevention and recovery often meant a few beers and a few stretches.

As his playing career faded, Tyzz began doing some junior coaching with Tony Roche, and something he had never considered before became the calling that would dominate his life. From Roche he learned care and trust, and how to work with individuals. Tyzz had been raised on a 'one size fits all' approach to coaching – if you didn't cut the mustard, there was something wrong with you – and now he was learning about the value of investigating each personality and investing in their identity. Coaching went from something he never thought he would do to the only thing he would consider doing.

His brother Roger coached Alicia Molik and Lleyton Hewitt, and was head of the Competitive Edge program at the John Newcombe Tennis Ranch in Texas. Tyzz joined him there running tennis academies, tennis vacations, tennis camps and *fantasy* tennis camps. The tagline: 'You take the best from down under, blend it with Texas flavor, and put it in the middle of the Hill Country. We call it "Aus-Tex" hospitality. You won't find that anywhere, mate!'

The main purpose, Tyzz told me once, was to get talented kids into college on tennis scholarships, and at that the ranch was incredibly successful. Tyzz stayed until he had experienced just enough of America – particularly that specific brand of southern conservativism you only find in Texas – and then decided to come home. He landed at a local Melbourne club, coaching people in the leafy eastern suburb of Glen Iris, while also working at schools like Wesley College and Presbyterian Ladies' College.

The first professional he worked with was Andrew Ilie. Ilie had been injured, and was desperate to return to his best. They started together from scratch, working with new doctors. Tyzz worked on changing his serve to overcome a troublesome back and get him firing on tour. Ilie never reached great heights but became a kind of cult figure, a fan favourite for his outrageous shots and outlandish celebrations, including a tradition of tearing his shirt after memorable wins. Together, they made it to number 38 in the world. Again, it's worth remembering what that means. The idea that there are 193 countries and 7.7 billion people on the planet, and yet there are only 37 people out there better than you at what you do? That's a ludicrous accomplishment.

Stolts played against Ilie quite often, so he got to know Tyzz too. That's how we came to work together briefly, and why I knew Tyzz well enough to say hello to him that day in February 2016 at Tennis Australia. I stopped to say g'day, wondering why he was at his desk at 10.30 in the morning, which is prime time for summer training sessions. Apparently, he had just finished up working with Daria Gavrilova, and was without an athlete. I was without a coach. They say timing is everything …

'Huh,' I said, thinking for a moment. 'You want to come out and hit a few balls?'

'Sure,' he replied. 'What are you doing here, anyway?'

'I'm gonna play a small doubles event in Perth in a few weeks. Do you maybe want to do some work with me?'

'Yeah, okay.'

We found a court, and hit and chatted, and laughed at the rusty hinges of my swing. Tyzz worked through all my shots and then shot me a look. 'How long has it been since you hit?' he asked.

'Yeah, yeah,' I acknowledged. 'Ease up. It's been a while.'

Then we talked about what I was doing and how I was feeling. I'd had time to think about what I wanted from this new phase of my life, and so I laid it all out for him, then and there.

'This time, I wanna do it my way,' I said. 'I want to make my own decisions. I want to pick the travel I do, and pick the tournaments that matter. I want time off when I need it. I want to choose the team around me. And I've got a very strong "no dickheads" policy.'

'I like it,' Tyzz said. 'In fact, I love it.'

I also needed to know what he saw in me – and I didn't mean the stuff he'd seen me do well. Tyzz's most valuable quality is his ability to pick prey apart and find their flaws, then communicate those cracks with clarity. I needed to know: what did he think I needed to improve? What weaknesses could others use to bring me down? It was the criticism and honesty I was craving.

Tyzz said I had more than a few areas for growth. 'You have to work on your serve,' he explained. 'You have to be taller.'

That might sound strange, as you can only be as big as you are. But it means finding full extension and using everything you can to get *up* to the ball. Learning to use your legs to drive and allow your body to move efficiently and effectively. The higher you are, the more space you have to clear the net. The lower you are, the less margin you have for error.

'You're not exactly tall,' Tyzz said. 'So you need drive to strike the ball higher.'

That wasn't all. I also needed to work on my accuracy and placement. The serve is the one shot in tennis that is in your full control. I wanted to do everything possible to make it a weapon. There's a mathematics to tennis that's undeniable. The more often you put the ball in the place it's meant to go, the fewer faults you'll have and the more chances you give your opponent to make mistakes. It's statistically incontrovertible that you'll win more points. Win more points and you will win more games. Win more games and you will win more matches.

There's even a psychological aspect. If your serve becomes relentless in its reliability, your opponents will wither in the face of it – they'll find ways to falter on their own. You don't need a cannon to blow up their game; you can kill them with precision.

My backhand needed plenty of work too. The slice backhand was always good – no need to tinker too much with that technique – but Tyzz had a question about my positioning. There are subtle differences in the set-up for a two-handed backhand and a slice backhand. It can be a delicate balance, but also a movement that you can be aggressive with. The tricky part is moving your feet fast enough, efficiently enough, so that you switch seamlessly between the double-hander and the slice. If you can master that, you can play the single-handed slice backhand more often.

'And that's a weapon,' Tyzz said. 'Nobody else plays it, so a lot of girls will just lose their marbles as soon as they see it.'

Picking the right ball to hit the slice is crucial too. With a lower and faster ball, I often chose to hit the slice, because I can get underneath it and use its pace. With a wider and slower ball, we worked on hitting the two-hander, because you have to get your body behind it and generate your own power and speed.

We also needed to work on perfecting different *kinds* of slices, Tyzz said. To really master the art. A faster, flatter slice. A spinny slice. A slow slice. A slice that floats and pops. Aggressive slice, defensive slice. No one will spot the variety because the adjustment is so subtle, so if you can perform each variant on command, you can wrong-foot your opponent with every strike.

We started a training block that would take us through
March, April, May and part of June, and during that time I
got to know Tyzz better. He is astute. He's also a clown. He's
emotionally intelligent. He's blunt. He says inappropriate
things. He's a Carlton supporter. His wife's name is Sue. His
favourite player of the past is Rod Laver, and his favourite of the
now is Rafael Nadal. He surfs to clear his mind, and is baffled
that airline travel hasn't improved in two decades.

But before I could trust this man and put his training into
practice, he had a little bad news for me. There was one thing
I needed before we could begin rehabilitating my game, Tyzz
said, and I wasn't going to like it.

'The first thing is fitness. We need to make sure you're
100 per cent fit, ready to utilise your speed and movement, and
able to stand up to the training,' he said. 'We need to get you
into shape – because right now, Ash, you're not.'

Simple, yet effective.

Zoom Zoom

Everyone needs a steak place, and mine is Moo Moo, in the Port Office building in Brisbane, not far from the Eagle Street pier and the Botanic Gardens. In early 2021, two days before I'm due to fly overseas on tour, I visit there with Crowey. We have a table. The waiters know us. We start the night with a Peroni each, and move onto a nice red. I order a medium-rare eye fillet with mushroom sauce, and he has his usual Scotch fillet, medium. We split a side of brussels sprouts, a pear and rocket salad and a bowl of fries.

The poor waiters have to ask for our order three times, however, because I'm caught up in talking and venting to my mindset coach and good mate. I'm worried, I tell him, because I'm leaving the country on tour this weekend, and I know there'll be no coming home this year – no agile ducking and weaving the standard obligations, no calling my own shots and picking my moments. Coming back to tennis, I had promised myself that I'd fly home the moment I felt I needed rest and respite, but freedom and flexibility aren't possible in a pandemic.

I'm thinking of Garry, too, knowing we will be apart for some time. He's now caddying for young golfer and good mate Louis Dobbelaar, and they'll be travelling too, meaning we'll need to try to align our schedules and find a balance. It's not as easy to move around for a week here and there in the current climate, yet there are moments I know that I'll need Garry by my side. Wimbledon is a non-negotiable. The US Open will be crucial, too.

'I'm shitting myself,' I tell Crowey. 'I'm scared. I don't know what this year is going to look like. I can't picture it.'

I've only ever travelled for three months at a time, and at the end of that kind of stretch I'm always fatigued and fed up. Every year I enter Wimbledon psychologically limping, emotionally deflated and physically spent, because it always comes when I've been away from home for the longest spell. When I can't reach my energy source – Mum and Dad, my sisters, my nieces and nephew, my dogs, my house and my country – I have no tickets left to spend. How do I function without that battery pack?

Crowey talks to me about Cotch, and his experience in 2020, when the Tigers trained and played – and succeeded – in a bubble, in specialist AFL hubs on the Gold Coast.

'It's no comparison,' I say. 'They went to Surfers Paradise with their best mates, and brought their families along. They're still in Australia and only a short flight away from home. It's not the same.'

'You're right. It's different,' he replies. 'But the philosophy and approach can be similar.'

Crowey points out that Cotch had wondered how he would live life in the hub, and whether it was worth it, and he battled doubts as that stay grew longer than expected. But he found his answer, too: *I love what I do, and now I get to go somewhere else and do what I love differently.*

I also have to acknowledge that I'm not alone in my discomfort. Other tennis players from all over the globe will be facing the same apprehension. Handling the situation better than them – if I can do that – will be an obvious advantage. As Richmond president Peggy O'Neal famously told coach Damien Hardwick, 'Whoever does this best … will win. And that can be us.'

I think back and remember what Cotch told me about that season – how it had been his hardest year of footy but definitely his most rewarding, all because of that difference and adversity, challenge and change.

'You need to think of this year as one big adventure,' says Crowey. 'It doesn't mean it'll be easy, but you never know what might come out of it. Treat this thing as unique – as something that's never going to happen again in the history of the world. This is an exploration – a hero's journey. Don't worry about comparing – focus on discovering.'

We work a little on establishing my values: Crowey asks me to cast my mind back to the really tough moments, and ask myself how I got through them. My answers keep coming back to grit, and courage. We settle on why those are so important to me, what they look like and feel like, and how I might hold myself to account through those values in all the tough moments in the approaching months.

It doesn't make this thing I'm about to do any easier, though. I haven't travelled in virtually a year, and I'm about to head off on the road with no end date in sight. These past weeks have been excruciating: I've been trying to pack and get organised and fight procrastination while pretending that my departure date isn't growing near. I'm supposed to be thinking about the Miami Open but all I dwell on is missing Lucy's first day of school.

I know my itinerary backwards. My bags are packed and checked, top to bottom. My travel app says the plane from Sydney to Los Angeles is delayed 12 hours, but I haven't received any alerts. That night in Brisbane becomes a flurry of phone calls between me and Tyzz and my travel agent. The booking system shows no delays. Qantas says no delays. But American Airlines says differently – their plane hasn't left the United States yet. Can Qantas reissue our connecting legs to Sydney? *Yes.* What happens if the flight to LA is delayed? *Hold, please.*

I get on the plane south, and in the domestic terminal at Sydney Airport I'm told that, because of Covid, there's no transfer bus to the international terminal anymore. I'll have to pick up my bags, get in a cab, go to international departures and check in for my flights – all in just 90 minutes. It's a fucking nightmare. *This is the world telling me to stay in Australia*, I think. *This is everything telling me: you are doing the wrong thing, you shouldn't be doing this.* Next I am told that one of my bags is lost: my tennis bag, containing my racquets, my string, my shoes, everything. I'm barely keeping it together when the bag is finally found.

I have a few minutes in this eerily abandoned terminal, and I decide I need a notebook, so I can write down all the stuff I need to know each week in each location. It's how I keep on top of my world. *What's the hotel address? Where is the laundry? Where do I get breakfast? What day do I need to do Covid testing? Who are the physios on this swing? How do I get in and out of this arena?* I need to write it all down.

But I can barely find a shop that's open in this usually bustling place. Thankfully, WHSmith is still trading, and I spy the only notebook they've got. It has cartoon cacti all over the cover. Perfect – I love it. I have an inkling everything is going to be a pain in the arse this year, like sitting on a prickly pear. Might as well get a laugh out of a tough situation, right?

On the first page I write 'Our COVID Cootie Adventure'. I have to take the seriousness out of the oncoming year, so I make it into an immature kids' game of dodging playground germs. I decide to count the days, marking them in sets of five, as if I'm in prison and counting down my sentence by scratching lines on the cell wall. I'll have my coffee every morning, and mark off another day in the COVID Cootie Adventure. I'll do the same with Covid tests. (I don't know it yet, but I'll end up marking 203 straight days away from home, along with 74 Covid tests.)

There are 22 people on our flight to California, and they're as annoyed as me at the already delayed trip and the lack of updates and information – and then we get word of a further one-hour delay. When they announce another hour's delay on top of that, you can almost see the steam coming out of people's ears. It's

9.30 pm now and there's a lockdown curfew in Sydney, so if we don't get on a flight by 11.30 pm we may need to check in to a hotel. A woman appears and tells us there's a mechanical issue with the plane, which should be fixed in time to beat curfew. But it is not fixed in time to beat curfew. The flight crew has also timed out of their shift. We'll need to fly tomorrow.

That won't work for me. The tournament rules in Miami mean we need to be there a full three days before it starts, so we can be tested and cleared. Tyzz and I try booking an early-morning Delta flight to get us there in time, and we stay in the airport hotel for a quick nap. I wake up and continue the most draining day of travel in my life so far. I'm 30 hours into this trip and still haven't left Australia.

Delta has issues at check-in, too, because my visa has a three-month limit. They won't let us check in because we don't yet have our flights booked from the United States to Europe – so how can we prove we won't overstay? I'm crying now, and that seems fair enough in this moment. My tears don't solve anything, however, so we book a ticket from Charleston to Stuttgart on the spot, to prove our intention to leave.

Finally, I sink into my seat on the plane, and begin watching a favourite movie (*The Imitation Game*), a sporting documentary (*Icarus*), and an ESPN *30 for 30* special about Lance Armstrong. I rewatch an episode or two of *The Last Dance*. When I'm not doing that, I read. Right now I'm into the Orphan X series, six books about assassins by Gregg Hurwitz. There's a Vince Flynn series of political thrillers I begin to devour too.

We land in Los Angeles and go through customs, and I learn that the private plane we booked to take us from LA to Miami is gone. We wanted to mitigate the Covid risk by flying with fewer people, but because of our 24-hour delay there are no planes available anymore. It's spring break in America, and wealthy teens have booked all the jets for trips to Tampa Bay and Corpus Christi and Cabo San Lucas and Playa del Carmen.

There are no seats on commercial airlines either, and if we don't leave soon we won't make the tournament cutoff. My manager, Nikki, who works behind the scenes with Pat Rafter, contacts actor Chris Hemsworth's travel agent, who puts us in touch with a private jet company, but there's also a chance we can use country singer Keith Urban's personal plane. Welcome to the greatest diva moment of my life, where my ability to play tennis rests on the good graces of a Grammy Award winner and Thor. Unfortunately, the jet company we're put in touch with by the God of Thunder is already fully booked, and the private Cessna of the singing *American Idol* host is being serviced. Someone has two tickets on a domestic flight, and we take them in an instant, and squish like sardines into economy.

We get tested upon arrival in Florida, get to our hotel room, and you might think relief would wash over me – but instead I break down completely, knowing that this is what the year ahead might look like. *I cannot do this*, I think. *This is not what I signed up for.*

But I have to snap out of it and look for some positives. I have to dig deep for the grit and courage I know are there, because I'm desperate to defend the biggest WTA title of my career to date. *Whoever does it best will win*, I remember. *This is the year of adventure*, I think.

*

There has been a lot of chatter about who deserves to be the WTA World No. 1. I don't follow it much, but I know a lot of people think I'm undeserving of the rank, particularly after Naomi Osaka wins the 2020 US Open and the 2021 Australian Open, two Slams in succession. This gets to me a little bit, and fires me up.

Now here I am in the first round, starting to cramp up and feeling emotional. I'm a bit underdone, and facing Kristína Kučová – an underrated ball striker with some funky patterns and a lot of fight. I haven't played outside of Australia in a long time, and the conditions are lively. Hot and bouncy is definitely not what I have been playing or practising in the last few months.

This match is another example of how people get it wrong when they look only at rankings. Kristina has come through the qualifiers, so the pundits figure she shouldn't trouble me, but she's beaten some very handy players – and right now she is hunting me hard. After a good start I lose my way, and soon I'm down in the third set, 5-2 and under stress. I'm tentative, unable to release the shackles and play freely.

On match point she rolls in a second serve at 115 kilometres per hour, into the middle of the service box. I move around and hit a forehand winner inside in, and that is the release. It's taken me until match point down, but the grit and courage is there when I need it most. *Fuck this*, I think. *She's not beating me today. If they want to see how a world number 1 fights, I'll show them. Take it on. Don't be afraid.* Saying that to myself, I walk a little taller and my chest comes out. I charge to a tie-breaker and finish her. It's a long time since I've come back from match point down, and it's satisfying as all hell.

The second round pits me against Jeļena Ostapenko, who brings some resistance, but by now I'm cruising and win 6-3, 6-2. The third round is a great test in Victoria Azarenka, who's a champion and always tough, but I find a way, 6-1, 1-6, 6-2. The quarter-finals is Aryna Sabalenka, traditionally a tricky match-up for me, but I'm calm now and refuse to let her break my serve even once. I kill her with consistency, and early in the third set she capitulates. I have completely broken her: the scoreline is 6-4, 6-7 (5-7), 6-3. The semi-final against Elina Svitolina is pure tennis, where I dance on that line between aggression and recklessness, and win 6-3, 6-3.

Screw the haters, I think. *I am world number 1, and I know I'm the best tennis player in the world at the moment.* I'm also into another final. To all those who don't believe in me, I send a silent message: *Shut your mouth, shove it and watch me play.*

I'm up against Bianca Andreescu, whom I've never played before, but I know her matches aren't stress-free. A lot of them are close and there's always drama. She creates and craves the drama, thrives on it, but she turns up for the big points. The conditions are brutal, with cold, gusting winds. At first I can't hit the side of a truck, but I adjust and she can't find the court. Whoever handles it better, right? It's an odd, muted finish, because I'm up a set and two breaks – 6-3, 4-0 – when she retires hurt.

I go into the press conference, and still want to unload on anyone talking me down. *Whether you think I deserve to be here or not, I know I deserve to be here – end of story*, I am thinking. But I don't need to say anything to them. I've retained the number 1 ranking, and extended my lead over Naomi. I have nothing I need to prove by making public comments like that. My tennis does it for me.

*

The feedback around the tournament in Stuttgart has always been great. It's consistently voted the best WTA 500 tournament, yet I've never been, despite the significant carrot they dangle. The city is described as 'the cradle of the automobile' – the home of Mercedes-Benz and Porsche – so the tournament offers a unique incentive. If you're a top five player in the world and you win a single round, you get a free Porsche. Win the entire thing, you get another free Porsche. I want to win a Porsche. Or two.

The contests are played on an indoor synthetic clay – the only surface I haven't yet won on – and I make my way through the early rounds, against Laura Siegemund and Karolína Plíšková and Elina Svitolina. That might sound as though I'm cruising through opposition with ease, like steel splitting wood, but each match takes grit and resilience, coping skills and consideration. More than once I come from a break down in the third set. I'm staying true to my values.

In the final, against Aryna Sabalenka, she's seeing the ball like a watermelon, and I lose the first set 3-6. In truth, I'm lucky it's that close. 'Tyzz,' I say. 'I'm not even in this. I'm getting rag-dolled here.' He tells me to find a way, and for me it becomes pressure on her serve, and pressure through my serve – getting on top of her at the start of every point, until she loses her head. The battle is mine.

And so, in the week of my 25th birthday, I end up winning two Porsches, which is completely mad – especially as I already have a Porsche at home, awarded to me in 2019 for finishing the year as the world number 1. I talked to Simona Halep about it at the time, because she has a few already, and she advised me to make it special and memorable, so my beautiful white Porsche 911 with black trim has a chrome foot step with 'WTA #1 2019' embossed on it, which you only see if you open the door. I barely ever drive it.

Still, the experience is fun, and all part of that spirit of adventure – the hero's journey of discovery. Before I move on to the next challenge of 2021, I think back to the moment straight after match point in this austere German city. I had turned to Tyzz with a cheeky smile and a few choice words: 'Zoom zoom, bitches.'

Pin the Body

In some sports you need endurance. In others you need speed. There are games where upper-body strength is your greatest asset, and others where strength through your base is more important. Flexibility might be everything in one form of athletic contest, or balance, or sheer toughness. The trouble with tennis is that it requires all of the above.

Tennis asks questions of you: *Do I have the raw power to overcome my opponent? Will my conditioning allow me to do so over and over again? Do I have the aerobic capacity to survive a*

25-shot rally? And the anaerobic capacity to compete in bursts?
Is my straight-line running fast enough? Is my lateral movement
efficient enough? Is my core capable of holding all these moving
pieces together?

And then the biggest question of all: *In a sport that's dominated*
by overuse injuries – including one nicknamed in its honour, tennis
elbow – am I durable enough to withstand everything as I follow
the longest competitive calendar in international sport?

That first year back in the game, the answer was no. I kept
getting injured. My recurring problem was humeral bone stress,
which affects the bone in the upper arm. My right arm was
not coping with the increase of pressure and impact, with the
muscles pulling around that humerus. It was invariably getting
more and more sore. Partly that's due to the way I play and the
strings I use. The co-polyester string I prefer gives me power,
control and touch, but it is still a hard string, and it takes
time and strength to be able to withstand the brutal impact of
repetitive training loads.

In the early days with Tyzz, I had to train and then rest,
train and then rest, with little continuity. We did 40 weeks of
training in that first year alone and suffered four injury setbacks
in that time, mostly inevitable, through sheer repetition.
Luckily, we had help – the very best. Strength and conditioning
coach Narelle Sibte, that is.

Narelle is a Melbourne girl – from the southeastern suburb
of South Oakleigh, to be specific. She calls herself a 'jack of all
trades, master of none' as an athlete, because she played netball
for Victoria but not quite for Australia, and because she competed
in athletics nationally but only as part of the second-string
teams, as a hurdler, shot-putter, javelin thrower, discus hurler

and heptathlete. Hyper-mobile, she contorted her body into compromising positions through teenage sport, and had suffered five stress fractures in her back by the time she was 17. She spent two years in rehab, which inspired in her a thirst to work out the technical and physical elements of athletic preparation.

Coming out of high school, Narelle wanted to be a physiotherapist, but missed out on the uni course by just one mark, which turned out to be the best thing. She did a physical education degree instead, then sports coaching and administration, and she won a scholarship position working at the Australian Institute of Sport in Canberra. Her strength and conditioning role was meant to be for 12 months but became permanent, meaning she was able to work with the Australian Olympic team ahead of the 2000 Games in Sydney, helping out in archery and boxing, women's basketball and men's water polo. She spent time at the English Institute of Sport in Loughborough, where English cricket is headquartered and the Formula 1 testing laboratory lives, and where she was also exposed to slalom canoe, triathlon and hockey.

Each new sport was a new learning opportunity. Narelle knew nothing about slalom canoe, for instance, but emerged an expert on shoulder movement range and how your hamstring can affect the rotation of your trunk. The triathletes she worked with couldn't understand why their maximal oxygen consumption – or VO_2 max – wasn't as good as that of international ten-kilometre runners, and so she ran a six-week course on diaphragmatic breathing, teaching athletes to sing in order to breathe. She knew hockey a little better, but still learned how to set up bodies so that they could lean over the stick all game long and not suffer lower back or abdominal problems.

Narelle moved to British Tennis next, and began to implement all the lessons she had learned from other sports. The biggest carry-over between other sports and tennis, she realised, was in boxing, through movement and control. There used to be this theory that you need to take short, sharp steps to get to the ball in tennis – but just look at Roger Federer, who moves like a cat, with a wide base and a still head. His movement is efficient and effective, saving him as much energy as possible for his shots. That's exactly what boxers do.

I met Narelle around 2010, when she had returned to Australia to take up a position as the national manager for an under-18s tennis program at the Australian Institute of Sport. I was playing at a tournament in Bundaberg, and Mum approached her to ask about my preparation. 'What's the right amount of exercise and training for a child?' Mum asked. 'What are your feelings and philosophies about elite sport in juniors?'

It just so happened that Narelle was about to start travelling with the Fed Cup team, which meant we would be crossing paths regularly, and she did some concentrated work with me as I made my run towards Junior Wimbledon in 2011. At Roehampton, the traditional lead-up event, I was about to face Madison Keys, and Narelle had questions for me, but they were more tactical than physical.

'You're on grass and you're playing Madison Keys,' she said. 'What are you going to expect?'

'She's got a big serve,' I replied. 'A very big serve.'

'Okay, so if you had that serve, what would you try to do to her.'

'Pin the body.'

'Okay,' she said, 'then that's what we'll prepare to face.'

Narelle found a wire fence and had me stand in front of it, between two wooden posts. She stood six metres away and told me she was going to smash balls right at me, and it was my job to get out of the way. 'And if you want to get out of the way properly,' she said, 'you've gotta use the ground. You've gotta read the approach from my hand and shoulder.'

The preparation didn't exactly help, as I lost the match, but I loved that Narelle thought differently and that our preparation was match-specific. I loved it.

I spent more time around her after that, right up until the time where I decided to quit. That dramatic meeting I had with Stolts at the National Tennis Centre, hugging on the couch? Narelle was right there too. When I finally considered coming back to the game, it made sense that she was one of the first people I called.

I had to be straight with her. 'I've been sitting on the couch,' I admitted. 'I haven't done anything. And I'll probably regret this – but do you want to help me give this thing another crack?'

'It'll be a grind,' she told me, 'but I'm keen to get stuck in.'

I was too, and so we began training back at Melbourne Park. Something wasn't quite right there, however. I felt watched, like I was under a microscope or inside a fishbowl, and in a way that's true. The National Tennis Centre has eight indoor plexicushion courts, in a space that feels like an aircraft hangar, but one wall is entirely glass – windows onto one of Tennis Australia's bustling thoroughfares, where peers and administrators mingle and move and glance out at who's having a hit. Taking my first tentative steps towards a comeback in this space, I felt judged.

My paranoia wasn't unfounded. Narelle had conversations with people from the tennis hierarchy in that first 12 months, and they often asked her about my fitness and my mental state. She earned my trust with her reply. 'I'm not employed to work with Ash by Tennis Australia,' she told them. 'Ash approached me in a private capacity. If you want that information you'll have to ask my boss, and that's Ash.' In the end, the solution was for me to travel to Narelle, who was living in bayside Mordialloc.

This is that part where the movie of my life would pause and become a training montage, set to music, like something out of *The Karate Kid* ('You're the Best' by Joe Esposito) or *Rocky* ('Eye of the Tiger' by Survivor). We got on bikes and rode to Braeside Park, or along the track by the Mordialloc Creek towards Patterson River. We did boxing sessions on the beach at Parkdale, and afterwards ran the stairs – up and down – between the foreshore and the sand.

Push-ups and standing leaps. Deadlifts and medicine ball rotations. I did rope courses at Clip and Climb – one of those places where kids have birthday parties and scale obstacles with names like Astroball and Spaghetti Junction and Red Square. And when it was wet and rainy and miserable, Narelle would drive me out to the Dandenong Mountains to run on slippery mud and gravel, climbing the 1000 Steps memorial walk at the foothills of a primordial forest.

She had warned me what it would be like. 'After two weeks, you're going to want to kill me, or not get out of bed,' she said. 'But by five weeks, you'll do less training and more recovery. You'll still feel terrible, but you'll know when to expect it.'

Narelle varied the work, so my body was constantly facing a barrage of new attacks, while my mind stayed nimble. She sat me on the very edge of overcooking, making real-time adjustments depending on what I could handle. She made sure I could keep up with other girls, then run past them. She helped me believe and trust that physicality could become a massive part of my game. She taught me to love training again and she began shaping my body into a weapon.

25 Per Cent Effort

This place is a treat, but it's one that I need. I'm tired and sore, and the 2021 French Open is coming. But I can't handle Paris too early, which is why we have flown to the south of France, to a place called Beaulieu-sur-Mer, just outside of Nice.

In little hamlets like this, the French Riviera is quaint but stunning, like a European dream. You go for a walk and it's all panoramic views of hillsides with homes slotted into them, and down at the base the land drops away into the Ligurian Sea. The water is azure, a reflection of the cloudless sky, and the beach is made of rocky pebbles that you can see through the clear saltwater. There's not a breath of wind, and middle-aged men and women wearing next to nothing sun themselves all day, until they're bronzed beyond belief, while their children rollerblade up and down the esplanade.

We've come here because it's quiet, but there's a little more activity this time. This is the week of the Formula 1 Grand Prix in nearby Monaco, so a parade of Ferraris and McLarens and Aston Martins prowl past.

It sounds glamorous but we keep things sensible. We are here to enjoy but we are here to work. We have a modest apartment, and we find a nearby rotisserie chicken joint, so we can get a hot chook to have with avocado on fresh baguettes for lunch. We train in the morning on one of five courts in a tiny tennis club that almost feels like someone's opulent backyard. I hit plenty of balls and physically I feel great. The days are long in the best way – languorous and full and stretching out in front of us. We have time on our side, and no need to rush – the perfect preparation for Roland-Garros. I have never felt more prepared for a Grand Slam.

All good things must end, and we head northwest to Paris. I'm back in the City of Love and staying in a nice hotel, but I'm also back in a Covid bubble, so I can't eat at my favourite little sushi shop near the stadium. I focus on what I want from this trip.

Sometimes you put your hopes and dreams out into the universe – I did that back in 2019 when I verbalised what I was seeking here. It worked that time, and I won my first ever Grand Slam. Subconsciously at least, I'm doing that again now. *Righto, Paris, what are you going to give?* I think to myself. *Are you going to be kind to me, or are you going to break my heart?*

I catch up with young Aussie player Olivia Gadecki, who's been in Turkey and Egypt, grinding away and doing an incredible job. We keep in touch regularly, but I haven't seen her in the flesh for months. She's into the French Open with a qualifier's wildcard, and I want to touch base with her. I feel like a bit of a mentor to Liv. Although I'm only 25 to her 19, it feels like a meaningful gap. I hope I can comfort her, because she energises me. It's her first time here, so we talk through the quirks and traditions of this place, and doing that helps me see it through fresh eyes.

I show her the locker room, where – because of Covid protocols – I'm expected to have a different locker every day, but I'm a creature of habit, so I ask the woman running the facility if I can keep locker 24, my normal locker, the one in the deepest corner of the room. We go into the gym and then I walk Liv onto Centre Court next, but I don't really recognise it – the whole place has had an upgrade, and there's a cavernous new roof. My heart begins beating faster all the same.

I point to the spot where I gave Tyzz my favourite ever post-match hug, and where I whispered to him, 'Mate, can I retire now?' We go upstairs to the players' boxes and my heart beats faster again, because I remember where everyone was sitting when I held up that trophy.

'It's a pretty cool view, isn't it?' I say to Liv.

She likes the view even more at ground level shortly after, when we start our practice together. It's my first time back here since 2019, and her first ever hit at Roland-Garros.

The hallowed French ground of Court Philippe Chatrier really is a beautiful place. It's grown to be one of my favourites. I have a wonderful hit the next day with Svetlana Kuznetsova, one of the best clay-courters I've ever seen. I finish up and tell my physiotherapist, 'This is the best I've felt in a month.' I hit with Naomi Osaka the next day, and feel great again. I'm firing on all cylinders – at least until the 45-minute mark of the session.

When I land after a serve, I feel a dull pain in the high adductor, the top of the hamstring. It doesn't feel quite right, and Naomi doesn't want to do much more anyway, so we cut it short and go inside to see if we can figure out what's happening with my leg. It doesn't feel as bad as I thought out there, so I hit the next day but the pain is there again on my serve – and this time it's immediate.

I'm rattled now. I've been doing physio sessions and we've tried to re-create the pain, to get more information, but serving is the only action that flares it up. I walk off court quickly and smash my racquet down on my tennis bag. *Fuck!* I think. *I'm meant to be playing in three days!*

I try to keep my cards close to my chest, though, and troubleshoot behind the scenes. I get a scan but it shows little except a little irritation of a nearby stabilising muscle and potential bony impingement in the hip joint. My team talks to hip specialists from all around the world, trying to find solutions. I try hitting with Maria Sakkari: playing a few points together is fine, and there's no pain – but when I attempt a serve, there it is again. And it has worsened. I finish the session and break down in tears.

We try something new the next day, taping four different areas of my leg – to the point that I can't fully straighten or bend it. I hit with Storm Sanders, who's just qualified, then I land on a serve and almost fall over, the pain is so intense. Storm knows something isn't right but doesn't say anything. She sits beside me and wraps her arm around me, and I have my head in my hands. My physio then adds more buckles and tape. Now it feels as though I'm preparing for an hour every day just to practise.

The conversation after the session is tough, too. I'm lucky I have a good person with me to talk things through. Her name is Melanie Omizzolo. I call her my physio but that's selling her short. She's the national physiotherapy manager for Tennis Australia, a role that means she's overseeing the physical wellbeing of a couple of dozen players at any one time. She's been doing that since 2014, which was when I first met her. I was living in Melbourne and not far away from giving the game away, which she saw coming. She's perceptive like that.

Mel and I are both introverts, so we only really interacted then when we had to, but her job took her to many major events on the WTA tour. She watched me play qualifiers at Wimbledon that year. They're held at Roehampton in the strangest setting. A series of big cricket ovals is connected, and they paint lines on the surface to make them into tennis courts. Mel sat on a grassy hill there near a court watching me play, as if she were in the outer watching a game of footy. She had the impression that I was unhappy. To her, I was that quintessential talented kid, doing something they're good at for all the wrong reasons. She could see it in the way I worked on my recovery, too: I wasn't particularly unprofessional, but nor was I particularly diligent.

After I came back to tennis, and as I got better and started winning more, I saw more and more of Mel. That's not because I was given extra attention, but rather that it's her job to be there throughout those major tournaments on the tour, and to stay until the last Australian is eliminated. The better I got, the more and more often I was the last Aussie to leave tournaments.

During Grand Slams in particular, the time we spent together bonded us. When I won the French Open in 2019, we spent hours together every day, with her supervising every aspect of my warm-up and cool-down and recovery, massaging and stretching and advising. She was at my side two hours a day, not counting coffees and lunches and dinner every night at that Japanese restaurant opposite Roland-Garros. Our working relationship quickly became a friendship and I absolutely loved spending time with her.

I came to know her, this girl who grew up in the northern suburbs of Melbourne and went to a Catholic girls' school in Northcote. She was a mad AFL fan, barracked for Carlton and wanted to work in football, as she was fascinated by the process of managing endurance athletes who play a brutal and ballistic contact sport on a weekly basis. After graduating from university, she worked with a VFL team, the Box Hill Hawks, and spent half of the calendar year working through the depths of winter with these young athletes.

While Mel was completing her post-graduate study, a lecturer took her aside and pointed out that the WTA was looking for physios. Mel replied as only she could or would: 'What's the WTA?' She had no understanding of or interest in tennis, but ended up working for eight years as a contractor physio for the WTA at tour events. She combined working in private practices in Melbourne with work at international events, including Grand Slams, with the world's best female tennis players. These were players with high profiles, high expectations and high pressures. Mel had to perform and travel and be independent, and work long hours and get things right.

So yeah, she's exactly the right person to manage me in this moment of pain and uncertainty. The conversation we're having now centres on whether I can still play, and what the risks might be if I decide to try.

'Something doesn't feel right,' Mel says. 'Something doesn't sit right with the pain, with the imaging. We're missing something.'

I can run and walk and play, but not serve, and once I have served I can barely climb a flight of stairs. This injury has come out of nothing, too – just playing against Naomi and landing on a serve like I've landed on a million other serves. In just 48 hours, it's become a major problem.

It's Monday morning now, and my tournament starts on Tuesday. We tape up again, and I practise at the Jean Bouin courts, trying to figure out a way to serve without using my legs. It gets to the point where my only option is an underarm serve, and I'm not willing to accept that.

The results of an ultrasound and an MRI come back, but neither helps with the diagnosis, and the discomfort is only worsening. I'm on heavy painkillers now, and they're barely dulling the sensation. I eventually work out that I can hit a second serve at about half-pace, without using my legs or jumping – a technique that players used 50 years ago, before the emergence of the power game. But I can't change the entire mechanics of my serve in the space of one day, can I?

By the time I'm ready to walk on court for my first-round match, I have my hamstring taped, my adductor taped, my glute taped and my hip taped – all on the left side. That should get me to the point that I can serve one of those old-timey arm balls with no leg power, and the pain should hover at a five instead of a nine. 'Tyzz,' I say. 'I'm gonna hit an ace today with a little arm ball.'

He looks unconvinced. 'No, you won't.'

I wink. 'Yeah, I will.'

And I hit an ace early and turn to him and smile, because sometimes you have to salvage joy from the wreckage.

I'm playing against Croatian-born American left-hander Bernarda Pera, and it's brutal out there. The pain ratchets up, and even though I feel I can endure it – I win the first set 6-3 – I'm also worried about doing more damage and jeopardising the rest of my season. Early in the second set, I move out to a ball on my forehand and my leg hits the ground. A full nerve shock shoots down the limb, and I groan without realising. Seeing this, Mel has her head in her hands. 'Stop, stop, stop,' she's saying. 'You can't play.'

I lose the second set but still feel close to winning. I just have to manufacture some pressure, find a service break and make Bernarda feel like she has to overplay her shots. That's exactly what happens, and I come off court half-laughing and half-crying.

'How did you do that?' Mel asks. 'I've never seen anything like that in my life.'

I decide I'm going to play the next day, and so we do everything we can. Painkillers. Laser treatment. Ultrasound treatment. I'm now spending two hours a day off court trying to mitigate my pain and bring it down to an acceptable level. I'm playing Magda Linette, a Polish counterpuncher, and the pain from the start is extreme. My abdomen is sore now too, because of the work it's doing to compensate for other areas, so we tape it up as well. I'm held together by Elastoplast and lose the first set 6-1.

I'm feeling the pain on every serve now, and I'm in danger of completely tearing an abdominal muscle. At 2-2 in the second set, I try to serve normally, and the pain in my leg when I land is so bad I simply buckle over. That's when I walk over to the chair umpire.

She sees my distress. 'Are you okay?'

'Nup,' I answer.

And that's how my 2021 French Open ends. I've run out of time. I take 15 minutes with my team in a treatment room. We don't know what to say. I sit on the floor and put my leg up, because it's the only way to get it free of pain, and I cry – not about the injury but the heartbreak. I have to do media now, and I don't know what I'm going to say. I don't want to look at my phone because I know messages are coming through, and sometimes all that beautiful support only makes the tough times harder.

I go back to the hotel and text our group – *Is it wine o'clock?* – and they all answer, *Yeah, it is.* We have a couple of bottles of red together, trying to have a laugh. I don't know what lessons or learnings or silver linings will come of this, and for now at least I don't bother looking for them.

*

There are 25 days to Wimbledon and we have to understand what's going on, and there it is – finally – in a scan the next morning. A ten-centimetre strain deep in my adductor. If I had played any longer at Roland-Garros, Wimbledon would definitely have been ruled out. I'm lucky there is even the slightest possibility.

I give myself some time to be upset, without lingering too much. We could have done things differently. In 2019, for instance, I played just 15 matches for the whole year on clay, whereas this year I've played more than 20 before the French Open even began. But there's no point in dwelling on that. If I'm going to dwell on anything, it should be the fact that I've only lost two matches in the past two and a half months. It's been an enjoyable and very successful trip, and you never know what's going to happen next.

The French Open has broken my heart, but I know that Wimbledon can put the pieces back together. A month on grass – I can't wait. We quarantine in London, wait for new scans and figure out a plan for the next three weeks, knowing we have to be malleable and tolerant, ready to overcome setbacks and play the cards we're dealt.

We start slowly with rehab in the house we've rented. The only equipment we have access to is a children's swing set so we buy therabands, a watt bike and any other gym gear we can cram into the backyard, which is no more than four metres square. We're in Southfields, not far from Wimbledon, and it's lovely. It feels like home. We have a BBQ out the back and an expansive kitchen. We have cooking competitions – my strength and conditioning man Matt Hayes and me versus Tyzz and Mel – to see who can come up with the best BBQ and salad dinner. It's the first time in months that we're able to cook our own meals on our own schedule.

But in another way, it drives us all mad. Tyzz, Mel, Matt and I are living together in a four-bedroom house, which is close enough quarters at the best of times, but during five days of quarantine it feels as though we're in each other's pockets. We do whatever we can to lighten the mood and keep our nerves from jangling. When you spend that kind of time together, you talk more, and you go beyond those surface-deep conversations you have with the people in the cubicle next to you at the office. You confide and debrief and laugh, and your relationships grow stronger.

I first got to know Matt in 2020, when I was at home a lot and needed someone to train with. He works under Tubs and often works with the younger kids, and I hadn't been home enough to get to know him, but I quickly saw that he's very good at what he does. He doesn't have a lot of travelling experience, but I knew I would need someone on the road this tour and asked Tubs if Matt might be the guy. 'Do you think he would want to come over, and would he be able to?' I asked. 'It's a big step to come into a team and run the gauntlet.'

He slots in like he's been one of us forever. I like him, too. He's a sports tragic, loves his AFL and NRL – the Brisbane Lions and the Brisbane Broncos. We're compatible as co-workers, able to slip out of easy conversation and jokes ('Ash, I'll get a tattoo if you win this Grand Slam') and into the discipline required. He communicates well when he isn't sure about something, and is firm with me when he is.

I need that certainty right now, because this injury cloud is forcing me to do things differently. I've always played a lead-up event before Wimbledon, so it's on my mind now that I might be a little underdone. Matt comforts me with his road map – his grand '21-day plan' that will take us through to that first Monday of Wimbledon. We started with those bands out the back, and the watt bike. Now he has me walking up and down the stairs to activate my hip. I buy a kids' scooter and, in our large house, I start scooting from room to room, building the load through my left leg. Childlike and fun – just how I like it.

Jumping is the hardest part. I'm terrified of landing after a serve. *I don't know if I'm ready for this*, I worry. *This movement I've been making for 20 years now brings on the most extraordinary pain of my career.*

We start by hopping, as if skipping over a crack in the footpath. A bilateral hop feels okay too, and then a small jump, but I'm favouring my right side. I'm terrified to go through the full motion on my left, but Matty encourages me.

'I don't think I'm ready!' I say. 'It's going to hurt!'

He keeps telling me just to give it a try.

Jump. Land. *PAIN*. Straightaway. 'Nup, I'm done,' I say.

I try to explain the pain a little better in the aftermath, suggesting I draw the pain on my body, like a colour-by-numbers book, showing where it hurts most. And Matt and Mel stay positive and patient with their patient, telling me I'm three days ahead of where they expected me to be. They're putting on brave faces, but I begin trusting myself more. I remind myself of the calibre of the experts I have on call here.

Eventually we're freed from quarantine – but rather than go our separate ways, we go out together, down to the local pub for a Sunday beef roast, Yorkshire pudding and a couple of beers while England plays Croatia in the UEFA Euro 2020, which has been postponed by a year because of the pandemic.

I tell Mel I don't want to know the detailed results of the new scan. I trust her implicitly and I want to go by feel. I want to treat the symptoms. What I don't want is a reverse placebo effect, where I'm told the medical extent of the injury and consequently crumble more quickly, succumbing to my own negative expectations. All I want to know from the medical team is whether the strain is a bit better than it was.

Even so, I'm shitting myself ahead of the scan results. I've been doing treatment and rehab every day, without giving too much away about how I'm feeling. When you're a professional athlete in international competition, you can't help but become this figure around which others orbit, and so the way your world turns has an effect on theirs. It's a responsibility I've never enjoyed, but one that I take seriously all the same, so I try to remain stoic.

For most of our time in quarantine, I had taken myself to bed early, trying to give myself space to think about what might happen, and to understand that my season could very quickly go one of two ways. Little did I know, Mel, Matt and Tyzz were all just as concerned. They were purposefully positive and energetic during our sessions, but as soon as I had gone to bed, it was as if they could finally stop holding their breath. Deep down, they knew how improbable our Wimbledon dream was.

The scan results arrive one night while I'm in bed curled up with *The Final Hour*, part of the Victor the Assassin series by Tom Wood. I don't learn the outcome until the morning. 'It's better,' Mel tells me. 'It's improved.' Time to crack on then, and get down to the All England Club. I call Mum straightaway to deliver the good news.

Fifteen days after retiring hurt in Paris, it's time for me to head to Court 3 at Aorangi. After my slow and meticulous rehab build-up, that first hit feels awesome. No pain. Beautiful setting. Cinematic. I step one way and then another, pushing it little by little, trying to feel out the threshold for pain so I can set my own limit.

Matt's holding me back, though. He says I need to stick to the plan. 'We are going to have a setback. We're going to have something that comes up,' he says. 'You're going to wake up sore in the morning, so we need to monitor what's happening.'

Next I'll try to serve, and I'm nervous. We decide to literally *walk* through the serve, with me keeping both feet on the ground and just rolling my arm over. I hit five or six that way and it feels fine.

'Can I try a little jump serve?' I ask Mel. 'Maybe 25 per cent effort?'

'Yeah, yeah,' she says. 'Try it.'

And in that moment, we all hold our breath. The serve is pain-free.

'Nice,' says Mel. 'Do it again.'

I serve another handful, and Mel cautions me: 'Just do ten serves – no more.'

I want to do more. I want to hit my serve at 50 per cent – even just once or twice – but the calm demeanour of my team belies the stress they're all eating.

Mel finally relents, giving in to my whingeing, just a touch. I can hit 15 serves at an easy half-strength swing. I feel no pain and smile, but now we're nearing the start of Wimbledon and the stress is mine, because I know that if I'm going to compete – to have any chance of winning – I need to be at my peak, and I haven't even reached 75 per cent of my capacity. Not even close.

Now it's the week before Wimbledon and I feel ready to play a practice set. I hit with Priscilla Hon, playing a few service games without trouble, but I'm still only at 70 per cent. I'm trying to bat away my doubts, and thankfully I see from the way Mel and Matt exhale that I've passed through another checkpoint along the recovery path they've been mapping for me. We push more and more through that week, serving at 75 per cent.

At this point we have to go into the Wimbledon bubble, moving into a hotel near Westminster. The hotel has about 2000 rooms, and I'm going to be in one of these for a while – depending on how far I go in this tournament. If I win, it could be 23 days going back and forth from this place. It's only 10 kilometres away from the courts, but you can't travel faster than 20 miles per hour, meaning it's a 45-minute drive at a minimum. Most days it takes over an hour. That means there are no short days, only long ones, accompanied by long nights in a hotel room. This doesn't feel like Wimbledon to me. It's unique, and challenging, and a good reason to remind myself of my motto for 2021: *Spirit of adventure.*

I find ways to make my lodgings my own. My room has a little fridge and a little stovetop. I go on to Amazon and buy myself a frying pan and a toaster, so I can make my own eggs and avocado and a toasted bagel each morning. I've brought my own coffee devices, too. Mel, Matt and Tyzz take the piss out of me, calling me 'the travelling house' – and, in fairness, I do have all those optional extras, plus my own tea towels, dishwashing liquid and a dish scrubber.

It's now two days before the tournament begins, and I'm finally allowed to hit a serve at 100 per cent – for two service games only, no more and no less. I'm all set. I'm about to embark on a two-week journey against the best players in the world, on our sport's grandest stage, and I haven't raised a sweat on court in a month.

Drovers and Drivers

My comeback to professional tennis began in fits and starts, in sputters and stutters. I qualified in Eastbourne at an ITF US$50,000 event and won my first match. I won six matches that week, in fact, and made it to the semi-finals, and I also made the semi-finals in doubles with Storm Sanders. I was back doing what I was supposed to do, playing this game on grass in perpetual summer, an hour from London in a seaside village with high white-chalk cliffs.

I was too sore to play the next tournament, though, so I adjusted my schedule and accepted a wildcard into a small WTA event in Nottingham, the midlands city of D. H. Lawrence and Robin Hood. This was where I'd won my first ITF event – US$50,000 and a wildcard entry into Wimbledon in 2012 – so I had fond memories of the place already, even if that early chance at Wimbledon had ended with Roberta Vinci giving me a severe lesson in how to manoeuvre a slice backhand.

Nottingham was just one of those spots where I always felt comfortable. I loved the way the courts played, and much of my extended family was from there. I liked the coffee shop 200 Degrees, a short walk from my hotel, with a fake fireplace and decent biscuits and slices. I even liked the laundromat around the corner, and it cleared my head to clean my own clothes. I made the quarter-finals there, which I hadn't done previously, and lost to a superior Karolína Plíšková in a tough one, 7-6, 7-6.

But my body wasn't yet prepared to play that many matches. I got injured at Wimbledon and came home nursing wounds. My new companion was back – distal humeral bone stress – that injury unique to tennis players and baseball pitchers, like shin splints for your arm. It's more common if you have a kick serve, as I do, because there's more torsion in your action. The pain would flare up with different balls, too. If you play in the mist at Roland-Garros, for instance, the ball gets heavier as it picks up clay and water, then all of a sudden you realise your arm is aching. But it's a mysterious injury, and hard to know if it's caused by your swing or the impact, the load or your technique, your equipment or the weather.

I tried to overcome it training back in Melbourne, where it's cold and wet, but that didn't help. We were putting together eight-week 'return to play' plans, but after six weeks the injury would invariably reappear. So we threw out the rule book and I played through the pain, entering a tournament in Taipei, in Taiwan, where I played really well. I did enough to get what I was after, anyway: a wildcard entry into the 2017 Australian Open, and I seized that chance too, winning through to the third round, the furthest I'd come so far in my home Grand Slam.

When I left tennis in 2014, I could have sought a 'protected ranking' – I was ranked 186 in the world at the time – but I didn't because I wanted the cleanest possible break. I wanted my leaving to be real, as if I had vanished from the sport altogether. Now I was back to that level of play anyway, rising from nothing to 180 in the world in a little more than a year. That felt significant, as though all my hard work had restored me to myself. I was ready to go further, to win more than mere ITF events.

I flew to Kuala Lumpur to play a qualifying match for the Malaysian Open. It's played at a resort with a gorgeous golf course where they stage a PGA event, but the tennis club is tiny, with temporary tents and grandstands. It was hot and humid – one of those tropical settings where you felt as though you could taste the rain in the air before it fell at 3 pm each day. I loved that rhythm, too: playing singles in the morning, resting during the daily deluge, then playing doubles by night.

On 5 March 2017, my comeback was complete when I breezed past Japanese baseliner Nao Hibino, 6-3, 6-2, to win my first ever WTA title. To cap things off, I won the doubles with Casey too. I'd played 12 matches in a week and won them all. I had finally cracked the top 100 – I was now ranked 92 in the world.

That tournament was the moment I broke the shackles of the past. *I've proven to myself I can do it, and now I've proven it to all of you, too,* I thought. *And I'm doing it on my terms. It's my journey now.*

*

The trophy I received for the Malaysian Open was a kind of crystal vase. I might have been justified in keeping it as a marker of my progress – my better-than-full-circle return to the game – but instead I gave it to someone special: my manager, Nikki Mathias.

Nikki grew up in Kyneton, in regional Victoria, where her parents were cattle and sheep farmers. When she was eight they moved north to Moulamein, over the border in New South Wales, to a rice farm in the middle of nowhere, but she loved it. Life on the land suits some people in that way – you have family, friends and the farm, nothing too complicated.

Nikki found her way in the world by leaning on those pillars, then she went to boarding school in Melbourne at 13, living in at Melbourne Girls Grammar, where she was into rowing and netball and playing the tenor saxophone. It was a setting where you had to learn to be independent and try new things, to know what you want and chase after it. It suited someone as clever and ambitious as her. She even coached rowing there after she left, overseeing 50 girls at the historic Merton Hall campus, teaching them how to be happy in themselves and get the best from their team.

Next, Nikki went to the University of Melbourne to study commerce, focusing on business law and finance through a degree that would keep a lot of doors open. She was the rowing coach of the daughter of the pioneering AFL journalist

Caroline Wilson, who became a sounding board. She found herself in bigger-name circles, babysitting the children of Essendon Football Club champion James Hird, and soon she began working in her first job at his sports management and strategy company, Gemba.

That was a joint venture with Ben Crowe, and his role as her senior manager was instructive. Crowey was already the one people listened to. You learned from him simply how to sit in a meeting, how to listen, how to notice people and treat them right, and how to shift things quietly. Nikki was put onto the Toyota account, which meant working in AFL circles, managing the likes of Hird and Brisbane Lions star Jonathan Brown – trying to understand what an outlet or brand or sponsor wanted from them before figuring out how to put them in their best light.

She lived in Sydney next, then in London, where she worked for a tech company on their sports sponsorships in tennis, golf, the NBA and NFL – global experience with enormous budgets and huge events. She came home and worked in the commercial team at Tennis Australia, signing partners for the Australian Open and managing those relationships. But it also finally felt like there was a chance to do her own thing, too, so she branched out and began representing her own clients, like football commentators and personalities Brian Taylor, Matthew Richardson and the late Danny Frawley. She began working with surfer Steph Gilmore, and later with AFLW star Daisy Pearce. But one of her earliest signings was me.

Nikki had been consulting for my old management agency, which was based in the United States. We met in early 2016, over lattes at Blackboard Coffee at Varsity Lakes on the Gold

Coast. She told me later that I stood out to her as gentle, and kind, and eager to please – as someone whom she could help to gain confidence. Nikki felt that I was smart and knew what I wanted, but that she could bring me out of my shell to recognise those traits.

She had this beautifully blasé, nonchalant attitude, but I could see in her eyes that she was driven and organised, and I instantly trusted her. She had prepared for our meeting but I didn't feel as though I had been studied by her in readiness for an exam. She asked me about my life – not my tennis – and told me a little about hers. I loved that she understood the global stage – that she had already swum in those waters in different roles – but also that she was Australian and knew the local market. She had never managed a tennis player before, so it would take a leap of faith for me to join forces with her – but when you know, you know.

I knew a few months later, around the time of the 2016 Wimbledon qualifiers. We went to one of her favourite pubs, the Anglesea Arms in Kensington. It was a stunning summer night, English blokes standing out on the street knocking back pints and us chatting deep inside the dark old bar. I asked her more about her personal life, and that was when I discovered that her partner was Ben Mathias, who had coached and chaperoned me on a few junior tours. As we sipped our way through a couple of bottles of wine and talked about life and boys, it felt as though our fates were intertwined. I quickly understood that she would make the effort to build relationships with everyone on my team. I knew she would be a vault for all of us. And I knew she would be a warrior for me. I wanted to start from scratch with her, and jump into this new unknown together.

I needed her, too, and right away. Ash Barty 2.0 became a meteoric journey, one that demanded steady hands at the helm. After finding my strength in 2016, it was in 2017 that I started taking down big names for the first time in my life. In June, I beat Garbiñe Muguruza and Barbora Strýcová and was ranked 54. In August I beat Venus Williams and was ranked 37. In September I beat Johanna Konta, Agnieszka Radwańska, Karolína Plíšková and Jeļena Ostapenko and was ranked 23. In November I beat Anastasia Pavlyuchenkova and Angelique Kerber and finished the year ranked 17 in the world, higher than any other Australian, male or female.

So many big things were yet to come. I was ready to attack 2018, but of course I had no idea that my Daria Kasatkina implosion at Wimbledon was just around the corner. I was yet to experience any of my greatest victories, highest pressures and toughest scrutiny. Through it all, Nikki did everything I could need. She was my chief strategist one day and my gopher the next. During the 2019 French Open, for instance, after winning my way through to my first ever Grand Slam semi-final, I learned that the RADO and Jaguar patches on my shirt were too big by two millimetres. Nikki became the world's finest carrier pigeon, flying immediately from Brisbane to Paris to hand-deliver my new strip.

She became that person who would jump on the phone and call everyone else if my sisters or Mum or Dad needed to know what was happening behind the scenes. Nikki coordinated, communicated and kept all the members of an expanding 'Team Ash' on the same page. There's a directness about her, too. It's not that Nikki is blunt, but you're never left wondering where things stand.

People in Australia generally get the word 'laconic' wrong. They think it means laid-back, and see it as representing our relaxed and easy-going national character. But they're wrong. Laconic actually means being succinct or economical with words. The national character it represents isn't the chilled-out surfer, it's the farmer on the land, the drover of few words, the doer and the dreamer who offers up wisdom and humour with brevity and concision. That's Nikki. She's laconic. She can put you in your place, quietly. She can put all the pieces in place, actually, without you even realising she's in total control.

Trophies don't mean a lot to me. I don't keep any in my house. The mementos I want most are photos of me with my team. But those stainless-steel plates and goblets and crystal ice buckets and vases do have value to others. I've known that all my life, or at least since I was 12 and Jim began urging me to donate my growing pile of prizes to tennis clubs that couldn't afford their own. Nikki didn't need my Malaysian Open trophy, but she deserved it.

She still has it, of course. It's in her home office in Runaway Bay, on the Gold Coast, alongside special winning racquets I've given to her, footies signed by her oldest client, Brian Taylor, a surfboard signed by her newest client, Molly Picklum, as well as jerseys and scarves and hats that have been given to her by so many other athletes, all grateful – as I am – for who she is and what she brings to the team.

I've proven to myself I can do it.

Triumph and Disaster

Wimbledon is the tournament that everybody knows. Whether you watch this sport or not, you understand the weight of its history. Even if you don't know that the playing surface is comprised of 54 million plants, each cut to a precise 8 millimetres high, you understand that there's a mystique around the surface. Whether or not you realise that there are no sponsorship signs wrapping every wall of the venue, you probably sense that the place is not driven by commercialisation. And whether or not you know the exact rules prohibiting colourful garments – or that they were established so that the unseemly sweat of the athletes could not be seen by spectators – you probably know that all players here wear all white.

But you don't need to know all of that, of course, because those are just distractions. And that's the thing about Wimbledon: no distractions are allowed. It's the blankest canvas, just the grass and the game. Elegance and purity.

Winning Wimbledon also means immortality. No one forgets what happens here. They celebrate and welcome past champions in the most special way, so you aren't just a winner here, you're absorbed into that history. The trophies have never changed, and the honour boards are displayed prominently around the grounds. You feel surrounded by those names – watched by them. As a kid, you think, *I can't be one of those.* It's so far beyond any kind of realistic imagining of the way your life might turn out. It's like thinking, *One day I'll be an astronaut*, or *When I grow up I want to be prime minister*. You know it's implausible, but in truth it feels impossible.

I've known for a long time that if I were to succeed here, I would be satisfied with my journey. Win one and I'm done. I thought playing my final match on the most beautiful Centre Court in the world would be perfect. It would be my end point, and perhaps always has been. There's something specific about the tournament that fits me right. 'The Championships' just get me. When I play here, I feel as though I grew up playing in the wrong era, like I'm suited to this place – to the restraint and the simplicity of the mood, to the green courts and the tops of the trees you can sometimes see peeking up above the tiered seating, and to the way the game is played here, with agility and elegance and grace. *Quiet, please.*

*

It's late June 2021. The London weather is awful and I really don't want to practise today. I don't want to hinder my leg or my hip. I don't want to deal with the traffic and the hassle, where 45 minutes of light practice becomes an eight-hour day.

Jamie Baker, the tournament director, sends me a message: *Ash, we would love you to open up Centre Court on Tuesday at 1.30 pm.* That changes my mood, lightening me up, until I realise why I've been chosen. Simona Halep, my good mate and the reigning champion, sends me a message too. She's woken up with back spasms and can't get out of bed without help. Centre Court was hers to open, and now her Wimbledon defence has ended before it's even begun.

I don't feel I deserve this position, and I'm unsure of my body, too. I'm playing against Carla Suárez Navarro, and I know this is her last Wimbledon. 'I've never played her,' I say to Tyzz, 'and with everything she's gone through' – she retired when she was diagnosed with Hodgkin's lymphoma, and two years later has come back to play – 'I don't know how to feel.' *Should I feel excited?* I wonder. *Scared?* I promise myself I will at least smile when walking onto court. I have good reason.

Mel is doing two hours of treatment on my leg every day, and finally I'm feeling no pain. But I ask her not to tape me as much as usual before this first-rounder because – for the first time in my life – I care a great deal about what I'm wearing.

I have a special outfit for this tournament. In early 2020, Nikki and I had noted that Wimbledon 2021 would be the 50th anniversary of Evonne's first victory here, and thought maybe an outfit reminiscent of the iconic scalloped white dress she had worn would be meaningful. I had looked through a variety of designs from FILA and chosen a shortlist, then asked my niece Lucy to narrow down the selections and make my final pick.

I had called Evonne and asked if I could wear a dress inspired by her, and she was taken aback and said yes. Deep down, I don't think she was ever going to say no, but I needed her permission all the same. The request felt both necessary and appropriate. Evonne saw the drawings and she loved the look. Unveiling it on Centre Court is too big a moment to ruin with a bunch of medical tape. I don't know if I'm going to win here, either, so topmost in my mind is that if I get eliminated and can only wear this outfit once, I don't want to spoil it by having a medically mummified leg peeking out the bottom of the skirt.

I'm in the hallway now, waiting to be welcomed into the public arena, and I see words in front of me. It's a couplet from Rudyard Kipling's poem 'If', which is always inscribed in view of competitors at Wimbledon before they begin their match:

If you can meet with Triumph and Disaster
And treat those two imposters just the same …

If you haven't read the poem in full, it's worth doing. Every line speaks to me. The messages aren't subtext – they're right there on the surface. Keep your head while others lose theirs in blame. Trust yourself when others doubt you. Don't hate or preen, or think yourself wiser than others. Dream, without letting those dreams become your master. Endure your truth being twisted by others. Risk all your winnings on one thing and be ready to win or lose. Walk with kings but stay true to your roots. If you can do all that, Kipling says, 'Yours is the earth, and everything that's in it.'

Yep, I think, *let's play some tennis.*

We do, but of course it rains. I stand with Carla while they close the roof, and we talk like practice partners. I'm thrilled to be able to test myself against this person. This is what tennis is about for me. It's not about the wins and losses, the triumph and disaster, it's the fact we're both sharing a special moment, but for different reasons. I win the first set, lose the second because I'm being too passive, and then flick a switch in the third set to end it. At least I'm off the mark and over the hump.

The next morning, I roll over in bed and I know I'm going to be sore, but it's not too bad. I wake up to messages from Mel and Matt: *How are you feeling?* I do a couple of exercises and everything is fine, but as the day wears on I grow more and more stiff. By the afternoon I can't bend over and touch my toes to do up my shoelaces. I can't sit on a chair because my glutes are so sore. My very light practice session with Tyzz is a comical disaster. We laugh and accept that it's more about recovery now – we won't stress over the tennis.

My second-round match is against Anna Blinkova. I know it's a match I can win while going through the motions, but my body is seriously hurting. I can barely push off to serve, and when I do, I can't find the court. But I find a way to win, and then I collapse in agony at the hotel.

A couple of days later, I work myself into my third-round clash in similar fashion, trying to take it up a level against Kateřina Siniaková. She's wiry and clever and therefore dangerous, so again I'm happy playing a cleaner match. I raise my level to take the opportunities in the big moments.

I'm aching, but my body feels as though it's finding its routine now. Long-distance runners talk about pain in this way. The lactic acid builds up in their legs far earlier in most races than you might imagine. And their lungs are on fire quickly too. They don't talk about making pain their friend exactly, but they do talk about 'settling in with the suffering' – enduring it, knowing that the pain is taking them in the right direction. I'm finding the middle of the racquet and my confidence is growing, so I'm not in the mood to focus on any potential mishap or injury. My team asks me time and time again, 'How are you feeling? Do you have pain?' Nothing. *Let's go.*

My opponent in the fourth round is Barbora Krejčíková, an all-court, accurate and aggressive player, as comfortable at the net as she is at the baseline. She has just won the French Open. I'd watched part of her semi-final there, in fact, in which she beat my good mate Maria Sakkari.

It's strange how and why some matches become personal, but I want this match-up badly. Maybe I'm feeling burnt by the French Open and what I missed out on there. I feel that dark desire taking hold – the mongrel inside of me. I want to prove something to myself, but also to everyone else. *I'm better than her – she's not beating me today.*

She makes me uncomfortable early, but I find a way to read her patterns and win the games that matter most. On match point, I offer a massive fist-pump to my team, and walk off court with purpose.

'Fuck,' I say to Tyzz, 'I wanted that.'

He nods. 'Oh, I could tell.'

It's getting closer now, my goal. It's 2021, three years since the Kasatkina meltdown, and three years since I met Crowey. I've been keeping a journal. I write in it every day, and I also write down goals at the start of every year. It makes me accountable. Sometimes the goals are specific and sometimes they're general.

For 2019, for instance, I specifically wanted to make the top ten, to beat Simo, and to beat Caro, but there were general development goals, too. *I want to play more carefree, fun tennis. I want to be accountable. I want to compete.* I conclude with a summary statement: *When I am at my best, I am CALM, CLEAR, PRESENT, CONFIDENT & SHARP.*

In 2020, one of my specific goals was to make the quarter-finals at Wimbledon. Then in mid-2020 I did an interview with wheelchair athlete Kurt Fearnley, and he's easy-going and disarming and so without realising it I said to him that I wanted to win Wimbledon. No one had heard me say that before, because I don't think I'd ever said it before, even to myself. But it had escaped from my lips, so at the beginning of 2021 I made it a firm target. 'Win Wimbledon' was the primary goal in my book – the one that sat at the top of the page circled in biro. And so the dream that had dared not speak its name had been both vocalised and inscribed, and now I'm here chasing it for real.

I'm sitting in my undies, strapped into an ice machine – a portable cold compression contraption called a Game Ready – and watching the tennis for once. My next opponent will be either Emma Raducanu or Ajla Tomljanović. I'm particularly interested to see Emma play, as she has burst onto the scene recently and I've never seen her strike a ball. I'm texting Tyzz about her throughout, talking tactics and the areas where we can expose her, and he texts me the same thing at the same time. *Ditto, mate. Ditto.* It's good that we're on the same page, but bad that the page reads clearly and emphatically: 'This chick is good.'

After spending this time observing and planning, we watch as Emma has to retire hurt. What seems to be breathing difficulties ends her dream, and forces me to shift my thinking. It's me and Ajla now – Aussie against Aussie. I can't even imagine the buzz back home.

I tell myself I want to play a stand-out match. I want to be respectful but assertive. In reality, this means too much to me to think in such ways. If I'm honest, I want to make Ajla feel tiny, thinner than a blade of grass. I want to use my experience playing on Centre Court and in Grand Slam finals to make her feel as though she doesn't belong.

And that's what I do. I'm clear about the areas of her game I want to exploit, and I find those openings and drive the dagger in. I intend to make her feel horrible out there – lost and drowning – and a 6-1, 6-3 win is how I make that happen. I couldn't allow the fact that she is Australian to factor into my thinking at all. Today, she was not a compatriot – at least, not until after match point.

My semi-final is against Angelique Kerber, whom I haven't played in a long time, and who has a winning record against me. I've always felt forced to go a little above myself to match her experience, and this year I believe she is the one to beat. Storm Sanders is still alive in doubles, but gives up her time to practise with me. I prefer to hit with a left-hander, to get my mind into an asymmetrical game. Stormy puts her own energy into my dream. Love that girl.

I play close to the best tennis of my life against Kerber. *CALM, CLEAR, PRESENT, CONFIDENT & SHARP.* My legs are burning the entire match and my energy is flagging, but I do as those runners do and settle in with my suffering. When you walk off the court with a win after spending yourself so thoroughly, the high is unlike anything else. Take the endorphins you feel on the couch after a long run and add the feeling you get when you ace an exam and you're somewhere near the heady, drowsy, utterly earned satisfaction I feel right now.

'I can't replicate that,' I say to Tyzz. 'That's as good as it gets for me.' I'm into the final at Wimbledon.

The 2000-room hotel, once chock-full of players and coaches and trainers and officials, is now surreally silent, and all the procedure and bureaucracy of this tournament, which had once seemed arduous and insurmountable, has lost all drama. The approach to the summit is quiet. There are no girls left to practise with, so I hit with Australian doubles specialist John Peers, which is ideal, because he can send down some big serves. I kick a footy around on the court a little too, keeping my routine. I keep reading on my Kindle – more spy thrillers. Seven books in total during the two-week event.

I toss and turn, and although I sleep relatively poorly, I wake up ready to go. It's the day I've always dreamed of.

*

It rains all morning, yet again. I'm meant to warm up on a practice court outside, but it's not going to happen. The sky is sodden, clouds hanging low and drooping like a big wet doona. My planned departure time, arrival time, treatment time and practice time are all shot.

I bump into Dylan Alcott, the Paralympian and star Grand Slam winner – and future Australian of the Year – and our teams have coffee together. He'll be playing his own Wimbledon final soon enough, but first we all have a laugh while watching some AFL that's being played back home.

We have a little bit of time before our warm-up, but we wander over to the practice site of Aorangi anyway to begin our preparation. We find the now vacant gym, and Tyzz sees a small sponge tennis ball, while Garry finds a broom handle. We can't stand around idly watching the time go by, we figure, so we may as well kill it with a cricket match, just like we did before the French Open in 2019. That worked out well, after all. Our pitch is the open-plan treatment area. Physio beds all around – extra fielders, of course. Game on. Mel is trying to warm me up and treat me, but I can't do it. It's more important to me now to loosen my mind than my body. 'It's my innings,' I plead. 'They've gotta bowl me out first.'

The gym supervisor cocks an eyebrow when she finds us, but there's news at least. I can have a practice hit on Court 1 … alongside my opponent. This has never been done before. Finalists in the greatest Grand Slam of all do not warm up next to one another on the morning of their match. They're like a bride and groom on the day of their wedding – kept apart until the moment they present themselves to everyone together at the big event that will change their lives forever.

Yet here we are, me hitting with Tyzz, and Karolína (Kaya) Plíšková hitting with her coach, Sascha Bajin. Tyzz and I are both wearing coloured clothes, because I wasn't planning to practise on a match court. This simply isn't allowed at Wimbledon. But due to the last-minute change, the All England Club allows us to play – just this once. I know it's a cardinal sin, so I'm embarrassed. Mortified, really.

Kaya and I are quite good friends, and we have a laugh about it all – and then a dozen cameras pop up, but they're late to the party. It's time for us to warm up, get changed and get ready.

As I walk out onto court, I do what I always do. Look up and smile.

The roof is open – this is good for me. Kaya's biggest weapon is her serve. If the roof is closed and she can launch at me all day with no elemental distractions, no gusts of wind or bursts of sunshine to throw off her rhythm, I'll be in trouble. An open court with the sky above is what I want. It also just feels more like Wimbledon should feel.

I win the toss and elect to serve. I always do. Give me the responsibility straightaway. I want the balls in my hand. My first service game is as good as I could have asked for. *Bang, bang, bang*, I think. *Yep, good.*

We expect Kaya to serve hard and fast in response, but the first one she sends down is slow and tentative. *What the hell?* I return it and look at the clock to check the speed, and sure enough it's just 84 miles per hour. I look at her face and see something there. I can see it in her arm, too. Kaya's nervous – and that relaxes me. I look at my box and smile. Tyzz has noticed it too.

When you're playing tennis, you're also playing mind games. All players have 'tells' – subtle cues that reveal how they're feeling about their place in the match, and what they have left in reserve. Right now, I read Kaya's face and sense an absence of energy. I know I can take control here. And when you're in a position of strength like this, you need to use it and push. Hard. You need to bully a little.

That's how it feels in my head, but on court it's as though we've simply swapped expected styles. She usually comes out on fire and I build into matches, but today she's so tentative that I don't need to do much to win the first four games. My big focus is to take away her aces and easy points – those cheap one-two, serve-and-first-strike winners. I can't let her establish any flow. I don't care if I have to chip back every single serve – I'm gonna force her to earn the winner. An extra ball, every time. I power through the first set, 6-3. She doesn't hit a single ace.

In the second set she changes her serving spots and it puts me in a bind. I can't cover both edges of the box, and she's stretching me on either side. She picks her spots well and finds her way back into the match. My legs are tiring now and I'm shaking a little. If I've worn any mask of deception – trying to convince her of my superior strength – it slips a little. Now we feel on equal footing. Now I just need to focus.

I walk as slowly as I can between points, trying to get oxygen into my limbs. It's 5-5 when I finally break her serve – she's 40-15 up and I have no right to win it, but I dig and dig and dig and it falls my way. Then I serve for the match, and she has no right to win it but she digs and digs and digs and finds a way to break back. We're both playing elite tennis, but she is more aggressive and finds a few points in the tie-breaker that I can't. We're going to a third set.

Naturally, you have doubts when you go into any decider, but it's different when you're playing from when you're spectating. A fan watching this final is likely sitting on the edge of their seat right now, wondering what happens next; having no control like that must be terrifying. I'm drawn to those thoughts sometimes too, wondering what everyone else must be thinking and feeling – considering all the points left on the table, the could-have-beens and should-have-beens – but such things are fleeting. Because this is my office. This is where I do my best work. Nerves? Nerves have no place here – not now, anyway.

I settle into the final set and make myself a promise: *I will play the rest of this match on my terms. I will walk off the court with zero regrets.*

I'm going to win this match, I think. *I'm gonna find a way. This is mine. I want it more than her.*

My heart beats quicker now, but my thoughts remain clear. *She's going to have to work her arse off for every single point. Nothing will be cheap. I will attack each point. I will be switched on for each return. I will be mindful when Kaya is on the back foot, because Kaya on the back foot is dangerous.*

The crowd is incredible, but it's not their fight – this is me against her. I have tunnel vision now, and am connected only to that competitive instinct I've had my whole life. There are so many tactical complexities in tennis – things I've learned from Jim and Stolts and Tyzz and others – but at the heart of a match like this lies the same question I've been asking myself for two decades: *What do I have to do to beat that girl down the other end of the court?*

I don't remember the last point, but I'm told Kaya hits a backhand into the bottom of the net, and the spectators rise with an almighty roar. That sound rushes through me. *Is this happening?* I think. *Can this be real?*

I cover my face and sink to my knees. I quickly hug Kaya and I forget to thank James Keothavong for umpiring the match – I later feel awful for failing to acknowledge him. I toss my racquet down and drop my head and crouch on the court once again, as though I'm simply not ready to open up to all the warmth and rapture raining down on Centre Court. My left leg almost buckles underneath me, and I look up with mist in my eyes. *What has just happened?* I'm incredulous. *Genuinely, what has just happened?* I thank the crowd but I know I need to get to my team.

I go straight to my box, thinking I'll climb up into it. I don't even remember that Pat Cash did exactly that in 1987 – I just don't want to be alone in this moment. At first I go the wrong way, and then the fans point me in the right direction to find them. I wrap Mel in my arms, and Matty next, and then Garry. I sink my head into his shoulder, smudging his shirt with my tears. 'This is so embarrassing,' I whisper. 'I'm crying in front of millions of people.' I hold Tyzz next, and I love the look on his face – a mix of pride and belief, while he's also humbled and wonderstruck. I give one final hug to Stormy, who has been there with me through thick and thin. I am so glad she is there to share this moment with us.

During the presentation, I'm shitting myself. It feels like too grand a stage. I try not to pay attention to the glow of celebrity or the glare of the public eye, but I also know that the stands in this past fortnight have hosted David Beckham and Benedict Cumberbatch and Sienna Miller and God knows who else. Watching this final, front and centre, are Prince William and the Duchess of Cambridge, Kate Middleton, who's presenting the trophy to me, and I suddenly realise I have no idea what the protocols are for dealing with the British royal family.

Kate is incredibly patient and kind with me as I present the Venus Rosewater Dish to the crowd. After the ceremony comes the traditional balcony presentation, but first I'm asked to walk through and briefly speak to those who were sitting in the royal box. Kate's smiling and so is William, and I have no idea what to say, so I find myself lost in relatable chitchat. Billie Jean King smiles at me and Martina Navratilova says, 'Welcome to the club,' and I sort of shake my head and nod all at once. *Holy shit, I'm now a member at Wimbledon – a member of the All England Club.*

That balcony moment is one I will never forget. A view that deserves to be a postcard – a sea of people, and my favourite lush green courts quietly resting in the background. Amazing.

The photographs are done, and the officials come to take the trophy away. And I finally get to see my team. 'Oh my God, I've just cried everywhere on international television,' I say to Tyzz. 'I don't remember what I've said in the last five minutes. This is the most embarrassing thing that's ever happened to me.'

Garry hands me a bottle of Stella Artois but I don't feel like drinking. I'm too exhausted. I give him one more hug as I try to hide from the cameras. I finally get back into the locker room and I just want to drop. I sit for five minutes, staring at my feet.

I open my phone and see messages from my family and friends. The texts continue to pour in as I stare down at the screen. The very first message on my phone was a little unexpected, but then I've always known that she's this type of person. *Congratulations, mate*, it reads. *I am so happy for you, my friend. You deserve it. It feels different, doesn't it? How good is the balcony. Enjoy, my friend.* It's from Simo. What a dead-set legend.

With my phone blowing up – alerts and notifications of all shapes and colours, blinking and blaring – I can't help but contrast it with the poise and tranquillity of the match itself. I knew exactly what was on the line, yet the contest itself – from the passages of untrammelled pure and untouchable tennis to the breaks of serve and losses and moments of pressure – felt lucid and transparent. Nothing rested on perception or emotion or momentum. Everything rested on process and mindset and belief. *CALM, CLEAR, PRESENT, CONFIDENT & SHARP.*

As a team, we find a quiet moment in the locker room over some Stellas, Haribos and chips. Now I finally feel able to ask Mel to tell me about my injury in detail. The strain was still there, she tells me now. It had improved, but only very, very marginally. She pulls out the report she's been keeping from me.

'Okay, this is what it was. You still had a ten-centimetre strain, which should have kept you out of competition altogether, and this is why we held you back,' she says. 'Bad luck that you were grumpy with us for the first week, but we did what we had to do.'

I can't believe what I'm hearing. I'll owe Mel, Tyzz and Matt forever. *How did we even get on the court?*

I have a few hours of press commitments ahead of me now, and it's 4.30 am in Australia, but it's my first chance to talk to Nikki and Crowey. They're two of the best phone calls of my life.

The All England Club organises a private dinner for my team – a beautiful five-course meal that is way too fancy for us. I sip a glass of champagne overlooking the Thames and realise that I haven't called Mum. I FaceTime her now, and I cry and she cries and everyone else does too. My body is wrecked and my heart is exhausted, and there's nothing more I can compute or experience or absorb.

Our exhausted and emotional celebrations end early, and I drift off to sleep and fall into my dreams, one unreality meeting another. I still don't understand today, this glorious day, and probably never will.

Trust
yourself.

Today, Love Won

The night before I won Wimbledon, I didn't feel stressed or excited. I felt present – existing fully in the moment as night fell on London. I was as professionally cool as it's possible to be, not exactly detached but certainly undisturbed. 'Primed' is probably the best descriptor. I felt ready in the most calm and composed way possible. And then I tried to sleep.

Normally I fall into bed early because I tend to rise early, and that's the way my circadian rhythms are, but the night before the final, slumber just wouldn't come. I rolled onto my side and my back and my front, looking for the perfect posture, searching out the warmest pocket under the sheets and the cool side of the pillow, but nothing felt right.

I tapped Garry on the shoulder. 'Are you still awake?'

He sniffed and yawned. 'Yeah, what's up?'

'I'm terrified.'

'What do you mean?'

'I'm terrified that I'm going to lose tomorrow,' I said. 'And I'm terrified that I'm going to win tomorrow.'

All that objectivity and serenity and self-possession I had been so proud of all day were gone in the darkness. For the first time in my life, I was scared by the outcome of a tennis match.

Garry turned to me. 'It doesn't matter,' he said, opening his half-shut eyes and smiling. 'Just play.'

It might sound trite to say this, but I needed to hear those words. I needed to hear that what happened on court wouldn't matter to him, or to anyone else in my family. There was no hesitation from him – no hedging or bullshit or working through each possibility and consideration. He made the matter clear: my worth to my loved ones wouldn't change a lick on the bounce of a few balls tomorrow.

We both rolled over into fitful sleep, but before we did, he hammered the point home one more time. 'Just go and win it,' he said. 'And if you don't, it doesn't matter.'

Garry and I met five years earlier, in late 2016, at the Brookwater Golf and Country Club – my local track. It's a great course, and new, too. Created in 2002, it's since been a regular in the top dozen or so courses in Australia. People like to describe it as an antipodean version of Augusta National, and I can see why. The undulating terrain and the tall trees make each fairway feel like a corridor within nature. With large greens, soft bunkers and shallow rough – and with doglegs and downhills and angled approaches – it has a manicured feel. And for 12 years this was Garry's office.

He spent his days here doing a traineeship as a golf pro, while also working as an irrigation technician. He loves grass, and gardens. He has a meticulous and bizarre love for every blade. He's the one who takes the time even now to tend to our own lawns with wetting agents to stimulate the soil and growth retardant to make sure it doesn't sprout too high while we're away. He has three garage cabinets filled with fertilisers and treatments.

Garry was born in Gladstone, way up the coast from me, somewhere between Bundy (Bundaberg) and Rocky (Rockhampton), but he grew up close, in Ipswich. My sister Ali's husband went to school with him, so we knew some of the same people, and trod some of the same territory, although we never crossed paths. There's a slight age difference: he's six years older than me. I remember asking Sara if she thought that was a big deal or a problem, but of course it isn't.

We met through the golf club, both playing. I found him to be instantly authentic and genuine. He's funny, too. In any list of traits that women find appealing in men, being funny is always in the top two, which makes sense. Would life be worth living if you weren't laughing along the way? Garry is that guy who makes people laugh. He can be incredibly inappropriate at times, but he knows when he's doing it and it's usually just to put people in stitches.

Our early days dating were as stress-free as it gets. We went out a few times, and then I went away to Europe on tour for

12 weeks. That meant we ended up messaging and calling, getting to know one another through messages and phone calls in different time zones. It was a different way to start a relationship, but nothing we've ever done has been normal.

We knew each other so well before we spent any real time together in person, but it was still nice to get to know him up close and personal, and to discover all his quirks. To learn that he's a big softie – but with an incredibly short fuse. To see him carry himself with strength and presence – but then lose his mind howling in pain when he stubs his toe.

I knew he had never been interested in tennis, but then I learned the depth of that blind spot. He didn't watch tennis. Didn't like tennis. Didn't understand the rules of tennis. The game had no meaning to him – and I liked that. In truth, I needed that. It shouldn't matter so much, but it seemed crucial in my mind that my partner be interested in me in spite of tennis and not because of it, and that was Garry. He's been with me since I had only just picked up a racquet again, when I was unranked, just a girl named Ash who apparently was decent at tennis a few years back. He loved me for me, and became the most important cog in the second phase of my career.

Garry threw himself into the deep end, too. He never seemed worried or concerned by the time I was spending away, and never pushed or insisted I cut anything back. I knew instantly that what mattered to me mattered to him. He would watch all of my matches, no matter where I was playing, no matter whether it meant sitting up late, alone in front of a flatscreen or squinting in the sunshine somewhere, trying to follow a live stream on his phone screen. And afterwards, he was always the first person to message me, win or lose.

He had no problem being at my beck and call either.

'Can you fly here tomorrow?' I might ask. 'I really need you.'

'No worries,' he would invariably reply.

I dragged him into a completely different world, but he handled it all with such a deft touch and good grace. Joining our team on the road, on match days, he would simply blend in, just another teammate looking for fun and trouble, wondering if that open space behind the court was big enough for a kick of the footy, or if this piece of gym equipment could be used as a cricket bat.

He quickly became someone I could turn to in my darkest moments – the one who would always make me laugh, taking the piss out of me way too soon. One of the worst moments of my life on tour came on a day when that harmony between us was broken by circumstance. In fact, it was perhaps the perfect example of a clash between Ash Barty the person and Ash Barty the persona.

I was playing in the Italian Open in Rome in 2019, and Garry was scheduled to fly home halfway through the tournament, as he had work commitments. As it happened, his departure date coincided with my match against Kristina Mladenovic.

The person I loved the most was leaving, at the very moment I was playing. I was supposed to be studying the tall French doubles specialist on the other side of the net, monitoring her heavy serve, but all I could picture was Garry in a cab, Garry at the airport, Garry on a plane, and me left here alone. I couldn't focus. I was crying on the court, and once I got off the court, my tears were out of control. Tyzz was a little confused that he couldn't calm me down.

I called Crowey, seeking some sort of calming influence or explanation.

'Ash,' he said, pausing. 'You're a lover. And you're a fighter. But today, love won.'

Garry made his own sacrifices, too. Anyone who's in a relationship with a professional athlete does. At the end of 2019, for instance, he deferred doing his PGA traineeship so he could follow me on the tennis tour more in 2020. Of course, Covid changed the entire world in early 2020, but I loved the fact that he wanted to be with me and share the journey of my career. He found a new love later with caddying, and is pursuing that now. The young golfer he's working with, Louis Dobbelaar, is still in the infancy of his career and is due to begin his PGA journey through the Korn Ferry Tour soon, but I love watching those two work together. It reminds me a lot of my relationship with my team, and I know it'll be a partnership that lasts.

Garry will be great standing beside Louis on the course. He knows how to flick that switch between being the strong and silent commander to the boisterous boy at the bar. Sport can be lonely on the road, and Garry is great company. And, of course, he knows his grass. Before each shot or each decision, he and Louis discuss how that particular patch of slow-growing zoysia will affect the way they play an approach shot, or how this type of kikuyu plays in the afternoon heat.

One of Garry's best traits is that he uses whatever he has at his disposal – whether it's knowledge or a nonchalant nod – to help people succeed. He never interfered in anything when it came to tennis, and not all partners are able to do that. Whether it was the business side of the Barty brand or the tennis complexities of Team Ash, he deferred to all others, understanding the value of an expert. I love that about him – that he can be opinionated but never outside his own lane. If he doesn't know something, he says so, and never tries to bluff his way through. That's an honourable characteristic in a person, and one that I think is in short supply these days.

In 2021, when he arrived in London and entered the tournament bubble at Wimbledon, it had been three months since I'd seen him. It was always our plan for him to join us at Wimbledon, but I didn't realise how much of a positive impact it would have on me. The environment can be intense, and filled with stresses major and minor, and everyone needs someone to lean on – sometimes as a sounding board, and other times so you can do a brain dump and let go of all your worries. I wanted someone to talk to about my injured leg – or, when my mood changed, to *not* talk about my injured leg. For the team, Garry was a fresh face and brought a new energy. He laughed, he took the piss, he did nothing at all and yet did everything that was needed of him. Sometimes showing up is everything.

After Wimbledon, we had some time booked in the Bahamas. Whatever the result, I knew I would need a rest before the Tokyo Olympics in July and August. I woke up the morning after the final and felt more tired than I ever had before. Apart from the champion's photo shoot, I stayed in my robe in my room the whole day. My limbs were heavy and my eyes stung. I was as depleted and drained as I could be. Rest and relaxation on a beach sounded ideal.

Once we got there, we went out for pizza and beers, and still I just wanted to go to sleep. The following day we went to the pool and did nothing, and went to bed early again. I had barely anything left to give, so we spent the week together eating hotel meals and overcoming our lethargy and trying to understand what had just happened.

The travel restrictions that were in place at the time didn't allow us to get back into Australia, and I regretted not being at home – denying my family and friends their chance to celebrate with me in person – but in truth I don't think I could have managed the procession of parties and BBQs and lunches that would have come my way. A week of forced relaxation was probably the best thing for me.

Garry and I have always had a normal and easy-going lifestyle when we're at home. We had been living together in the house in Augustine Heights that I built in 2017, but now we were ready to move into our new home – our forever home – which was perched on a hill with a view of the golf course.

I love what we've built together. I love that when Liverpool is playing, I know Garry will be wearing one of his 50-odd jerseys. I love that if I give him any chance at all to control the sound system at home, DJ Dillon Francis will be blaring. I love that when we're near an In-N-Out Burger in the United States, I can guarantee that he'll be popping in to get a 'Double-Double' with fries. I love that – despite my tendency towards obsessive-compulsive disorder – Garry shows not even a flickering desire to place his socks in the sock drawer, and instead simply sheds his clothes at the end of the day, letting them fall wherever they are removed. I love that he's compassionate and tolerant but has no patience at all for people who bullshit or outright lie or who don't do what they say they're going to do. I love that – as a Queenslander – Garry's sporting hero could be anyone from Adam Scott to Allan Border, Mick Doohan to Mal Meninga, but he fell the hardest for the hardest hitter: left-handed opening batsman Matthew Hayden. I love that Garry's dogs and my dogs – our dogs – are the most important thing in his day, most of the time even more than me. I love that he sits on the steps with my youngest nephew and talks dinosaurs until the kid is exhausted, and that if Lucy wants to kick a ball she need only look in his direction. He has always fitted into our family and has never changed who he is. That's what I love the most.

The Last Summer

A new summer is coming and I'm not feeling it. The desire is gone. It's the end of 2021 and the idea of slaving in the sun and hitting a few thousand tennis balls and going from home to car to airport to flight lounge to plane to terminal to transport to hotel to practice court, in one city and then another city and then another city, all within a matter of weeks, has never felt so pointless.

I see now that all sport is mountain climbing. We set our sights on a summit and, step by step, we trudge towards that peak. We look at nothing else, ignoring all other concerns, and once we're on the mountain and making our careful ascent, there's no coming down until the climb is done. We slip and fall sometimes. Other times we freeze on the spot. We live a spartan journey, too, filled with order and sacrifice. We reach dizzying heights, where the air is thin, and we get delirious over how far up above the world we're perched.

But what do we do when we reach the pinnacle – when we finally win our Grand Final or our World Cup or our Wimbledon? Do we stop, sit, enjoy the view and breathe? Do we take the time to appreciate what we've done, and move on to something new? No. In sport, we simply return to base camp every year and begin the journey of attempting to summit once again.

Do you know the myth of Sisyphus? He was condemned to push a gigantic rock up a hill, only to watch it roll down to the bottom, and to repeat that action for all eternity. That was his *punishment*, handed down by the god Zeus. Professional athletes serve that same life sentence – push that same rock up that same hill – only we hand this punishment to ourselves. Train, play, rest, travel, rinse, repeat.

I start with my favourite hard 30-minute bike session to use as a reference point: five sets of a four-minute time trial, then two minutes of rest. Usually I love taking myself to this dark place. Today, I quit the session during the second rep. Something I have never done before. I don't quit. Ever. I'm physically capable but cannot be knackered. This sounds like a little thing, but it's not – it's a clear red flag. Pre-season training is always a slog but there's a rhythm, too, where the hard work turns from something arduous into something you eat up. This isn't that, though.

Soon I begin cracking tongue-in-cheek jokes – 'Think this'll be my last summer, guys' – and people laugh, because they think it couldn't be true ... could it? *She couldn't quit, as the number 1 player in the world and reigning Wimbledon champion, could she?*

Tyzz knows it's a possibility, though. He saw my enthusiasm flagging months ago in Cincinnati, where we went ahead of the US Open. We chatted in a library off the lobby of the hotel where we were staying, in yet another middle-sized city of the world. He could see writ large on my face that I didn't want to be there. 'So why are we here, then?' he had asked. 'If we're going all this way, shouldn't we put it all together and make it count?'

'Yeah,' I replied. 'You're probably right.'

I won the Cincinnati Masters that week but I was still exhausted. All I wanted was to be home, and now that's where I am, trying to force myself back into my groove. I do so with some hitting practice with Ben Mathias. He's Nikki's husband, but he's also been a coach of mine and my hitting partner for the past couple of years, particularly during Covid lockdowns and border closures, when Tyzz couldn't come north from Melbourne.

A normal practice hit in our first week back is 60–90 minutes long, with a bit of everything. Up and down the middle of the court. Volleys. Serves and returns. Lobs and smashes. It's basically an extended match warm-up designed for the off-season, to start a cool engine and turn it over once or twice. You're not trying to reinvent the wheel so much as get your eye back in and your workload up. But it can be a shock to the system after a break – even after just one month off.

Ben knows that my coordination returns more quickly than for other players, and that he doesn't have to overplay me. He says I'm a freak when I'm fresh, but he also says that a rusty Ash Barty is a moody bitch. He tells me that Tyzz is always secretly happy when Ben takes over that first week of pre-season hitting, because he knows I'll be in a shitty mood.

Ben thinks he knows why, too. When I've had a break and come back and start hitting tennis balls, I have to start getting my head around the oncoming year. The tour becomes a reality. Add some physicality and soreness to the equation and it puts me in an even worse mood. He says it with a smile, of course.

Ben's known me for a long time, and hit tennis balls for a long time himself. He played a lot as a junior and was good, but he stopped at 15 to live as a normal kid. Sounds like a smart move to me. He came back to the game when he was 18 and had finished school, but a professional playing career wasn't to be. At 25, he started working for Tennis Australia's National Academy, followed by the AIS and then the Davis Cup squad, coaching Australia's top male players.

He met me when I was just 13. I was at the national academy, and he was looking after the elite boys from Queensland. TA changed their structure soon after and assigned different players to certain coaches, and Ben worked with me for a year in Brisbane. Like others back then, he used to say that I had variety, and talent, and that I could volley and slice. He loved my ability to hit a kick serve too. I was the girl he could 'coach like a boy', he said. Ben was the chaperone on my first overseas playing trip, to New Zealand. I got homesick quickly on that tour and he saw that immediately. We had spent enough time together talking sports trash with one another, arguing over whose rugby league team was better – my Wests Tigers or his Manly Sea Eagles – for him to spot that my spark was missing.

These days, Ben is one of those people who makes training days fun. We have the stupidest arguments, about whether BBQ sauce or tomato sauce is better – and the debate never ends in a win, just an exhausting and exhaustive flurry of points and counterpoints. (Although tomato sauce is clearly better.) He likes to tease me – 'Bet you can't hit that ball can with a serve' – and then when I miss and he's right, he'll say, 'Good try, sunshine!' He's a smug bastard.

Ben is a 'no bullshit' individual, and that comes in handy because he knows when I'm lying to myself or hedging or dodging. He calls me out and challenges me, even though he knows I hate being called out and challenged. We have always had that type of relationship: the permission and trust to be honest, no matter what. He forces conversations with me that others can't. Put it this way: if Nikki is a protective surrogate mum, Ben is another of my surrogate dads. She's gentle and he's blunt. She stays away from tennis lessons but he charges in.

Ben knows he doesn't have to beat around the bush when he needs to set me straight. He did that for me in 2018, after my loss to Kasatkina at Wimbledon. I went back to the London townhouse after that match, sat down on the porch and asked him to tell me what I needed to hear.

'You need to go and apologise to Tyzz, and you need to come up with a plan,' he told me. 'You don't wanna behave that way. That's not you. And you're not dealing with the pressure – you need to address this.'

That honesty is a two-way street, however, and so now, facing a new pre-season, I go down to his and Nikki's house in Runaway Bay. Ostensibly I'm there to do some signings – posters and hats. It's only late morning but we're having a beer anyway, a Balter XPA, and I'm sitting in his office signing, and then I'm venting, and before I know it the whole truth comes tumbling out of me – about how hard the year has been, and how I'm not sure I can do it all again.

'I don't know what I'm playing for anymore,' I say. 'I think I'm done.'

'Yeah, I get it,' he replies. 'But to be honest, you haven't won a hardcourt Slam yet.'

There's a silence, and he's the one to fill it first. 'I think if you were to go racquets down right now, there would be something hanging over your head – there would be unfinished business.'

'Benny, I've got nothing left, no spark.'

'But you don't have an Australian Open, and you want one,' he says, winking, poking the bear. 'Just go and win the Aussie Open. And then retire.'

I'm quiet after that. I don't like this conversation. I especially don't like that he's right.

Win one and then stop. I can do that, I think. *Set me a challenge? Fine. Game on.*

*

Melbourne was, for a time, the most locked-down city in the world, and so Melburnians have been waiting longer than most for their 'hot vax summer'. Over 57,000 people pour into the Melbourne Cricket Ground on day one of the Boxing Day Test match between Australia and England – including me and Crowey. We haven't caught up in almost a year, since our steaks at Moo Moo ahead of the year of adventure. It's nice to give him a hug again. Crowey gives great hugs.

The cricket is a sight to behold. England are skittled for 185 runs, with a nice contribution by a big, bustling 32-year-old debutant, Scott Boland, a Gulidjan man, but we don't see enough of that as we have too much to catch up on. Crowey and I speak and message almost every day, but it's never the same as catching up in person. In person, the face tells the story. You can recognise when they're beaming with pride, or spot the furrows that belie their worry. In person, you laugh more loudly and reminisce more deeply.

We talk through the past year in the space of an afternoon, reliving it all, and Crowey sums me up as only he can. 'More money, more titles, more fame does nothing for you,' he says. 'They call that extrinsic motivation. You need intrinsic motivation.' That means different things to different people, he explains – it might mean finding purpose in your work, helping others, being part of a team or realising your potential. As he sees it, I still have two main motivations. 'One, you want to know where you're at, and whether you can and have realised your absolute full potential,' he says. 'And two, you like the fight – you need the hunt, whether you're playing pool or in a putting competition.'

He's right. I'm curious about the upper limits of my ability, and how far they stretch. And the desire to compete is always there – when I play you, I don't just want to beat you, I want to kill you. I decide to serve both those motivations in the new year at the 2022 Adelaide International, and in the first round I draw an even-keeled prodigy on a mission, Coco Gauff – but

again there's no bloody spark, no fire at all. I'm flat and frazzled
and don't even know why I'm here. Before I know it I'm down a
set against her, and down 4-2 in the second, and it's break point
on my serve. In my head, I'm already conceding the match.
Ah well, I think. *Standard first-round loss of the year.*

And then there's this rally. No one writes anything about it
later, but something pivotal shifts in this single point. We go at
one another shot after shot, and Coco might only be 17 but she's
one of the purest athletic beasts on the tour already, a predator
chasing down every ball. She's been making me feel old. But
after 20 shots, 25 shots, maybe 30 shots, I win the point. *Not
today*, I think. *Not today.* I win 11 of the next 13 games and take
her down. And this is the start of my summer surge.

I talk with Tyzz later about what I felt out there – this sense
of playing without emotion. I have never been overly emotional
on court, but I always played with fire in the belly, so this is
something I've never experienced before. It almost worries me –
except that, right now, nothing at all worries me. You could call
it cavalier or nonchalant but it feels cooler than that. Robotic,
almost. And the tennis it produces is imperious.

I start with Sofia Kenin, whom I want revenge on for
the 2020 Australian Open semi-final, when I butchered the
outcome. I deliver her one of the best serving days of my life,
and I feel nothing. The next day I go out and play Iga Świątek,
and I love the way she plays so I wanted to get up and motivated
for the match – but something's missing, something's missing,
something's missing. It doesn't matter because I dismantle her
game anyway, and again I feel nothing.

I go for a swim as recovery that night at midnight, and then
close to 1 am I have a chat with Tyzz and Nikki. They're gently

trying to talk me out of retirement, telling me how I can pick and choose my tournaments, how I can stay even closer to home this time, but they're not really hearing me.

I play the final in Adelaide and pick apart Elena Rybakina's game and take the title for the second time. *Yay*, I think limply. *I guess?*

Storm and I play doubles that week, too. She brings so much energy and joy to the court, and we combine so well together, that we finish the week as doubles champions. It's our first WTA title together – and for both of us our first WTA doubles title on home soil. To be honest, I enjoy playing doubles with Storm that week more than I enjoy my singles – the five-year-old Ash is back again, loving the creativity of the doubles court and the opportunity to play the game with one of her best mates.

I don't know how to explain this new attitude, but I think of it as careless: I know I'm about to quit the game, so I know the next big loss is the last loss, the last point in the last game of the last match of the last summer of my career. Crowey doesn't call it careless, though. He calls it carefree. I may not feel the excitement to play matches or the thrill of the fight, but I'm also without any distraction or distress. People in my team keep asking, 'Is she okay? Are you okay, Ash?' – and I am more than okay. I'm dialled in to the task at hand. *Is this my flow state?* I begin to like this way of being.

We head to the Australian Open and stay in the house of a friend of a friend, just behind the Royal South Yarra Lawn Tennis Club, and I'm reading more crime books, maybe one a day, and having the odd BBQ with steak or chicken from the local butcher and a bunch of veggies or salad from the supermarket, and I'm looking forward to playing.

Usually I'm jangled by now, reliving my history in this tournament, which is filled with regret. But none of it troubles me as much as it once did. In 2017, the first time I got to the third round, I had no idea what I was doing. In 2018, I made another third round – fine. In 2019, I beat Sharapova in the fourth round and lost to Petra in the quarters, another stepping stone. In 2020, there was the semi-final loss to Kenin – these things happen. (That match taught me a lesson, after all: you don't get what you deserve, you get only what you earn.) In 2021, I screwed up royally against Muchová, but now I have a chance to atone. I have a chance to finish all that unfinished business on my terms and within my own timeline, through my own boring build-up to one of the biggest tournaments of my life.

In my opening match I'll be playing a qualifier, so I look through the list of who that might be. There's only one name that makes me pause: Lesia Tsurenko. I've lost to her previously and had some bad memories. I just want a comfortable match-up, and would prefer to avoid her, but of course that's who I draw. *Fuck.* She's coming off an injury, but she's tricky and she does that thing I hate, putting a lot of balls in awkward places. She doesn't so much dominate as frustrate.

First round. Rod Laver Arena. Dry mouth. But it's over in 50 minutes. Do I need a physio? Nup. Just home for a sleep, ready for the next round.

I've never played Lucia Bronzetti before, and never watched her play – to be quite honest, I've never even heard her name. But Tyzz does what he does best – he analyses her game, picking it apart, and then writes me a long and detailed plan, which I glance at between snippets of vision. I see her at the coin toss, and although she's 22 she looks 17, and I can tell she's completely overawed here. She has nothing that can hurt me, and it's over in 57 minutes.

On my day off, I go for a walk with Crowey and his spanador, Molly, and we talk about how this is it for me – and how I need everyone to accept that. I know they have my interests at heart, and only the very best intentions, but I can't have people trying to talk me out of quitting.

'I'm not going to regret this,' I tell him. 'I'm tired of people telling me I can play one or two tournaments a year, that I can do Wimbledon and the Australian Open and avoid all the others. I *can't* pick and choose, because there's all the work in between.' I don't want to train half-arsed for six months just to play a few rounds at a Slam, and then do it all again. I'm done.

He understands and he gives me a hug. This is the end, the line in the sand, and now everyone knows for sure.

I play Camila Giorgi in the third round, and I like this match-up. She's very structured, and smacks the ball hard. Pound for pound, given her body type, she might be the hardest hitter in tennis. She looks like a gymnast and her side hustle is as a lingerie model, but she just *smokes* the ball ... as long as it's in her hip pocket. I can deny her the hip pocket. I can get the ball up, and down, and change the pace, and loop it, and constantly change her contact point. Her pace doesn't bother me either – I can use that against her.

There's all this extra hype, as usual at a Grand Slam, but we muffle that with silly games in our warm-up. I've got some electrical tape so we draw a little net on the wall and start playing soccer. We play cricket, too, and Tyzz bats first. We bowl seamers at him, and he always finds a way to get hit in the nuts, probably on purpose, because it makes me laugh. I love him for making the effort to lighten the mood but I don't even need it this time. There are no nerves and no adrenaline. I'm numb, and the match is over in an hour. Someone points out to me that no one has broken my serve yet this year, a streak now stretching to 52 consecutive service games.

I'm up against Amanda Anisimova in the fourth round, which is a shock to some, because the media has been talking all week about the prospect of me playing Naomi Osaka, but Naomi loses and I'm annoyed that Amanda hasn't been respected. 'You guys always predict this stuff will happen,' I tell the press, chiding them. 'But it *never* happens.'

Tyzz offers me his notes about Amanda's damaging first-serve speed, and tricky second-serve location. She likes to return through the middle, he says, and if I go wide to her backhand it needs to be with quality or she'll punish me. 'You need to expose her movement,' he says, 'because any time she's able to establish a good position on the ball, she's dangerous.'

The last thing Tyzz tells me before any match is about attitude rather than mechanics, and this is what he texts me today: *Must be ready to compete in this one. She's gonna be up and about after beating Naomi. Look to stick to your plans and break down the forehand side.* It feels like a dangerous match but it's over in an hour and 15 minutes, straight sets again.

Tick, move on. *I'm into the quarters but I've done nothing,* I think. *I haven't* needed *to do anything.*

The quarter-finals continue the theme of the tournament so far. I'm up against Jess Pegula, whose billionaire father owns NFL club the Buffalo Bills, and they've just lost a playoff game to Kansas City. There's volume in the grandstands but I can't quite make out what people are cheering and jeering; later, I learn that some of them are trying to put her off by yelling, 'Go Chiefs!' It's a good burn – the Chiefs just broke the Bills' hearts in overtime – but I'm not sure it's necessary.

I start well anyway, and Jess completely hands me the match. Sometimes, if you don't think it's your day, a slow start is all the confirmation you need to retreat, and that's what she does. This match falls into her too-hard basket and is done in 63 minutes. Afterwards, she admits as much, telling the media she felt 'helpless' out there. 'When she gets into a rhythm, she can kind of run away,' Jess says. 'It doesn't feel good.'

I've played six matches in barely more than six hours, and I'm into the semi-finals. Now I'm starting to laugh at how the mountain comes to you when you decide that you're done climbing. At the beginning of the fortnight, for something different and to completely lighten up, I begin doing something now that I never do – I listen to the outside world.

*

A couple of years ago, Crowey told me a story about Cathy Freeman and the 2000 Sydney Olympic Games. She was asked at a press conference how she was dealing with the pressure, and her answer was simple: 'I'm not.' Every journalist in the room perked up after that comment, thinking a story was breaking about an athlete about to crack under the strain, but then Cathy clarified what she meant: 'I'm not dealing with the pressure, because it's not even entering my attention.' She was like a little girl in a house, she said, and she could see a storm brewing outside but couldn't hear any of the howling winds or thunderclaps. She simply closed the doors and windows. She refused to let the whirlwind of global expectation into her mind. I loved that analogy.

But now I'm going a different way. I want to laugh at it all, and let it all in, the wind and rain and lightning. The TV is usually on mute, but now I crank up the volume. *If it's there, it's there*, I think. *What will be will be.* I begin listening to the pundits, curious about what they think they know about me, and my eyes widen. *They're talking useless crap*, I realise. *They're analysing but have no idea what's happening – and no idea what I'm feeling.* They only see me on court, when I'm not even really there – when I'm so far into my own head or wired into the flow of the contest that there's nothing they could possibly read in my expression – yet they sound so *sure* of themselves. They see me at press conferences, too, when I'm never going to tell them anything, yet they believe I'm revealing all.

I see an advertisement on one station and the script is wild. 'Ash Barty! Our world number 1! Our Grand Slam champion! The queen of Wimbledon! But can she win the one that counts?' I'm pretty sure the one that counted was Wimbledon, so I just laugh, shake my head and turn it off. That's enough.

For a few years now, Garry and I have been playing a game. Whenever we're watching TV or listening to the radio and someone says my name, we let out a little 'Woo!' and do a high-five. (Watching the morning news at the wrong time of year can make your hand sore.) We take it to a new level at the 2022 Australian Open, starting a new team WhatsApp group called 'Where's Ash?' The rule is simple: if you spot my image or name in any context, send in a picture, draw a face on it, have fun with it.

Soon the photos start rolling in. Me on bus stops and tram stops and train station platforms. Someone sees my name on the news ticker crawling across the bottom of a television at JB Hi-Fi. There I am on a skyscraper in the city. Is that me on a billboard on the side of a brothel? We open up every window and door, embrace the weirdness and laugh about it all.

A strange thing happens, too – I begin to understand that I'm not playing for me anymore. I'm playing for everyone else. I'm playing for this country. I want them all in my tent.

The semi-final is against Maddie Keys, whom I love. We've played against one another at Roehampton and Junior Wimbledon and in Fed Cup, and I love the contests. I'm happy if this is as far as my tournament goes. *If I lose to Maddie, that's okay*, I think, *because I'd be genuinely happy for her to get into a Grand Slam final.*

Tyzz gives me his instructions, and I go out on court and perform as instructed. That's the way it works in Slams, of course. You need all your advice up front because there's no direct coaching allowed on court. You can look at your box and, mostly, I look to Tyzz for reassurance.

I don't look at him at all in this semi-final – in fact, I haven't all tournament. My player's box has ballooned into comfortably more than a dozen friends and family, but I don't see any of them either. Right now it's just me and Maddie, and then when match point falls my way it's just me, with a single fist-pump for company. I'm into the final of the Australian Open.

Who I'll be playing against is decided the next day. Iga Świątek is playing Danielle Collins, and for me the equation is simple. I love Iga, and I have a rocky relationship with Danielle. I want to play Iga. I want to share it with her. But Danielle wins, and I think back to the matches we've had in the past and how they were never fun. I never walk off court after playing Danielle thinking, *That was good tennis*. Each match has been an ugly, tiring scrap.

On my day off, we go out as a team for a light practice. It turns into more of a classic catches afternoon, with balls flying everywhere – everyone's a target for a cheap shot. We use the session more to keep my body moving, and we don't stress too much about the tennis balls struck. We touch briefly on some tactics for the final and keep it all very relaxed.

Later that evening, Tyzz sends me his long tactical text, and I scroll through it, trying to remember a few salient points, but it's always the emotional insights that I retain best. *She is weird, and hard to read, but is vulnerable when up in the score, and definitely guilty of getting a little bit tight*, Tyzz writes. *At times, when feeling anxious, she will lose composure and get angry and loud. This is a big win for you.*

For the whole tournament I've been warming up in a loading dock, and moments before I'm due on court for the final I see Casey, who stops for a chat and a hug, then I go back to waiting for my team to come together. We coalesce, and then comes that moment when it's all left to me, and I'm ready to walk out alone.

Danielle enters the arena first, while I wait at the top of the stairs. The crowd is restless, the murmuring audible even to me in the shadows. I make a promise to myself – *Look up and take it all in, and walk out with a smile*, because wearing a smile onto the court is what I've done since I was a little girl. It's my way of reminding myself to have fun – to enjoy the game and not let it control or consume me. I do the coin toss, and consider it my duty to make the kid flipping the coin smile and laugh, and then I feel immediately settled.

Things go smoothly in the first set, although there is one moment when Collins has break point and I'm against the ropes. I hit a big second serve, find my forehand with the first ball and pull it inside in – my go-to pattern when it matters. That gets the game back to deuce, and I play two more solid points to win. Holding my serve is massive for me. I win the first set 6-3, rounding it out with an ace. *Yep*, I think, nodding. *This is good*.

But in the second set I get a little passive and things start to go south. My slice is no longer crisply chipped. My powerful first serve is a little loose. I run to the wrong places. I double-fault. Danielle has court position and is controlling the centre. She's crunching second serves and being assertive early in rallies. Before I can blink I'm down 1-5 and spectating, and I don't know how I can get back into this contest.

Crowey always says that in such moments you draw down on your values. This isn't something you do consciously – it's more instinctive. You're reminded of who you are in the dark moments because you *know* yourself – because you've done the work to determine what it is you stand for in life. Remember the three words Richmond legend Dustin Martin uses on the football field to centre himself? 'Strong. Aggressive. Unstoppable.' Those are his key words – his courage mantra. I often use 'I'm imperfect but I'm worthy' or 'I am enough', but the reminders don't have to be serious. Cotch has four words to bring him back to his best, and although the first three are serious – 'Strong', 'Clear' and 'Calm' – the fourth is 'Jokey'. He needs that nudge to not take himself too seriously on the field, and maybe I do too.

I think of a few words that take me back to my earliest times in tennis: 'Happy', 'Excited', 'Loved'. How do I stay calm under pressure? I try to remember the little girl who fell in love with the game. Because she was the story before the narrative was packaged up and sold. And she was just thrilled to be in the contest, and grateful for the opportunity, and not in the least bit fucking nervous.

There is a moment in the second set that snaps me back into the right process. Danielle breaks to lead 5-1, turns to her team and screams, 'Come on!' It's loud – very loud. It's the first time she really tries to assert any positive energy into the match. I'm a little confused as to why she chooses this moment to impose herself, as she's all over me. It's unnecessary. The crowd sense this and get a little fired up. I smile and think, *Fucking game on – one break back here and it's on.*

That won't get me back into this match entirely, though, so I also call to mind the tactics Tyzz has drilled into me. I can see that he wants this one badly – for him, for me, for us – so I forget none of his tips and fundamentals.

Find forehands, I think. *Find forehands and be aggressive.*

I know in this moment, too, that this is the only match of the summer where I will not be able to accept a loss. I can't accept losing to her here and now. I won't. It's not an option. Right now I need some grit. I need to take her out of this, and take control of the match.

Find your feet. Find forehands. Be aggressive. Every point.

I tell myself that if there's a ball that I'd hit with a backhand 65 per cent of the time, I'll run around and hit it with a forehand – and I'll do that again and again and again. Why? Because if Danielle looks over the net and sees me hitting forehand after forehand, she'll think she's doing something wrong. She'll think she needs to do something different – something *extra* – and that's when she'll make a mistake.

We go to 3-5 and I can see her wavering now. The crowd is as loud as I've ever heard them. We get to 5-5, and I can feel the control spilling back my way. Rod Laver Arena is deafening. Danielle looks unnerved as she holds serve, and I feel unassailable as I hold serve. Then it's 6-6 and we're going to a tie-breaker – a buster – but the momentum is all mine. She's vulnerable. She's tightening. She's angry. *This is a big win for you*.

For the first half of the tie-breaker, I'm playing into the wind. *No cheapies*, I think. *Make her earn every point*. I want to continue to be aggressive off the first serve, but also to make sure I'm involved after every return. *Get. Into. Every. Single. Point*.

First point, she serves and we get into a rally, but she's impatient and presses too hard for an advantage, and her forehand goes long. 1-0.

Second point, I serve, and fault. I put heavy topspin on my second serve, and just a fraction quicker than normal, and it cramps her left hip. She gets aggressive and doesn't respect it enough, and misses her backhand return long. 2-0.

Third point, I hit my go-to serve – flat down the T – and she makes the return but I work hard to find a forehand and the court is open for my inside-out forehand. She doesn't get near it. *Bang*. 3-0. Now the tie-breaker is a completely different proposition. The psychology of the leader is mine.

Fourth point, she serves and I find a short slice backhand return that is just *nasty*. It gets me in the rally, and when I get the second slice I place it short and low, because I know that with Danielle's forehand grip she can't do damage when the ball is below her knees. The slice forces her down and in, and all she can offer is a cross-court forehand. I drop my reply over the net, and she flicks it high to buy herself some time. I hit a routine smash into the open court and the crowd goes nuts. 4-0. I give them a little fist-pump.

Fifth point, she serves and I miss the return, barely connecting with the racquet. *C'mon, mate*, I think. *No cheapies!* 4-1.

Sixth point, I'm serving again, and with my second serve I go slow and high into the wind. It catches her off-guard and so she smothers it, dumping the ball into the net. There's something about the way the arena cheers now – I can almost hear every guttural bellow and squeal. 5-1.

I've lost track of the score but I don't want to look up at the scoreboard because I know the eyes of everyone inside Rod Laver Arena are on me, not to mention the 4,261,000 people watching at home, and I know they'll take that as me getting ahead of myself. I sneak a quick glance to check as we change ends.

Seventh point, I have the wind behind me now, and all of Australia too. She presses with a double-handed backhand hard and flat, and my return is long. 5-2.

Eighth point, she serves and pushes hard in the long rally that follows. I use my defensive slice to keep me in the point until I can find forehands that gain me control, and *then* use my slice low and slow down the middle. It's a ball she thinks she can hurt me with, but she doesn't adjust to the pace and is way too early on it. She shanks it wide. 6-2.

Ninth point. Match point. Championship point. *No cheapies. Get yourself into the point.*

Danielle goes for a big free winner, a flat serve down the T, but I love this because there's no risk, and I can chip that ball back just past the service line. She rips a backhand cross-court and I neutralise with my slice. It's not the big deep slice that gives me time, but the short slice that brings her in, taking her away from the baseline. She wants to control the point from the back of the court, but I've forced her to approach. Now she only has one option – my forehand – and it leaves her in the wrong position, a sitting duck.

I see my spot, my favourite shot, the cross-court winner, and there is no hesitation. I don't nurse it, I *crunch* it – and as soon as I do, I know the shape is perfect. I know exactly where it's going to land. I know it's going past her, and that she'll barely get her racquet up to swing. I don't even bother recovering for the next shot because I know the ball isn't coming back. I take one step and spin on my heels, turning to my box, and it's all over. 7-2. I've won the 2022 Australian Open.

I'm screaming now, letting everything out, flexing my forearms and roaring again and again, exhaling every emotion. I'm aware that my hands are sweaty, and in that moment the world is vibrating, pulsing, surging. It's not so much surreal as hyper-real. I forget my surroundings. Have I shaken the umpire's hand? Have I thanked the crowd? Have I put my gear away? I don't know what I've done or what I'm supposed to do. Casey is at the side of the court and I run to hug her first. 'Thank God you're here,' I say. 'I love you.'

Evonne presenting me the Daphne Akhurst Memorial Cup is one of the best surprises and one of my favourite moments. My dear friend, my mentor and my family. It couldn't have been more perfect.

Next there are speeches to make. *Compose yourself*, I think. *Tell them what it means. Thank them for everything – don't stuff that up.* After that there are questions to answer and photos to smile for, and these commitments stretch out before me into the night, and it's not until five hours later, well beyond midnight, that a car takes me into the city, to the party where all my people are gathered. It's held in a private upstairs bar at Garden State in Flinders Lane, and I enter through a back door off one of Melbourne's best grimy dark alleys. I take the elevator up and walk out in a rush, and love is everywhere. So many people who have meant so much to me – it would be impossible to name them all.

I see my fitness team – Tubs and Narelle, Matty and Mel – the people who built me up and kept me going and made me strong. I see my teammate and my captain – Casey and Mol – who held me close and demanded more of me. I see my manager, Nikki, and Benny – the couple who kept me on track. I see my mindset coach and my first coach – Crowey and Jim – the boys who taught me the right life lessons at the right time. I see my tennis gurus – Stolts and Tyzz – who took me to tennis school and helped me graduate with honours. I see my fiancé and my family – Garry and Ali and Sara and Mum and Dad – the ones who picked me up when I fell to pieces, and sacrificed everything so that I might chase a lofty dream. It's the first time all five have been together to see me play, and the first time in a long time – maybe the only time in a professional setting – that all six of us have been together.

These are the people who brought me to this place, who have been a part of the journey and have brought so much energy. They party hard and go all night long, gulping Peronis and sipping espresso martinis and munching on chips with aioli. I can only muster the energy for a single beer. I am the first to leave the party. It's time for the people I love the most to enjoy this together. It's time for me to take it all in and get some sleep.

Strings Away

The morning after the 2022 Australian Open, I wake up in the house where we've been staying, in the leafy inner east of Melbourne. I rise slowly and walk to the window, pull apart the curtains and look out over the grounds of the Royal South Yarra Lawn Tennis Club in Toorak, one of the wealthiest postcodes in Australia. My eyes are scratchy, almost dry, and a feeling of tiredness overwhelms me, but I've been expecting this. I always do after a long tournament, because two weeks of Grand Slam tennis demands so much of your body.

It demands that you press and hold, that you sprint and stop, jump and stoop, charge and change direction. Your mind tells you to ignore the discomfort all these competing actions are causing in your muscles and joints, and the end result is a fortnight of tension deferred and pain put off. When it's all over, your body finally relaxes – and only then do you fully feel all that soreness you've been carrying, hiding and denying. *Hello, old friend.*

I'd arrived home at 2 am and gone to bed at 4.30 am, and now it's 7 am and Nikki is coming over with coffees. Hair and makeup are required before I do a photo shoot in a park somewhere. I do what I'm told – *Stand here, turn your head, hold up the trophy … and smile!* – but really I want to get back to the business at hand. I want to get back to packing.

My suitcase is small and simple to fill. I pack light and with a spartan efficiency I've honed over my years on the tour. The only tricky part is fitting in all the Australian Open towels. I bring these souvenirs home for everyone I know, so I have to fold each one and find a way to get them in the suitcase. Still, I like folding. I like most methodical things. It might as well be meditation.

Next I take the rubbish out of my tennis bag, and repack it. I'm packing it very differently now from how I usually would, because I know I'm not preparing to play again. I put my strings away. I put my energy gels and hydration tablets in ziplock bags. I pack my orthotics into their special case.

I've donated my shoes already. They have charity bins at all the major tournaments where players can put pairs they don't need anymore – when the shoes have lost just enough traction that they're no longer effective, but they're still in good enough nick for others to wear. I'm hard on my tennis shoes. On average, I go through a pair every eight days on court. I used four different pairs alone at the Australian Open. I should probably have kept a pair – someone might want them one day. The shoes I wore when I won the 2019 French Open are in a museum somewhere. Oh well, it's nice to think there are now four people out there getting around in a pair of size 9 red FILA tennis shoes, footwear that carried me to a third and final Grand Slam victory.

It's time to exhale now, and the relief begins to wash over me. Not relief at having won the tournament, nor at the idea that this is it for my career. The monkey off my back was performing in an Australian Open on my terms, win or lose. So often the outcome at my home Slam has been dictated by factors beyond my control, or by slips of my own making, but I feel as though I've played the tournament my way, as I'd always wanted to do.

Garry and I have some friends over for lunch – steak sandwiches and salad. I drop him off at the airport that evening, so he can head to Saudi Arabia for a golf tournament with Louis. It's the most bizarre thing, heading to Melbourne International Airport at Tullamarine to send him off into the world for his work, while I stay put. Roles reversed. *I could get used to this.*

*

I fly home to Brisbane the next day, taking a private flight. I want to avoid being around people for a short while, but people find me anyway. The press are waiting at the terminal in Brisbane. It's a 40-minute drive home, and when I get there five cars are parked in front of my house – the house I haven't yet lived in. I lock myself inside alone and begin unpacking.

I have at least a dozen boxes that require urgent attention, and key rooms to settle and structure. My laundry. My library. My shed, underneath my gym. As the days come and go, tradies come and go, finishing off unfinished surfaces. I've given myself two weeks with no commitments at all. My family will bring groceries so I don't need to venture out. This is my forced solitary lockdown, my hermit crab moment, and I spend it making my new house into a home.

At night I sit in front of the iMac in my office and transfer my photos across from my phone. I get stuck there, staring at the screen. I want to select a handful of images to print and frame – tennis photos to put up on the wall alongside the pictures of Garry and Mum and Dad and Sara and Ali and the kids. I've never put up photos from my career before, and it's hard to decide. I guess I didn't realise there would be so many.

Every night I sit quietly for a couple of hours, scrolling through thousands of images. I'm deep in digital reminiscence, looking at myself as a child and a teenager and a young adult. There I am in Belgium on that first European trip, the one that scared me and scarred me. I smile at the memory, though, knowing that you learn as much through trauma – maybe more – than through joy.

There are baby photos in there too, in an album labelled 'Home'. I'm meticulous with my photo albums. I label them all. Cairns and Cincinnati and Doha and Eastbourne are there. I have 11 separate Fed Cup albums alone, and 217 albums in total, all heavily curated.

Eventually I settle on the images I want on my walls, and not one of them is an action shot. They're pictures of the people I've met, the faces and days that remind me of the funny things I've seen, the bizarre places we've been together and the stupid shit we've done to enjoy this thing I called a career. I am kissing Casey's forehead after the Australian Open final. I am flanked by Cathy Freeman and Evonne Goolagong Cawley a little later that same night. I am arm in arm with Tyzz, holding the Venus Rosewater Dish after winning Wimbledon. I am hugging Rod Laver – *Rocket knows my name!* – after the 2019 French Open. I am with Tyzz and Stolts and Jim, each of whom led me to where I am now. We all have a beer in hand.

Where am I now? I'm at peace. I'm content.

I get up early, because I always get up early. As a WTA professional, once you hit the top 100 in singles, you need to make yourself available to the WADA drug testing authorities every day of the year, meaning you need to supply an address and an hour of the day in which you would prefer to be tested. My hour is 5 am to 6 am, because I know the testers will wake me up, and because I can go to the bathroom right away. Urine supplied, blood taken, done and done. In 2019, I was tested almost 30 times. It becomes as routine as making your morning coffee. But the testers don't come during this fortnight of seclusion, and so I simply start my day.

After a strong skinny latte, I play on the grass with Affie and Chino, my Maltese cross shih tzu boys. At 6 am we take a 45-minute walk, and once the pups are tired I can do other things. I answer emails, make a sandwich for lunch, unpack a few more boxes – and I clean. I like vacuuming most of all. In the late afternoon, when the Queensland heat has receded,

I throw the ball out the back with our border collie, Origi. I eat dinner and I'm tucked into bed by 8.30 pm. Unless some sport is on, the TV is off, so I read a couple of chapters of something and then drift off to sleep – 9.30 pm counts as a very late night for Ash Barty.

It sounds fairly plain, and uneventful. Boring, even. But at this moment it's what I need. I need no one else around, so I'm not distracted by what's next, by who's coming over – *Where are we going, what are you doing, what am I doing?* Directionless days like this are everything I've dreamed of – and everything I want.

Nothing is official yet, of course. Technically, I'm committed to playing in an upcoming tournament. There's a Fed Cup tie scheduled for April, and although it's not public knowledge yet, it's going to be held in Brisbane. I've told Mol I'll be there. What a way to finish things – playing at home, playing with the team, playing for Australia. I couldn't have scripted it better.

I haven't been doing much other than jumping on my stationary bike. I love my bike and I love routine. I think I'll always work out, even if not with the same strict regimentation. I begin hitting again in the first week of March, a little more than a month after the Australian Open. I drive down to Queens Park on the Gold Coast to hit with Ben, knowing the first real workout in a while will kick my arse. And that's when the rumours start circulating: Russia and Belarus might be disqualified from the Fed Cup – which has been renamed as the Billie Jean King Cup.

If that happens, the tie in Brisbane might not go ahead. Australia is set to play Slovakia, but as we're the highest-ranked qualifier, we might take Russia's spot and walk directly into the finals. But the final is in Glasgow, in November, and there is no way I will be playing tennis in Glasgow, or in November. For me, it's now or nevermore. Basically, if the International Tennis Federation condemns Russia's invasion of Ukraine by banning the Russian and Belarusian teams from international tournaments, then my tennis career is quite likely over already. They say all politics is personal, but I don't think this is what they meant.

The news comes out overnight on Tuesday, 1 March – Russia and Belarus are out – so now I wait. It's the morning of Saturday, 12 March, when I wake up to a text message from Mol. Australia will advance to the finals. The tie in Brisbane has been cancelled. And just like that, my career is over.

I'd like to tell you I feel stunned or shocked or just spun on a top, but I feel good. Great, even. All day long there's a kind of pulsing wave rushing through me, not of excitement or fear or adrenaline or even relief – just the sense that something important and right and true is happening. Something is starting and something is finishing. It's done. I'm done. I'm retired. It is what it is.

All of a sudden, this thing that's been a part of my life for 20 years is no longer, and yet I feel no sadness, and no great happiness either. It feels natural and normal. I don't need to chase anything anymore. I don't need a farewell either. When a chapter in a book ends, you don't stop reading. Maybe you pause a moment, dwell a little on what you've just learned, but then you turn the page and keep going.

That night I go into the garage, where I keep my racquets. I've always protected my racquets fiercely, as if they're more than my property but rather an extension of myself. I know them intimately. How to store them, how to string them and when to string them, so they can be evenly rotated.

I have a stringing machine of my own, and do them all myself when I'm here. Some people employ masters to do this for them, believing in the alchemy of the artisan, putting their faith in only one stringer. Whenever I can, I like doing things myself. Like I said, I enjoy methodical moments. Folding towels. Packing bags. Stringing racquets. It's all therapeutic.

But I know right now that I don't need to string these racquets anymore. I don't need to rotate them anymore. I take them out of their bag and look at them, and I find the racquet I was holding for that final point of my competitive career – *Cross-court winner, 7-2 in the tie-breaker, crunched it! Fuck yeah! Game, set, match, tournament!* – and I put it aside. It's special. And the others? I take them apart, piece by piece.

I'm accustomed to this process. I've kept one racquet of every model and design that I've ever played with, and when I store them away I always remove the string and the grip, so they're just a frame. I have dozens of them – one of every animal from throughout my career – stowed away in suitcases.

The best way to explain why I do this is that I like finality in things. I like a clean cut, a complete list, a box checked, a door closed. It reminds me of when I quit playing as a teenager and decided not to protect my ranking. When you're out, you're out. Blank slate. Clean page. New day.

Today I hold one of those spare racquets in my hand, and I take out a pair of scissors. I start in the middle, snipping the strings in a big cross – *north, south, east, west on the racquet face* – and then I pull the strings from the outside edge of the frame and drop them in the bin.

I pull the red plastic tape from the top of each handle, and from there I unpeel the grip and toss it in the rubbish too. I pick the Australian Open sticker off the throat. And then I do it all again for nine more racquets, one by one, until they're all completely stripped. I wipe down the bare frames, slide them into my tennis bag and zip it shut. I lean it against the wall for the time being, and think about where I might store it in this house I'm still trying to decorate and organise and fill.

I switch off the light. I walk out of the garage, and back into my life.

Why, Not When

It's time to tell the world about my decision to leave tennis, but first I need to tell *my* world. I sit down with Tyzz and Nikki at home in Brisbane on Tuesday, 15 March 2022. They already know this moment is coming, of course, but I need to make them appreciate the finality of the decision – my 100 per cent commitment to giving the game away.

We sit at the dining table at home, having sushi for lunch and coffee afterwards. It's now that I cry about my choice for the first time, although not because I'm sad about leaving tennis but rather because this is the end of something. The second phase of my career was something we started together, seven long years ago. I was dipping my toe back in the game, while Nikki was going out on her own and Tyzz was taking a chance on me, and now we're going out, on top, together. That's a momentous thing to share.

It's one of the most difficult conversations I've ever had, letting the words tumble out of my mouth and trying to read their faces as I stumble through each thought. It's funny, but when I'm sharing this with the people to whom I'm closest, I'm scared of their reaction most of all.

I want to make sure they understand why I am doing this. I want them to have that clarity. I want them to know there's just no greed or need or want or desire to chase things left inside me anymore. An extra title or a few more dollars aren't going to make any difference in my life.

'I've achieved my dreams,' I say. 'Not many people in their life get to live out all their dreams.'

I wait for a response, and my heart catches in my throat when they smile – when they don't question me for a second, when they don't say 'What if ...' or 'How about ...', when they just wrap their arms around me.

Don't cry 'cos it's over, I think. *Smile because it happened.*

Garry knows already, and he loves me for my decision. Crowey knows, and he supports me. My family know, and they know it's the right thing, too. The kids are pumped, of course, although Lucy especially needs to confirm it with me.

'But ... when are you going back to play tennis?' she asks.

'I'm not, darling.'

'But ... when are you going away again?'

'I'm not.'

'Oh … cool,' she says. 'So we can have some tennis lessons?'

I watch the cogs turn in her brain as she begins to grasp that I'm no longer going to be on the other side of the world for the majority of every year. Aunty Ash is gonna be around a lot more.

On Friday, 18 March, I sit down with Casey to film an interview about my choice, a few days before it will be released to the world. This chat is Nikki's idea – one she's been considering since the Australian Open, when the idea of me moving on began to gather serious momentum within our circle. She knew that I wouldn't want to do a press conference – that I would want to describe my reasons in my own words before the inevitable questions came. She knew I would want it to be an exciting and comfortable and *real* way of revealing my truth.

Before we start the interview, while the film crew are setting up their gear, Casey flicks through her notes.

'Shit, this is getting real,' she says, and her eyes go glassy. 'You know we don't have to do this.'

'Don't you do it to me, mate,' I say, looking at her as she wells up. 'If you cry, I'll cry.'

We can't look at one another now. Our relationship has always been this way. We're always soft and relaxed – we don't do hard and heartbreaking.

The filming begins and we get very serious very quickly, and we can't stop. It's a strange balance of sad but animated, painful tears and happy tears, talking to one another and talking over one another. The video the public will see is cut down to six minutes and six seconds, but actually we've talked on camera for two and a half hours.

The dissemination of this message needs to be handled with utmost care, and with that in mind Nikki grows ever more protective, planning the exact days that specific people will be told. 'The more people who know,' she warns, 'the more it's going to get out.'

On 22 March, the day before we release the video, there are phone calls I need to make to people who I want to hear this message from me and me alone. The people I love the most. And who have shared every moment of my journey with me. It's the least I can do for them. Narelle. Mol. Mel. Tubs. Storm. Carolyn Broderick, a TA doctor. Chris Mahony, from the national academy in Brisbane. Adam Schuhmacher, my physio at home. Donna Kelso, from the WTA. Micky Lawler, president of the WTA.

The first one is Stolts, and it's hard. He's taken aback. 'Shit, mate,' he says. 'I feel like we've had this conversation before.'

Jim is one of the last, and he says he knew already, in his gut. 'I had a feeling,' he says. 'I had a feeling after Wimby, and after AO I knew.'

These are the toughest phone calls I've ever had to make, and yet really the hard part is dialling the numbers. When we get to talking, they're easy, because no one is upset or angry with me, or sceptical or confused. Mol cries, and Mel cries, and Stormy is close, so by the end I'm emotionally ruined, but I'm also restored. I'm happy to have this time with each of them, not even to break the news but to thank them for pushing me and putting up with my shit. I wouldn't have grown into the person I am without them.

On the morning of Wednesday, 23 March, I tell my sponsors and formally inform the tour, and let particular journalists know what is happening. Garry and I go grocery shopping before the video drops, to make sure we have enough food, knowing we won't be leaving the house for the day. We know to close all the blinds, too, because people will come. We don't go into our backyard either, because photographers will no doubt train long lenses on our home from the adjacent golf course. Other than that, there's nothing to do but wait.

This feels effortless. Light. Natural. It doesn't feel like a break with the past but a continuation of the present. My life is going to be exactly the way it has been during the two blissful months since the Australian Open. The only difference is that everyone else will get to know what I'm thinking, and why I'm thinking it, and I'm eager for them to have that understanding. If I'm scared at all by anything, it's by my own comfort. *It's almost too easy*, I think. *Too calm*.

Most athletes don't get to retire on such terms, although there have been a few. Ian Thorpe left the pool at 24. Shane Gould was only 16. In my sport, Tyzz says, I remind him most of Björn Borg. He was 25 at the time he retired, and imperious on the court. Everyone was confused by his decision, but the tour was changing then, adding tournaments and making many of them mandatory, and he just didn't want to play that often or that far away. He made the same choice I'm making, and at the same age, too.

I listen to a lot of athletes talk about their decision to stop competing, because it's a decision most of them will have to make. 'When you know, you know,' they say. And I know.

I've heard others describe the alternative, too, which is going out when your body gives way, or when you despise the game you once loved, or when a coach makes the decision for you, with you clinging on tightly and unable to see that the time has come.

There's a line I like about this: 'Retire when they ask *Why?*, not *When?*'

Give it away when everyone will ask *Why did you?* rather than *Why don't you?*

That's what I'm doing.

Nikki finally shoots my goodbye into the ether. She hits send from my social media accounts, and I watch as the messages flow in. This happens whenever I'm prominent on court, whether I'm winning a tournament or losing in dramatic fashion. The messages came like a raging river after the French Open. Like the sea after Wimbledon. Like the ocean after the Australian Open. But this is more like rain – a seemingly infinite summer storm, showering over this one place in time.

I set my phone to DO NOT DISTURB, because it's too hard to absorb the torrent as it roars – too hard to figure out whether I should respond to this one or that one. Do I get back to Scott Morrison and Anthony Albanese right away? In what order do I reply to Cathy Freeman and Hugh Jackman, Mark Webber and Adam Scott? My best mates from the tour – Jules and Kiki and Coco and Simo and Caro and Petra – will understand if I wait a little while before getting back to them. As will every girl I played cricket with at the Brisbane Heat and the Queensland Fire, and the men and women and boys and girls I played with in social competitions as a teenager and child.

The only phone call I take is from Evonne.

'You okay?' she asks.

'Yeah, I'm great.'

'That's all that matters.'

I shut off the news, too. I try to keep myself occupied and pretend to be ignorant of and oblivious to the biggest announcement of my life so far. In the next few days I'll sit down to reply to every single message I've received via text and

WhatsApp and Messenger, because it's important to me to acknowledge their time and their gestures. One by one I reply to them all with my phone in airplane mode, without the data on – and then I reconnect to send them all at once.

What makes me breathe easiest is a simple grab Ali sends me from Twitter. It's not written by her but by someone else, someone I don't know. 'The day I retire,' it reads, 'I hope people talk about me the way they're talking about Ash Barty right now.'

That's cool. I've always wanted to make people proud for the right reasons, and in the tributes I begin to slowly absorb I can see that the world has received me in exactly that way. The things people are saying about me now have nothing to do with the accolades, the trophies, the rankings, the matches or even the shots. They're about the behaviour for which I wanted to be known – the friends and the lessons and the memories they have of me.

Ash Barty the tennis player made this announcement, but the responses to it were for Ash Barty the person. It's proof positive yet again that the two can coexist, overlap and ultimately coalesce. The story and the self are finally together, singular and side by side.

Postscript

Reaching this point in my life – retiring at 25, as the number 1 female tennis player in the world, coming off victory in the 2022 Australian Open – feels like absurd good fortune. *Seriously, pinch me.* But it's also worth noting that none of this happens – not one bit of it – without that match against Daria Kasatkina at Wimbledon in 2018. That collapse was ground zero, or rock bottom, or whatever you want to call it.

I'll call it base camp – a low vantage point from which I could study the terrain, before attempting to scale the summit.

Clambering up from the bottom – being forced to understand what I wanted from my tennis – helped me understand what I wanted out of life, too. And I understand so many things now that I didn't back then.

I understand that it requires not only work, but the constant reinforcement of checking your decisions and interrogating your motivations. More importantly, I understand that tennis doesn't define me, and that I have different dreams outside of the lines of the court.

What I'm going to do with my time isn't settled yet, and in truth I hope it will always remain fluid. I know I want to talk to children through books, and to corporate leaders through speaking engagements. I don't think I want to coach, but I definitely want to mentor. Enough people have helped me find my path – the very least I can do is work on the guidance and growth of others through the lessons I've learned from so many great minds.

I've set up a charitable trust: The Ash Barty Foundation. I want to help people bring out the best in themselves, and be comfortable within themselves, through the pillars of youth, education and sport. I want to help all kids – girls and boys, kids and teens, from the city and country – all across Australia, by giving them opportunities to live out their dreams.

Maybe there's a teenage girl in remote Western Australia who thinks she's fast enough to win the Stawell Gift, but needs some new running spikes and a return flight east to test her mettle. Maybe there's a young golfer in Sydney who wants to play in America, but it'll cost $15,000 for him to chase that dream. I'm hoping they can apply for funding and sponsorship, and we can look at those applications – reading stories both heartbreaking and inspiring – and find a few new ways to expand horizons through resources and opportunities. I can't wait.

But I'm also retired, and I want to take my new-found freedom out for a spin, to see what it can do. When I gave up tennis the first time, Evonne called me and told me it was a good decision, and to 'Go and wet a line'. But I never did. I haven't been fishing in years, but I'd like to. I'd like to go pump the flats somewhere for yabbies, fish off the beach and then see if I can land a big reef fish out off the Great Barrier Reef.

I don't go out a lot, but I'd like to visit the pub with Jim. One of the things he said when I told him it was over was that we've finally got one more reason to go to the Brekky Creek Hotel and celebrate with a steak and a beer, because they serve XXXX 'off the wood' there, where they have to put a spike in a barrel to drain out each drop. Jim's excited about that, and I am too.

In the months after my Australian Open win and my retirement, many people wondered aloud if I'd go back to the game someday, or maybe have another go at cricket. 'Maybe you should try AFLW,' they suggested. 'You're big into golf – are you going to go pro and join the LPGA Tour?' I'm not, but I do travel a little in those first few months, to play a golf tournament at Liberty National Golf Course in New Jersey, and then at a pro-am event on the Old Course at St Andrews in Scotland before the British Open. For a weekend hacker, I'm spoiled rotten.

I have no desire to play golf professionally – I'm just playing the sport that's always been closest to my family's heart. Mum and Dad met through golf, just as Garry and I did. It doesn't stir my competitive juices – to me it's about having a stroll and having a hit and maybe a laugh, too. It's been funny trying to get people to understand that.

The simple things in life still draw me in. I still love to train and I suspect I always will. I get in the gym and on my bike and I run, doing the kinds of workouts I hadn't been able to do before, either because they weren't part of my highly regimented program, or because my very specifically trained body wouldn't allow it at the time. Now I feel a freedom to move that's both metaphorical and literal. I need the sweat, too, and that sense of clearing my head through physical exhaustion while listening to random playlists – the trashier the better. After 20 years of training, I get antsy if I do nothing for too long. Maybe I'm addicted to the endorphins.

I'll continue to grapple with the idea that tennis is not who I am but what I did for a while, and that now it's time to do something else for a while. I get questions about that from others, too – 'How's the transition been?' – and the way they ask is always tinged with suspicion, as if I must have some kernel of regret. But this ending is not something that happened to me – it's something I made happen. It's not a breakup, or a breaking point. It's not a tragedy. The circle is complete. My life is as it was and should be. I just don't hit tennis balls for a few hours every day anymore. *I'm good, mate. I'm good.*

I love to relax at home most of all, lingering in my lounge, the dogs chilling on the floor and barking at the wind. I love seeing Garry at the BBQ on the back deck, and me on salad duty in the kitchen. We don't do big dinners or big parties – a quiet night in is a good time. I love cleaning my house, making it spotless and doing it myself. I vacuum the floors last because

that's the most satisfying part of the job for me. I always light a
scented candle afterwards.

The kids come over all the time. Lucy calls and asks the
inevitable question – 'Can I have a sleepover?' – and I respond
the same way every time – 'Of course you can, babe – come on
over!' What I love most about those moments is that they're no
longer special. They are special, of course, but now they're also
normal, not the exception.

*

For Lucy's sixth birthday, she wants a tennis party, so we take
her and three best friends back to the West Brisbane Tennis
Centre. Mum and Dad and Ali and Sara come down as well.
It's 30 minutes of games and then pizza and cake.

'Have a look at Luce,' I say to Jim. 'She's had three lessons.'

He nods, and takes her over to the side of Court 4, just like
he did with me 20 years ago. He throws her a ball and – *bang* –
she middles it perfectly. Jim's jaw just about hits the ground,
and his eyes go as big as I've ever seen. He tries a few combos –
forehand, backhand, switch-switch-switch – to see what she can
do, and we all laugh and shake our heads at the thought.

Jim is selling the centre soon, though, so I come back one
weekend before it changes hands. I bring my trophies and we
sit them all on a glass outdoor table, and we have a BBQ with
beers on the grassy hill in the shade of the tall palms and big
jacarandas and giant poincianas. Jim and I have a final hit
together on Court 4. We play a few points, and he shows me
a thing or two. I'll never stop wanting to learn. I'll never stop
loving the game.

Our last shot each is a slice backhand, then Jim walks to the net and rolls it up for the final time. And that's when I lose it, stifling a sob session at the thought of everything that has come to pass since I first set foot here as a baby girl. He gives me the net, because he can see that I need it as a keepsake.

I don't think I'll ever be able to drive back down this road now, because I can't bear the thought that this place, my home, won't be here anymore. I don't want to see it as anything other than how it exists in my mind. When I walked onto those courts as a kid, I felt so small, as if I was lost in this big, scary place, and then the world got bigger and scarier – brighter and wilder and more confusing and more wonderful – while those courts only felt more and more comforting and safe.

I walk each one of them now, and the memories pop back into my mind. I'm practising the slice and mastering the hopper. I'm spitting the dummy and cracking the shits. I'm gloating and crying. I'm laughing and roaring.

I'm breathing deeply and sweating in the Brisbane sun, chasing yet another ball deep into the corner, turning on the scratchy surface in the shadows and unleashing a final shot. I watch the ball clear the net and land – just within the lines – before it bounces, and bounces, and rolls, and stops.

The circle is complete.

Thank You

My tennis journey and the story I have shared with you in this book would not have been possible without the love and support, belief and talent of so many people –

Mum & Dad • Sara, Lucy & Oscar • Ali, Nick & Olivia • Garry • Steve & Jenny-Lee Kissick • Nikki & Ben Mathias • Jim Joyce • Rob & Sarah Joyce • Craig & Sue Tyzzer • Jason & Andrea Stoltenberg • Narelle Sibte & Shannon Nettle • Casey Dellacqua & Amanda Judd • Mark Taylor • Matthew Hayes • Ben & Sally Crowe • Alicia Molik • Adam Schuhmacher • Melanie Omizzolo • Dr Carolyn Broderick • Dr Robyn Shirlaw • Evonne Goolagong Cawley & Roger Cawley • Cathy Freeman • Matt Hornsby • Trent & Brooke Cotchin • Andrew Roberts • Darren McMurtrie • Pat Rafter • Donna Kelso • Micky Lawler • Neil Robinson • Victoria Bush • Chris Mahoney • Mark Woolley • John Hamilton • Damien McKern • Luisa Braun • Bill & Elizabeth Peers • John & Sally Peers • Andy Richards • Ian & Karin Codd • Martin Mulligan Sr, Thomas Bischof & my wonderful sponsors • Konrad Marshall, Leo Schlink & the team at HarperCollins

To my playing peers, thank you for pushing me to become the best I could be. Especially to my closest friends: Julia Goerges • Kiki Bertens • Petra Kvitova • Storm Sanders • Simona Halep • Coco Vandeweghe • Victoria Azarenka • Caroline Garcia • Caroline Wozniaki • Demi Schuurs • Iga Świątek

And to my fans, thank you for being part of this story too.

Australian tennis superstar ASH BARTY teams up with Jasmin McGaughey and Jade Goodwin to bring young readers this fun and exciting new illustrated series about school, sport, friendship and family.

THE WORLD OF Little ASH

BOOK 1
Ash tries EVERYTHING, but which SPORT will she choose?

BOOK 2
A FRIEND in need? Ash to the RESCUE!

BOOK 3
Ash is in TROUBLE. Will she make her match in TIME?

BOOK 4
Ash is WORRIED she won't WIN ever again!

BOOK 5
Dress-up is FUN but will Ash find her MISSING racquet?

BOOK 6
Ash is having no LUCK. Will she still PLAY hockey?

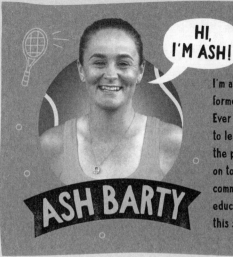

HI, I'M ASH!

I'm a three-time Grand Slam singles champion and former WTA World No. 1! I have always loved reading. Ever since I was a little girl, reading has been a way to learn, and has brought me great enjoyment. Over the past few years, reading was a huge part of my life on tour with tennis. I'm a proud First Nations woman, committed to supporting kids through sport and education around Australia. I'm thrilled to bring you this series of books about a sporty kid, just like me!

ASH BARTY

HI, I'M JASMIN!

I'm a Torres Strait Islander and African American writer and editor. I've always loved storytelling, and I'm proud to be able to work and learn in this field. It has been really exciting to write the Little Ash series. I really hope you enjoy Little Ash's adventures!

JASMIN McGAUGHEY

HI, I'M JADE!

JADE GOODWIN

I'm an illustrator, letterer and arts worker. I loved spending time in my grandparents' screen-printing studio when I was growing up. That's why I'm passionate about creating unique and colourful artwork. I use traditional and digital mediums to make my art and I enjoy exploring new ways to connect to my Gamilaraay heritage. I hope you like my drawings in this book!